Other books by Marilyn Catherine McDonald, MA

Little Girl Lost
A True Story of a Tragic Death

Mother of Eight Survives Population Explosion
"Just Between Us" Column Selection

Alert the Media
How the American Indian Movement used the Mass Media

Adapted from 1977 University of Portland Master's Thesis
The Interrelationship between the
American Indian Movement (AIM) and the Mass Media

Snowbirds Unlimited
Tales from the Restless Traveler

An Unforgettably Marvelous Chicken Named Oscar
(Children's e-book on Kindle only)

Read. Reflect. Respond. Rest.
366 Daily Reflections on Random Selections from Scripture

ISBN: 13-978-1500886400
ISBN: 10-1500886408
Library of Congress Control Number: 2014915202
CreateSpace Independent Publishing Platform
North Charleston, South Carolina

Front and back cover design by Alexandria N Smith
Front cover "self-photo" by Cody Cheng and Alexandria Smith
Author photo on back cover by Christina Eddy

Dedication

To all my friends in recovery,
no matter what you are recovering from,
where you come from or where you are going.
I love, honor and respect each and every one of you.
Together we can change ourselves and make the world a better place.
Thank you, God, for all the awesome people in my life
– and, for this remarkable journey.

Acknowledgements

People often ask of writers, "Where do you get your ideas?" The answer may be, "It's complicated, and yet very simple – it's all about connectivity.

In prayer and meditation we know when we quit talking, or when we quit asking for guidance, and when the guiding thoughts emerge, and take us to a higher place. If we pray to a God of our understanding, then why not acknowledge the feedback we get as coming from the source for our petitioning. So, I say, "Thank you God for prompting me to embark on this journey, and thank you for helping me to see it through to its completion."

I acknowledge the fine education, including Bible study that I received from the nuns, priests and lay teachers during my 11 years at St. James Catholic School in Ferndale, Michigan. And, I thank the Confraternity of Christian Doctrine (CCD) for their teachers' guides and instruction that helped me teach Christian faith, hope and love to seventh and eighth graders on Saturday afternoons for nine years. I thank the Carmelite sisters at the Sacred Heart Retreat House in Alhambra, California, for their guidance to those of us who served as Retreat Captains for our parishes. I thank them for guiding me on my path to becoming a professed Third (Secular) Order Discalced Carmelite on July 18, 1967. Although "Isolated" (meaning not affiliated or attending meetings) I still have the soul of a contemplative, and a commitment to prayer and meditation.

I thank my dear friend Doris Gauthier for her willingness to read everything I wrote for this book. Most of all, I appreciate her encouragement for me to continue when my faith in my own ability lagged. Many thanks as well to my husband Harry Taylor, who is still, as I write this acknowledgement, giving my manuscript a word for word and page by page reading. Not so much because he is looking for errors, but mostly because he wants to read what I have finished writing.

My son Tom's wife, Dr. Jan Smith has reviewed my previous books after publication, but this one has her in its grasp prior to publication. As a writer, author and successful Bestlight Creative Co-Owner and Managing Director, Jan's review on the back cover is most welcome.

Rev. Guy Lynch, Unity of Beaverton pastor, has helped me believe in myself. He represents the spirit of truth and support I have received from calling the prayer support team at Silent Unity in Unity Village, Missouri, and from reading and meditating on the *Daily Word* every morning for more than 30 years.

In addition, I want to thank Associate Director Mary Elizabeth Sperry, Confraternity of Christian Doctrine (CCD), Washington, DC, for helping me resolve the copyright and legal fair use issues concerning the excerpts used for this book that came from the 1970 Saint Joseph Edition of *The New American Bible*, allowing me to maintain the integrity of my manuscript.

Thanks, once again, to Amazon, CreateSpace and Kindle Direct Publishing (KDP) for their technical support teams' patience and advice, and for making "self-publishing" respectable.

Introduction

Daily meditation has been part of my life for decades, and the thought of writing a book of daily reflections was an infrequent occurrence. As often as I dismissed the notion, it returned. On January 1, 2011, the writing began – I started my commentary on random selections from Scripture.

In the beginning years of our wintering in Mexico, we held non-denominational Sunday services at our clubhouse. A semi-retired Lutheran minister frequently provided a service, and a retired Anglican priest from Canada began to fill in as well. When the priest needed a missal or bible for his Sunday readings I asked around.

One of our neighbors gave me *The New American Bible, Saint Joseph Edition* left in her house by the previous owner. I acquired the thick Bible with its heavy, warped and faded green cover. That Bible became my reading, reflecting, responding and writing resource for this project.

I began where the Hebrew Bible began, "In the beginning…" from the "First Story of Creation," (Genesis 1:1, page 4), fully expecting to complete the writing by the end of December 2011.

Four years later, after entering 366 (1 extra for February 29) hand written pages in three separate college ruled 8x10.5 notebooks, I completed the first computer draft.

Most of the time, I opened to a page in the Bible; pointed to a place on the page and started reading. When I found something that struck a chord, I wrote the quote for the day, noted the page, cross-referenced a date in the Bible, took a few minutes to reflect, and began writing my commentary.

Lectio Divina

Near the beginning, I told a friend about my project. And she said it sounded like "Lectio Divina," a Latin term meaning "divine reading." During the 12th century, Guigo, a Carthusian monk, described his spiritual practice in the following stages:

Lectio (read) Read a Scripture passage slowly and reflectively.

Meditatio (reflect) Think deeply about the text.

Orato (respond) Open our hearts and minds to the Divine.

Contemplatio (rest) Let go of our own thoughts and listen.

In the 16th century, St. Teresa of Avila founded a religious order based on the tradition of Carmel, and the practice of deeply theological prayer and contemplation. Christine Valters Paintner, in her beautiful book *Lectio Divina—the Sacred Art: Transforming Words and Images into the Heart-Centered Prayer*, applies the Lectio Divina process to a variety of sacred texts. She explains the Haggadah, Judaism's method of studying and memorizing Scripture that was a part of the life of Jesus and his followers.

Although, the traditional, expressed purpose of Lectio Divina is to draw closer to the Divine, my personal and original intent was a writing exercise based in Scripture. Had I known in advance the difficulty of the task and the number of years involved, I might never have begun. Finishing what I start does matter, and the exercise is rewarding on so many levels.

My commentaries are meant to demonstrate the results of staying with the practice of reading, reflecting, and responding to the words in the holy books of your choice. This introduction is about the process of honoring my own inspiration and following it through. If you seek guidance to do what I did, then I direct you to books and studies using the Lectio Divina method.

Legal Fair Use

During year three, I contacted the Catholic Publishing Company, New York, NY, and was referred to the Confraternity of Christian Doctrine, regarding copyright for *THE NEW AMERICAN BIBLE*, 1970.

In the initial email from the Associate Director, Permissions and Bible Utilization, I was informed that "If your proposed work uses more than 5,000 words from the NAB (New American Bible) or if the NAB quotes are more than 40% of your book, we need to review the manuscript before permission may be granted. Such permission should be requested once you have identified a publisher for this work.

"Please note," she continued, "that all citations must be verbatim and follow the capitalization of the original printed text. The verse structure of petic text must be retained. Permission is no longer granted for the 1970 New Testament."

My estimates followed: "I expect my Scripture passages will average 25 words x 365 daily entries to equal about 9,000 words. My commentary will average 300 words per page, or 300 x 365, about 109,500 words. I chose this edition because I could cross-reference the dates.

Email response: "Since you use more than 5,000 words from NAB, permission will be required. We need to review the pages of your manuscript that include the NAB text. In addition, there will be a permissions fee. That fee is based on the print run and list price of your book.

"The 1970 NAB New Testament is still under copyright, so permission would still be required for its use. However, we no longer grant that permission. Instead, we require that authors and others use the superior 1986 New Testament translation."

Six months later, having completed the computer entry and a first edit, I sent my manuscript as an attachment to the Confraternity of Christian Doctrine (CCD). In two weeks, the review came back with nearly every scripture entry red-lined. New Testament words were changed to the 1986 edition of the NAB. After careful count, the words in the scripture passages represented 9.4 percent of my manuscript. Changing the wording to the 1986 edition of NAB would destroy my continuity, my commentary. Finally, I asked "Can we agree on what constitutes legal fair use determination"

Final email: "The NAB's gratis use limit is 5,000 words. Your work exceeds that limit. The limit looks at the whole Bible, both Old and New Testaments. The approved policy requires a permissions fee beyond this limit. These points were made in my November correspondence." (May 27, 2014)

I took great pains to reduce my word count for scripture quotes from *The New American Bible, St. Joseph Edition*, 1970, to just below 5,000 words. The quotes are brief, and I encourage readers to go to their Bibles and read on. As a result of this process I am enlightened and grateful.

Book Title

The working title for this project was *The Day Book.* I went from the working title to several other attempts to be original. My next choice was *Out of Context,* until I put the words into my Kindle search and found several books with that in the title.

I really liked *Out of Context* because; every word we read, hear or write is taken out of its original context and becomes integrated with other thoughts or words to become our own personal creation. Every thought is recycled or released back into the wild. Every word or thought I express in writing is coming out of my individual context and released into the wild – so that you – my readers may integrate my thoughts into your individual humanness – or release those thoughts into the wild. Thoughts are energy. All we think, see or do is energy. In my concept of energy there is but one source. That source, I choose to call God. But, whomever or whatever you believe is the source of all energy, I honor that.

I looked at titles around the Lectio Divina method of reading, reflecting, responding and rest. My conclusion was the title I chose for the cover of this book: *Read. Reflect. Respond. Rest: 366 Daily Reflections on Random Selections from Scripture.*

My Amen!

The Bible, Old and New Testaments combined, is often referred to as the "Word of God." Not, the "words" of God. I take that to mean the "Spirit" of the entire collection of words. Those words have been translated and re-translated over and over again, in an attempt to find the most relevant meaning for the current times. The words are translated into different languages – without changing the Spirit of the words that express the relationship of humans to the God of their understanding at the time the words were first put in place – cast in stone, or written on paper.

My purpose in starting this project four years ago was a spiritual, not religious, reading and writing exercise. I believe that the "kingdom of God is within." And, I believe that kingdom is within every human being. The deeper we go (reflect) into our own kingdom (spirit), the better we will be able to recognize that kingdom (spirit) in everyone we meet. Seek, and you will find the questions you need to ask yourself – and sometimes, answers.

What is time?
—The shadow on the dial, the striking of the clock,
the running of the sand, day and night,
summer and winter, months, years, centuries
—these are but arbitrary and outward signs
—the measure of time, not time itself.
Time is the life of the soul.

– Henry Wadsworth Longfellow -1807-1882

Quote from *The New Dictionary of Thoughts,* Standard Book Company, 1959, Brown and Bigelow, Saint Paul, Minnesota, page 675.

January

❧

Janus
Roman god of doors,
beginnings,
sunset and sunrise.
One face looking forward,
one looking backward.

January 1

In the beginning. – Genesis 1:1

Right there, the discussion and the disagreement, and the diversity start. The people and the nations of planet Earth, by someone's definition, cannot agree about how, when, where and by what force it all began.

Sensible, intelligent people have difficulty understanding how it could have all been accomplished in the allotted Biblical time of – just short of seven days. No wonder that the "literal or allegorical" creator of the entire universe – not just the Earth planet – felt the need to rest.

My question is, "Why does such an all-powerful being or force feel a need to rest? Are we to assume this force of nature somehow found the creation process tiresome?"

Today is the first day of a new year, for us, the western part of the planet. For the Asian people the New Year comes later – and has unusual names that vary by some other calculation than our western calendar. Strange names for years, such as The Year of the Dragon, or The Year of the Turkey, or The Year of the Rabbit mark the Asian calendar.

Then again, the people who put together the Hebrew Bible have their own calendar. Sometimes Hanukkah and Christmas fall on the same day. The Druids no doubt had another idea about the first day of a new year.

So, we use whatever gives us humans a sense of purpose, knowing and direction; serves our needs, answers our questions, and establishes our right to exist on this planet called Earth. If it works for you, use it.

January 2

There is an appointed time for everything. – Ecclesiastes 3:1

The man at the gas station said, "If everyone would start their day 10 minutes earlier they wouldn't be in such a hurry." Why are we always so busy? We wear our busyness like a badge of honor.

The old saying goes, "If you want to get something done, ask a busy person." But, sometimes that's the only way the busy person can say "no" when asked to take on another commitment.

Just say, "I'm busy." And usually, we are – busy already.

When we were kids there seemed to be plenty of down time, plenty of play time. But, as we age, take on jobs and family responsibilities – we get very busy. Then, into retirement we are challenged once again by down time, play time.

We are fortunate to spend our winters in Mexico. Not only do we enjoy the warm weather and get away from the hustle and bustle of all our trappings stateside, but we also adopt the mañana mentality.

Our neighbor in Mexico, when asked what he does here, says, "I don't know, but it takes all day to do it."

There may be an appointed time for everything – however, sometimes we simply miss those appointments.

January 3

An unremitting war was waged. – 1 Samuel 14:52

It hardly makes a difference about who started or who finished the war – the point is the never relaxing, never letting up, never slackening, and increasing and continuous nature of Samuel's war against the Philistines.

A man's entire life and legacy was measured by an endless war. And, if that particular part of ancient history was written by the Philistines – we would be hearing a different story, about a different set of heroes. I don't understand. I never will understand – Why war?

My entire lifetime, my entire generation, has known war, major war – primarily fought in other countries – on land, on sea, and in the air. And we ask, too late, why?

I've long been a supporter of a peace academy – a place to study conflict resolution, and how to make it work. How can Switzerland exist in a constant state of neutrality? Why can't that work for other countries – all countries? Doesn't anyone get tired of territorial or ideological conflict and killing?

Tolerance is much more than putting up with someone's snoring at night – it is that internal struggle to live in peace with people where our differences overshadow our similarities.

I once saw a bumper sticker that spoke volumes.

Peace is Possible. Amen!

January 4

Turning your ear to wisdom, inclining your heart to understanding; – Proverbs 2:2

I opened and closed the Bible several times before I found something to trigger my thoughts. I'm looking for a way to continue these daily mental exercises. My goal is to write 366 daily thoughts – one day at a time. At the end of this current year I will assess and edit.

Not forging ahead and not falling behind is my only guideline. I'm using phrases from the Bible. I am trying to have meaningful dialogue with you, who read what I am writing. I can't totally cut God out of the deal, because, I am a "believer."

I believe in something greater than myself, and I am not quite sure what that means. I only know that I use the Bible because it is the most historically reliable and available resource. The books of the old and new testaments have been studied, interpreted and misinterpreted to death.

In my vocabulary, "wisdom" is something and someone greater than me. I can't invent wisdom, or create wisdom. It's there, but I don't always recognize wisdom at first glance. My ear, my inner ear or still, small voice turns toward wisdom, and I am listening.

Somehow, the inner ear, the inner voice of the spirit, the soul, moves the heart and mind to understand.

January 5

Every day is miserable for the depressed, but a lighthearted man has a continual feast. – Proverbs 15:15

We all know about the yellow smiley faces that we use on the closing of our emails. The modern version was introduced by commercial artist Harvey Ball in 1963. Not unique, but uniquely presented.

Smile! Haven't we all doodled smiles from preschool into adulthood? Seeing a smile makes us smile, whether it's a drawing or on a human face of someone we love, or a stranger on the street.

Behind our protective masks we may want to be recognized, cared about, and loved. We joke to get a rise out of someone wearing a somber face. Stand-up comics fill rooms with people who dare them to "Make me laugh. Say something funny. Help me change my mood."

Sometimes our hearts are breaking and we want someone to help us laugh, to get over and get on with life the way we want it to be. Sometimes our neighbor or loved one is in pain, and all we have to offer is a smile and a glad or hopeful word.

A smile uses fewer face muscles and is uplifting for the face as well as our hearts, and the hearts of others.

January 6

As for the classes of gatekeepers, – 1 Chronicles 26:1

The implication in the introduction to this book of the Old Testament indicates that it is "less concerned with reporting in precise detail the facts of a situation than with explaining the meaning of the facts." This sounds a good deal like how we gather and report our news today.

No longer do we receive objective fact, but rather "interpretative" commentary. Gatekeeper in this particular passage has to do with the families assigned with guarding the gates into the temple area. Where there are gates, there are people coming in and going out – and walls.

Now, why are the Pearly Gates assigned to St. Peter for the purpose of preventing people from entering – by selection of the fittest? And, we seldom hear of the gate swinging in both directions. Either souls can't get back out or they don't want to return to this place called Earth. Except when Clarence gets his angel wings in the movie "It's a Wonderful Life."

Gatekeepers are everywhere: checking us out at airports and checking us out at grocery stores. As part of an orderly universe we need gatekeepers, and guards. We need to keep some people in and others out – for whatever reason suits our purpose.

Unlike walls at least gates allow us options.

I ask myself if I have a gate or a wall around me. Am I accessible or am I selective?

January 7

Is not man's life on earth drudgery? – Job 7:1

My poor old friend Job – he's always thinking about himself. What about woman's life on Earth? If you don't think nine months of getting ready to go into hard labor and delivery of a baby is drudgery, then you are probably a man.

Sure, nine to five jobs, with only an hour for lunch may be drudgery. But, I'll match you with 24-7 for the rest of a child's life. We women never retire from parenting – it's in the blood, in the bones, in the heart, and in the umbilical cord.

So, the race is on, who has the short end of the stick. Who drew the short straw? And really, does anyone care? Let's not get into the chicken and the egg thing, or the indoor versus outdoor human plumbing hazards or conveniences. We are what we are. It's the way the genetics crumble. Most of us accept who and what we are genetically – or pay the price and the pain for the physical changes.

Speaking of changes – what about that not often enough discussed "change of life" for men, as well as women?

Yes, life on Earth is drudgery. But, what else do we have to do if we weren't here, doing this – playing the cards we've been dealt.

January 8

And when your time comes and you rest with your ancestors. – 2 Samuel 7:12

God assures David that his lineage is secure no matter what, no matter his own death. Do we wonder about our children, our children's children, and on and on?

Of course we do.

Whether pregnancies are planned or accidental, we hope for the best for our children. Whether our children are natural off spring or adopted, we want the best for them, even better than what we received. All that we hope for is out of our control, as each follows his or her own path in life.

Today, January 8, would be my mother's birthday had she not died in 1996. All we have left when our loved one's die is the memory, the photographs, the image in the mirror.

When I look in the mirror I see my mother – her features and evidence of my aging. The breath I breathe is a continuation of my mother's life. I am her gift to me.

When I breathe my last breath I know that my eight children have passed along that life and spirit to their children. And their children will be doing the same.

Ancestors came before us, and someday we will become ancestors. That is life as we have come to know it.

January 9

Everyone who enters the registered group must pay a half-shekel... The rich need not give more, nor shall the poor give less, than a half-shekel. – Exodus 30:13-15

In the days of Moses, the religious law ruled, and those who spoke for the Lord levied the census tax and made the laws. Many places in the world still mix the rules and customs of dominant religions into the laws of governing diverse populations.

The founding framers of the Constitution of the United States of America went to great lengths to separate the influence of specific organized religions from the laws that govern our country. By trying to simplify the law they also left it open to formation, implementation and interpretation by the three branches of government. There is nothing simple about the U.S. Constitution.

There is nothing simple about the "registering" of "citizens" or the levying of taxes. There is nothing simple about anything anymore. Life in the civilized modern world is very complex.

I subscribe to Henry David Thoreau's philosophy of "Simplify. Simplify. Simplify." I try to get by on less of everything, including money.

I developed a budget, a system, and discovered peace of mind in the process. If I needed shopping therapy, I left the tabs on clothes, hung them in the closet and a week later, could, if I chose; go through the painful task of returning merchandise to the store.

January 10

The prophet is a fool, the man of spirit is mad! – Hosea 9:7

Who declares a man, or a woman, a prophet? During the lifetime of a person who speaks prophetically – about the future – we are told to be aware, alert to falsehood.

Like beauty, which is in the eye of the beholder, does our belief about what a person says depend on our belief or suspended belief – our faith? How do we know, with certainty that someone speaks the truth? The history books – Bible included – speak volumes from those who in their own times were visionaries, prophets. Step out of line and you may be the next fool, or the next prophet.

Most visionaries were considered "mad" at one time or another. From Thomas Edison to Steve Jobs, and many before, during and after their times, were, and will be considered different, odd, or strange because they saw the world and things as more than they were – beyond imagination.

The "mad scientist," strikes us as a harsh judgment, because we can't see into their future. We couldn't have seen into the future of a Christopher Columbus, or Jonas Salk. These visionaries saw what we could not see, went where we could not have gone. We each are born with a dream and a longing in our heart and in our souls. To each, his or her own path.

January 11

He has sent me to bring glad tidings to the lowly,
to heal the broken hearted. – Isaiah 61:1

The books of the Bible are filled with the ups and downs of generations. They frequently are in the business of rescuing and restoring. Nothing ever runs smoothly forever.

Are we in the best of times or the worst of times? It never will be perfect times. Based on percentages – are we living in the top or bottom portion of good or bad times? On a scale of one to ten, how are we doing?

The constant polling of the public in the United States attempts to get a feel for how people think, and how they spend their money.

What are the glad tidings that Isaiah is bringing to the lowly; to rebuild a society that is broken, to heal the broken hearted?

Times are always tough for some, and better for others. When you claim to be the "Chosen" people then you have greater expectations about the future. The lowly and broken hearted may not feel they are chosen for better, even great happenings in their lives.

Are they lowly and brokenhearted by their own or some-one else's declaration?

January 12

Wearisome comforters are you all! Is there no end to windy words? – Job 16:3

Blah, blah, blah – don't tell me what I already know. Hearing what you have to say makes me feel worse. I know I have to solve my own problems. I appreciate your concern, sharing your experience of how you overcame a similar problem, but you can't possibly know what I am going through. You can't feel my pain – no matter how you try.

Poor Job, he can't stand the attention of his friends. They can't possibly understand his difficulties.

When I first read Job, looking for answers, about 50 years ago, I identified with his pain. My friend! I could wallow in my self-pity as long as I wanted. The only way out was to let the sun shine in. It was all a matter of re-thinking.

Like the "Little Engine That Could;" I had to change my point of view. I had to flatten out the hill or mountain in front of me. Make it a smooth highway, a slick, straight track for my engine.

I Can! Take the "t" off the end of the word "can't."

Turning the other cheek can mean seeing the future as brighter rather than gloomy. Tolerance serves us well as the "capacity to withstand pain and hardship."

Tolerance also asks us to recognize and respect the opinions, beliefs or actions of others. Granted, they can't feel our pain but they care.

January 13

I am my father's only daughter and he has no other child to make his heir. – Tobit 3:15

Sarah, daughter of Raguel, would have hung herself and died, but considered it to be an insult against her father. Instead she pleaded with God to have her die.

How sad, a woman who produced no children was considered useless. At least she considered herself a failure in the business of leaving an heir for her father.

How far have we come from that sort of thinking?

I was the survivor in my family. There were no McDonald males left to carry on the family name. The long, fine line of Scots would end with me.

When my first marriage failed, I took my "maiden" name back, and so it will be until I die. My eldest son has McDonald as his middle name, and passed that on to his son. Will it end there? I haven't a clue. It's a fine old name, but we are more than our names. We are more than our heritage.

We are unique individuals, with body, heart and soul. Although we are part of a long chain of other humans – we are bound to set out on our own path – to be all we can be here and now.

January 14

Render to everyone according to his conduct, for you alone know the hearts of men. – 2 Chronicles 6:30

Solomon's prayer at the dedication of the temple in Jerusalem speaks of many things that speak to us – both in and out of context. He places the responsibility – out of our hands – to judge the conduct of others.

So, are we to give up our favorite pastime – judging and criticizing others? Must we now look to ourselves only regarding conduct? How unfair is that – wouldn't I rather look for the speck in your eye than in mine?

On the other hand, Solomon may be giving us permission to judiciously and lawfully render decisions regarding the conduct of those who go against the laws and decrees set down by the ruling or legislative branches of government. Orderly conduct is expected in an orderly society.

Lady Justice is usually blindfolded because she is supposed to be blind to all those elements that have no bearing on the judgment of an individual's actions. Nor, can she know what is in the hearts of men, with certainty.

Judgments at all levels leave us wondering if we know all there is to know. Judges and juries have the burden of proving to themselves beyond reasonable doubt the guilt or innocence of people who come before them.

We can only try our best to know the hearts of men. We can only try.

Only God knows!

January 15

Even though you cannot curse them... at least do not bless them. – Numbers 23:25

This one makes me laugh. So much of the Bible speaks of prayers and curses and blessings and conflict and revenge. And, who gets the credit or the blame – God, of course.

If you are going to bring a curse upon someone, then at least have the dignity and honesty to admit to what you are doing. Blessings can be more private because we don't need to take credit for blessings that come to another person. Just be happy for them in their good news.

Being a coward by wishing others an ill fate is beneath us. Taking credit for someone else's blessings is above us, beyond our powers. We want good things for those we care about. What small effort does it take to want good things to happen for everyone? We don't know what that good may be, but we are capable of wishing everyone good in their lives.

In the end, there will be little difference between cursing someone and asking God to deny them blessings. What kind of God wants to do our dirty work?

What kind of person are we if we seek to deny others blessings – or curse them?

That doesn't seem to be what prayers are for.

January 16

Be firm and steadfast. Do not fear nor be dismayed. –Joshua 1:9

Moses never reached the Promised Land, but his son Joshua did – and there, he fought the battle of Jericho.

Sometimes we set goals for ourselves, prepare the way, but are unable to realize the achievement of those goals. But, if the goals are worthy then someone else will see them through.

These passages teach us the importance of letting go, when the time comes. It teaches us that the power is often in the journey itself, and not in the destination. Goals are important, but everything that happens on the way to a goal is also important.

We sometimes forget to enjoy and appreciate every day that we move closer to our goal – our promised land. Whatever that may be?

Identifying a goal often causes us more of a headache than the speed bumps on the way. I meet people who tell me they want to write a book. They know they have a great story to tell. Yes, as a matter of fact, I believe everyone has a great story to tell.

My happiest times as a reporter, a journalist, was helping people tell their stories, providing the unknown with recognition.

January 17

Terribly and swiftly shall he come against you because judgment is stern for the exalted – for the lowly may be pardoned out of mercy. – Wisdom 6:5-6

The more educated, the wealthier, the more privileged we are, then the more we have to give to each other. The only real rule is whatever the conscience demands.

I can't tell anyone else how much to give, how much of their wealth to share. Everything looks different when viewing from outside. Thinking our neighbor should be giving more back to our society borders on envy. Each of us has a pool of resources and each of us is responsible for managing those resources.

While raising my eight children they often referred to what someone else had, hinting that they should have the same. We learned to negotiate their needs and wants.

Rich people, powerful people, don't rob banks – but they may have other issues to deal with – such as greed, and cheating on income tax. There may be different judgments for the exalted, the powerful, and the wealthy.

What we do with what we have or have been given is between the individual and his conscience.

If power corrupts then the powerful are responsible for that corruption. However, that doesn't necessarily mean that the poor are totally responsible for their poverty.

January 18

Adorn yourself with grandeur and majesty, and array yourself with glory and splendor. –Job 40:10

Like Job, we spend far too much time dwelling on our pain and troubles. But the dawn of a new day brings hope for a brighter future. We put on the cloak of joy, of dignity.

Being grateful for who we are and for what we have is putting on a garment of glory and splendor. It's so much easier to stay in our gloom and doom. It takes real effort to feel good about ourselves.

Once a year the movie "It's a Wonderful Life" shows up on television. Every year I can watch that movie and feel good. When our character comes out of his deep depression he realizes how much he has in his family and friends. He is saved from the depths of despair by a "would-be" angel.

There are many angels in our lives to remind us of how important we are to them. Even on a cloudy day, the sun shines, although hidden. We believe in sunshine.

We have hope. We pray. We reach deep into our souls for the glory and the splendor. We all are children of the same God. Our dignity and majesty abounds.

January 19

I am confident and unafraid. – Isaiah 12:2

Confidence and self-confidence are two different qualities in our human experience. Self confidence says "I" can do this. Confidence says "we" can do this. When we have some concept of a power greater than ourselves – whether as a member of a group or with a God as a spiritual teammate – we know someone, something, has our back.

Even in the darkest corner of my mind, I know I am not there alone. Every step forward signals a new experience. Fear freezes us in motion. With the confidence that comes from knowing we are not alone comes the ability to move forward – unafraid.

Though fear may overshadow us, we are secure in a faith that we are not alone. We may have to feel the fear – and move forward anyway. Staying in an uncomfortable place means nothing changes.

Action moves us out of our fear. Taking the most logical next step, or doing nothing, both represent action. One is forward movement and the other is simply a delay of action.

Nothing changes until something changes. We can face life like a deer in the headlights of an oncoming car – or we can take control of a situation by doing what human beings are capable of doing – move to one side or the other to avoid annihilation.

January 20

Moreover, one goat shall be offered as a sin offering in atonement for yourselves. – Numbers 29:5

According to the preface, The Book of Numbers is a combination of law and history. Reading the passages makes me wonder if it was written by the lawmakers or bookkeepers during the 38-year journey from Sinai to Jericho.

This is a census report of the Twelve Tribes that crossed the desert. Of the descendants of Simeon alone – one tribe – "all the males of twenty years or more who were fit for military service were polled – 59 thousand three hundred were enrolled."

The total number of males fit for military service over the age of 20 – omitting the Tribe of Levi, for they had other duties – amounted to 603,550.

What an incredible task, to move that number of people, plus all the women and children, and animals – across the barren desert. Granted, many of the nations and peoples of those times were primarily nomadic, wandering tribes to begin with.

How did Moses keep all those people under control? First, they all were convinced their leader spoke for God. If they did what they were told to do they would survive the journey – or die in peace.

There were laws in the Garden of Eden. There were laws – in abundance – for hundreds of thousands of the people crossing the desert. How can we possibly expect to be totally free of binding and protective law?

January 21

For gracious and merciful is he, slow to anger, rich in kindness, and relenting in punishment. – Joel 2:13

Probably one of the shortest books of the Hebrew Bible, Joel predicts the coming of the Lord – or the end of times as he knows it. Bringing his people to repentance through fasting and weeping and mourning – Joel gives us a new vision of who God is.

We have, now, a God of mercy and kindness. The God who helps people win wars over their enemies is temporarily set aside for this God who is "slow to anger and relenting in punishment."

In assigning these qualities to God, we can only assume we are meant to imitate the graciousness, kindness and serenity that appear to be the hallmark of God.

So often, in reading the Old Testament we see an angry and vengeful God. This God of Joel, I like. Here is a God capable of loving me and caring for me in the manner to which I choose to become accustomed.

No longer a God to fear and hide from, but someone we can call our friend. Here is someone who knows all about us – our deepest secrets – and loves us unconditionally.

What a relief to be free of the chains that bind us and separate us from our one true source of comfort – our one true source of love.

January 22

She stealthily approached him and drove the tent peg through his temple down into the ground, so that he perished in death. – Judges 4:21

The judges of this era were not magistrates, but military leaders. The woman whose actions are described above was Jael, wife of Heber. The man she did in thought he was entering the tent of his friend, but to his demise found out otherwise.

So much of the Old Testament describes the battles fought among friends as well as neighbors and enemies. Are we to assume from these books that the Israelites were the only tribes with a God on their side, since we have no other writings to compare with their accounts?

So Jael knew she was doing the military leader Barak a favor by getting rid of an enemy – even though, not really her enemy. Certainly a woman to be reckoned with, capable of pulling the wool, or the rug, over the eyes of Sisera, who thought he was in a place of refuge, and fell asleep.

The woman actually went out to meet him, and lured him into her tent, "Come in, my lord, come in with me, and do not be afraid."

Who would have thought a woman would be capable of such a violent act. He slept while she got a tent peg and took a mallet in her hand and pinned his head to the ground.

January 23

Gray hair is a crown of glory; it is gained by virtuous living. – Proverbs 16:31

My hair is white by virtue of the number of years I have lived – and the fact that my mother had white hair by the time she was my age.

I was raised to respect my elders – now I am one of those elders. What kind of respect do I expect? I don't want anyone to do for me what I can still do for myself.

I don't expect people to expect me to solve their problems for them. When I was young it was "speak when you are spoken to." That didn't mean to "talk back," as in being disrespectful.

I don't want to give advice unless I am asked. Sometimes I give it, thinking I heard a request somewhere in the conversation.

I'm old enough to know what I don't know – or maybe forgot. And that sometimes causes some sadness. Knowing that my mind is not as quick as it used to be – that I can't always find the word I'm looking for in my mental filing cabinet – is cause for concern.

Being true to who I am and who I want to be is ever challenging. Sometimes no one really wants to hear what I have to say. That's when I pray for the wisdom to keep my mouth shut.

January 24

Sorrow is better than laughter, because when the face is sad the heart grows wiser – Ecclesiastes 7:3

The prelude to this book describes life as "an enigma beyond human ability to solve." We are constantly weighing and deciding right or wrong, true or false, dark or light, thick or thin, heavy or weightless. Contrasts and compromises? We are told that our best guess at any twist or turn of events is simply our best guess.

So many people claim to know the answers to life's problems and pop quizzes. They can't all be correct. I suppose we are most content or happy when we believe in our ability to make correct choices – the best automobile, the best house, the best neighborhood the best job, the best school, the best career, the best investments.

The passage we quote today tells us that there is nothing wrong with laughing and being happy, even though we may learn more from the more serious events. There is something about being down rather than up that forces us to think deeply.

Perhaps the sadness we seek is a compassionate and caring attitude and emotion that helps us identify more closely with our friends, relatives and distant fellow man.

Sometimes deep thinking hurts the head, but it apparently teaches the heart, and feeds the hearts hunger.

January 25

How long, O LORD? Will you hide yourself forever? Remember how short my life is; how frail you created all the children of men! – Psalms 89:47-48

We are born seeking – we know not what. St. Augustine said, "The heart is restless until it rests in you O Lord." We may never reach that place of rest in this life. Without hunger we would not eat.

We are born with a curiosity, a desire, and emptiness. The needs of the soul are ever present. We venture up and down many paths. Our careers and talents take us to places, sometimes – where no one has ventured before.

The human experience is a human adventure. The poorest and the wealthiest can all seek the splendor of a contented wanderer who comes to an oasis in the desert. The dry, parched soul thirsts and quenches that thirst.

The writer must write, the builder must build, the leader must lead, the healer must heal, the preacher must preach and the teacher must teach.

Often, we are many seekers – either at different times or all at once.

A pause in our seeking may give that which we seek an opportunity to catch up with us.

January 26

How wise you were when you were young, overflowing with instruction, like the Nile in a flood! – Sirach 47:14

This is meant to be a complement to Solomon, who, with God's help, ruled in an era of peace and secure borders. It must have been easier to be wise when times were less stressful, during a time of peace – no wars.

How often do we, and do our leaders, create unnecessary stress. War and the threat of wars keep everyone on their toes and at the ready.

The parallel might be that youth has fewer worries or concerns, and can make sweeping pronouncements without the accompanying consequences. In our youth we think ourselves wise, and bullet proof, at least for appearance sake.

We join the debating team in college and tell the audience how it can or should be done, offering sufficient proof. Hopefully, our youth will work with words and not get physical in making their point.

Then again, it is the youth we send to war, to fight the battles our elder statesmen determine need to be fought.

We may have been overflowing with instruction in our youth, but how often sidetracked or discouraged from seeing our dreams fulfilled.

We all are capable of wise thinking, but how wise are our actions?

January 27

They refused to obey and no longer remembered the miracles you had worked for them. – Nehemiah 9:17

When life is going well we forget what got us here. We tend to think we did it all on our own, that we are self-made men or woman. We forget those dark nights when we couldn't sleep and we prayed for God to answer our prayers.

When we were children, our mothers sent us off to school. They told us to look to the left and then to the right before we crossed the street. We did what we were told because we believed our mothers cared about our safety, and we felt responsible.

God's direction and approval is less obvious. The subtle prodding, guiding and satisfaction come to us without shouts and flashes of light. But, these miracles, large and small, do come to us. The daily miracle of waking up and standing on our own two feet escapes our attention.

Obey God and do good, my mother said. My mother had many wise sayings that I took to heart. When I got out of line she had me sit in front of a poster she put on the wall. It was something about how a good child behaves, some kind of commandments for children.

And, I haven't a clue, now, as to what they were. But they helped me be a better child according to my mother.

January 28

Let everything that has breath praise the LORD! Alleluia. – Psalms 150:6

Every living thing? We know what that means. We watch the seeds we plant grow and blossom, and provide us with beauty and nourishment. We watch small animals grow and provide us with companionship, transportation in the fields, and nourishment for our bodies.

None of those living things ask how they can praise God. They know. It's in their genes, their DNA. We humans are the only breathing things that question – not only how to praise – but most often ask why we should. Our free will offers proof that we have decision making mechanisms that can often steer us in the wrong direction. Our acts of praise are just as deliberate as our acts of rebellion or meanness.

Making a decision can take an instant or a lifetime – depending on our willingness to acknowledge something greater than ourselves directing and guiding our decisions. Those decisions – whether they come early or late in life – have their "ah ha!" qualities.

Praise comes without much fanfare. It comes when we know we are being, acting and speaking the way we know we are meant to do.

Our actions always speak louder than our words. We praise God by doing God's bidding and God's work. Alleluia!

January 29

May the humble not retire in confusion. – Psalms 74:21

Don't give up your ideas and your ideals because others have convinced you they have the only correct answers or solutions.

The problem with the meek or the humble is that their faith wavers in the presence of power. Are we so humbled by life that we give up and give in too soon? It takes a tremendous amount of courage to go against trends and the charismatic leaders. You can only defer so long to others, and then you begin to waver and wither in your resolve.

It can happen to anyone, on any side of an issue. Everyone believes they are being true to who they are and what they believe. Who can shout the loudest and get the most media attention? Who has written a book proclaiming their truth? Be brave. Be true to yourself. There are no guarantees we will be on the right side of the argument or the outcome – but we must stay true to ourselves.

Principles, although good, may be at odds with each other. Step back from the edge and give it time. Rest does not mean permanent retirement.

Everyone gets confused when they are bombarded with arguments or negative information. Pause, pray, meditate – and know yourself well enough to act or not act, to speak or not speak.

Sometimes giving up a fight is the more correct action.

January 30

With string music before the altar, providing sweet melody for psalms, – Sirach 47:9

I tried to learn piano as a child, but the teacher made life miserable for me. I couldn't arch my little fingers to suit her, and could not reach the keys when I tried. We didn't have a piano at home, so I could only practice at the neighbor's house, and occasionally at school.

Some learning is too difficult, and not meant to be. No matter how much I wanted to learn to play the piano, I didn't have the talent or the drive to make music. I acted in plays and sang in the chorus for musicals all the way through grade school and high school. I could follow the notes on the page and blend in with the others by following directions. I had a good time participating in making music.

The same thing happened with learning a language, or the chemical symbols chart, or my times tables, or free-hand drawing. There are some things I do better than others. Some, not so good. I am a great admirer of music makers of all kinds. I appreciate what the talented people can accomplish. That is my lot in life – to appreciate the sweet melody of the psalms. I particularly like string music. I weep when the violin notes pull on my heart strings.

We each have our own talents, and music in our hearts and souls. We do what we can with what we have been given. I hope my words on paper find their own melody and sing my songs.

January 31

And for your own sake, O Lord, let your face shine upon your desolate sanctuary. – Daniel 9:17

I'm not sure I feel secure enough to address God by saying, "for your own sake." It seems quite presumptuous to think I would know what God needs. In this passage it seems to have something to do with keeping the temple intact.

Buildings for worship are important to demonstrate our faith and have a place to gather for worship – but, I believe these beautiful buildings are more for showing God and our friends and family what we can do in God's name.

How can we possibly know what the creator of the universe wants or needs? We remember what happened to the people of God when they built the Tower of Babel in their attempt to reach him. We have been forever since divided by language. And the glorious temple of Jerusalem – subject to destruction by the enemy of the people of God – why wouldn't a God of their understanding save his own place of worship from destruction?

Our expectations of a God are of our own making. God's face shines on the lowly as well as the mighty. Haven't we seen enough history to know that God doesn't take sides in a war or in a football game, or in a crap shoot?

So much of what happens in this life is just dumb luck or lack thereof.

February

Februare,
Latin, to purify.
On February 15
Romans celebrated
Festival of Forgiveness for Sins.

February 1

I will restore you to health. – Jeremiah 30:17

Promises! God is always making promises. And, beseeching! Man is always beseeching.

Please, make life better for me. Heal me. Feed me. Clothe me. How does God respond? Subtly!

The means to feed and clothe ourselves will present themselves. The means for healing ourselves is often right under our noses. It's called a mouth.

Whatever we put into our mouths finds its way throughout our body. Depending upon the quantity and quality of what enters our mouths – determines the benefit to all our organs and systems. There is only one logical way for nourishment to enter our bodies – through the oral cavity.

But, what does the mouth want? It wants whatever it decides tastes good. Sweet or salty – a little goes a long way. Much of our illness and discomfort can be traced back to what and how much we ate or drank.

And, what comes out of our mouths? That's another story about what we can say to make us and others wish we were kinder regarding what we regurgitate. The mouth is a marvelous channel to allow nourishment to enter and to expel wisdom, loving words, kindness, information, song, and helpfulness.

One of my teachers once told the class that the tongue can be a vicious weapon. That is why we have teeth and lips to stop it from doing harm.

February 2

For the wicked man glories in his greed. – Psalms 10:3

Ouch! Is there no middle road? Must we be either greedy or covetous? It's not a matter of the have or the have not, but rather, I have it and you don't – or you have it and I want it. Whatever "it" is.

Those who have plenty can live comfortably without considering the lowly. The lowly can't live comfortably because they have to be concerned about the basics. Those who have just enough of everything they need are probably more likely to be willing to share with the less fortunate than those who have plenty and overflowing.

Greed is such an awful judgment. It's a matter of conscience. How much is enough and how much is too much? Thieves are born out of need and want. There is little or no virtue in trying to take what rightfully belongs to others. Those who lack the basics in life are more likely to curse God and a fellow man for the lack of fairness in the universe.

The greedy enjoy their riches and sometimes share their wealth. Only the wealthy can say "How great I am." The poor want something better and they can say, "Poor me."

How much is enough? Neither the rich nor the poor know the answer to that question.

February 3

Pleasing words are a honey-comb. – Proverbs 16:24

I received an email today with words in the subject line that were politically offensive and I was going to dump it in SPAM. It was from a person I know and thought again about reading the message. The email surprisingly went into detail to explain the facts behind the subject line, and I found it interesting.

So, instead of dumping the message I read it, and responded, "Great information. Thanks."

I imagine the sender was scratching his head wondering why I thought it was good information. I'm sure my response was puzzling rather than pleasing.

Sometimes people mean to hurt us, or shake us up, or try to influence us with some shocking information – something much less than pleasing. I've worked with words all my life and know how much power is in the printed and spoken word.

We love to hear pleasing words from our loved ones. I finally learned how to accept a compliment.

We love to have people agree with us. How sweet it is to have kind words in our ears, and also dripping off our tongues.

The words of the poet are most often pleasing – but sometimes the poet's truth can cut deep and hurt our conscience.

February 4

A wise son makes his father glad, but a foolish son is a grief to his mother. – Proverbs 10:1

Once again, the value of sons is defined but the value of daughters is ignored. What is a wise son? One, who pleases his father, does what is expected of him, stays out of trouble, and brings blessings upon the house of his parents, probably with a good and productive wife and male children.

The foolish son is probably the one who does not follow the instructions, expectations and career choices of the father. The mother of the wise son appears to have no credit for that son, but suffers some kind of guilt or responsibility for the actions of the foolish son.

Where is the fairness here? Father's get all the credit for the efforts of the sons who succeed in school, in sports, in business, and with career and family. However, the mother bears the brunt of the wayward son who messes up in school, on the farm and, in general, in life.

The Bible tells us that the sins of the father should not be visited upon the son – and yet the sins or shortcomings of the son are visited upon the mother. The father apparently has rejected the unwise son and leaves him to the care of his mother.

Once again, women seem to be short changed in the area of credit for having good children, or forgiven for having children who don't quite measure up to the expectations of their fathers.

February 5

There is a group that is pure in its own eyes. – Proverbs 30:12

These people are described as proud. Not me, of course. I have never given the impression that I am one of those referred to in this proverb.

Basically, Proverbs leaves no one untouched, no one unscathed by its words. None among us can claim to be so pure that there isn't something lurking or hiding in our closet.

There was a song sung at the church service this morning, "How Great Thou Art." It's not about how great I am. Few of us can say, how great I am, or, what great things I have done. On a scale from one to ten, where are we? With pure on one end of the scale and filth at the other end, most of us register somewhere in the center. Hopefully, we are more balanced than the Proverb spells out.

Can we take much credit for our purity of heart and soul, our accomplishments and power? Now it becomes a scale with honesty at one end and illusion on the other. There will always be someone less than me, and someone greater than me.

I bow my head in humility, and must admit – I am not much better or much worse than the majority of people.

However, I try to be the best me I know how to be.

February 6

Lo, I will send you Elijah, the prophet. – Malachi 3:23

Amen! Come, Lord Jesus! – Revelation 22:20

Both the Hebrew Bible and the New Testament end on a similar note. They promise the return of a prophet, who will make all things right and good. It will be a time of clarity, understanding and peace. It will be a time when all who are on the earth will have their doubts satisfied and the truth will be made known to all. And, that truth will set all spirits living within all human form free. There will be a freedom never known before to mankind.

Elijah appears to be the returning prophet and savior of all who followed God's law of the Old Testament. Jesus appears to be the returning savior and prophet of the New Testament. Elijah and Jesus have much in common.

Time will tell how closely Elijah and Jesus are linked and how recognizable each will be, and whether they come at different times or at the same – end of time.

Both of the "last books" of each of the testaments prefer to end on a note of hope that God will indeed send someone back to recover the remainder of humans and move them onward or upward, or both.

Something to look forward to!

February 7

He causes the changes of the times and seasons, makes kings and unmakes them. – Daniel 2:21

When I was walking in the desert this morning I stopped and surveyed all that surrounded me. The mountain peaks to the west, the sun attempting to break through the clouds hanging over the Sea of Cortez. How can anyone doubt that some greater intelligence has set this in motion, as the nearly full moon remainder was quietly setting in the west?

Just like clockwork. In fact we do set out clocks and date our calendars based on what is happening around the sun and the moon. This God we know, love and serve is not made in our image. The tides and the sunrises and sunsets are nothing the human being can regulate. How the world turns or spins is beyond human control.

We are told, and for the most part believe, we are made in God's image. A God who is neither male nor female, and lacking in skin color. How can we put a body on wisdom, energy, intelligence, and beauty?

Something magnificent makes the world go round, and causes all things living to re-create themselves. All I ask of that power source is to keep me alive and well.

February 8

The LORD is my shepherd; I shall not want. – Psalms 23:1

When I was traveling in the Holy Land we went to Jordan – to Petra. Just before the call to prayer our group watched in amazement as a young Bedouin edged along the hillside toward a lamb, and carefully scooped it up in his arms and began his descent. A wandering lamb was separated from the flock and was returned. How sweet!

The above Psalm is most often heard at funerals or memorial services – because we associate death with the peaceful afterlife. But the story of the shepherd rescuing the lamb seems to be more about living – welcoming back the stray, the one who has journeyed afar and returned.

All of the talk of not wanting, but desiring verdant pastures, repose, restful waters and refreshing the soul – that is what the living seek. We want that feeling of peacefulness and serenity in our lives, now.

Today, my friend's best friend died. She is comforted by believing. God speaks to her about peace and refreshment. She knows her friend is in a better place, a different place. Those of us who believe in an afterlife also believe that the soul of our loved one is alive and well – just not in this dimension of life.

The soul of that loved one is vibrant and alive somewhere, somehow – watching, guiding, caring, comforting us in our loss.

February 9

Take up the shield and buckler, and rise up in my defense. – Psalms 35:2

Were the ancients always at war and seeking God's protection? Or were they subtly and allegorically aware of their inner struggles. The enemy within can be far more dangerous to us than the so called forces of evil outside ourselves.

The shield we seek protects us against our own inclinations to do harm to ourselves or others. Hatred and resentment, anger and bitterness, cause our good nature a greater harm than what others say or do to us.

The inner battle, the inner victory may not be visible to others, and will not win us trophies or rewards, but we know when we are winning. Becoming the person we are meant to be has its own rewards. Peace of mind, joy, and contentment can be with us all the days of our lives.

The shield may be our awareness of that protective energy we call God. The buckler may be the small round shield of our still small inner voice that remembers and prompts us to keep moving forward with confidence that we are on the correct path.

Fear of what is outside our area of influence, beyond our control, can only harm us. Attentions to our inner battles and successes can only strengthen us.

February 10

Has not the one God created us? – Malachi 2:10

The universe wasn't as large as it is today when this book of the Old Testament was written – but the sentiments are worth considering. Are we not, after all, children of the same God? Consider God's definition, not ours!

In the so called "Garden of Eden," there was one God, one man, one woman, and lots of animal, plant life and fruit trees. No theological conflict yet! The covenant generally referred to in ancient times is the law handed down to Moses from the God of the Israelites – and, we assume – the same God of all humankind.

The covenant of the New Testament is one of brotherly love, the "do onto others as you would have them do on to you" variety. We owe care and respect to each other as children of the same Father.

Why is it so hard to be good and kind and respectful? Because our universe is so widespread and we know what happens on the other side of the world 24 hours a day, seven days a week, via the marvelous inventions and discoveries of cable television, cell phones, computers, and GPS.

We live in an age like no other before ours. All the tools for communicating with each other can be used for our good, or ill.

A blind man doesn't see skin color. A deaf man doesn't hear accents and experience the barriers of language. A warm handshake or comforting touch feels the same, no matter the person's religion, or lack thereof.

February 11

Like snow in summer, or rain in harvest, honor for a fool is out of place. – Proverbs 26:1

Most of the Proverbs have interesting contrasts and allegories. Much like the contrasts in real life, we have some crazy ups and downs and dark comedy moments. I can only imagine people sitting around the hearth fire and telling stories and joking with each other.

Reference to fools is common in ancient times. According to Webster, a fool is "deficient in good sense or judgment, a court jester, or one who can be tricked or duped." That is certainly not me, or you. Just when we have life figured out, we do something foolish, just because we took a leap before we had all the information we needed, or we were under the influence of someone or something.

An occasional foolish act keeps us humble. Something that seems like a good idea at the time can turn upside down. Perhaps, that is why honors and praise are as rare as snow in summer – out of sync, out of season; like those times we feel that things simply do not fall into place. Plans don't work out. Meetings are delayed. The information doesn't get to us in time to make critical choices, important decisions.

Sometimes the job doesn't get done. Our part is lacking something. The play goes on, even when the actor forgets his lines. He feels foolish but the play is a success.

February 12

Where two or three are gathered in my name, there am I in their midst. – Matthew 18:20

This particular passage follows the story of the brother, or friend, who has wronged you, and how to deal with such a situation. Rather than call the authorities down on the person or talk about him behind his back, we are told to approach the wrongdoer by ourselves. If that doesn't work then we may need to bring a church elder.

Therefore, the message about two or three being gathered makes more sense. If the person who has wronged us responds favorably on the first, second or third try, then the amends have been made and we hold no resentments. We have forgiven, and essentially we forget and move on.

Church goers may use this passage to, not only require attendance at their congregational services, but also to demand participation and almsgiving. Gathering together is not a requirement for God's presence. However, there are times when a group thinking and praying together may be more beneficial and comforting.

God is as present in the life of the hermit as in the cathedral filled with the faithful. Wherever we are, as individuals or as a group, God is indivisible and omnipresent.

February 13

He who loves correction loves knowledge, but he who hates reproach is stupid – Proverbs 12:1.

You've got to be joking – no one loves to be corrected. Even when asked. Our lives are rift with people correcting us. Just imagine not correcting our babies as they crawl near an open door, or stopping them from falling down a flight of stairs.

People, especially those close to us, can't possibly appreciate our correcting their use or abuse of language – in public or in private.

But, then, there are those moments when we are enlightened by an observer – someone who cares – to correct course, change direction. We may not appreciate or love the advice we get at the time. But, the idea grows on us as we see we are getting results.

Insanity is described as doing the same thing over and over again and expecting different results. So, a sign of sanity is then to recognize this foolishness, and finding a new and different way to tackle the problem. We then avoid self-destructing.

Going down the same road every day can become boring. Variety adds flavor and spice to life. There are many changes I have made in my life at the suggestion of a mentor or a trusted friend. I love them for pointing me in a new direction.

February 14

For you are a refuge to the poor, a refuge to the needy in distress; Shelter from the rain, shade from the heat. – Isaiah 25:4

There are people in our lives to whom we go when seeking refuge. People we love. People who demonstrate godlike characteristics. People we depend on. People who shine like the sun breaking through on a cloudy day.

We see how others act and we wish to be like them. Imitation of goodness is a good thing. I want to be a refuge to the poor but my resources are limited. The needy in distress are everywhere. Giving of our time to listen to those in need of support is shelter from the rain and shade from the heat.

An umbrella is shelter from rain, and a roof over our head keeps us dry when the heavens open and clouds burst. Our needs are always met by a loving God who watches over us when it is sunny, cloudy, rainy or dry.

All days are good. All that nature gives us is good. All that our friends and loved ones give us is good. We stay forever in the goodness of the creator of us all.

We avoid negative influences and reach out to hold hands with all people of good will. God bless us, everyone!

February 15

Why is one day more important than another? – Sirach 33:7.

People say they are having a bad day, a bad hair day, and a day when they want to go back to bed and start the whole thing over again. What makes one day better or worse than another? God only knows.

Events outside of us can cause us pain or discomfort. Health issues can get us off to a bad start. A phone call with news that makes us sad. A bill that needs to be paid a week before payday.

Just as days take a wrong turn they can also take a good turn. We complete a project successfully. Our children get good grades, make the team, say they love us, or clean their rooms.

Special days, holidays, holy days, birthdays, anniversaries, the celebration of numerous things and events bring joy to us or others. Or, we make the day happy for ourselves and others.

A gift can make our day. Giving a gift can make our day. Taking an early morning walk can make our day. An exercise class, a good breakfast, reading a daily meditation – one or all of these things make it a good day. Spending quiet time in prayer. Watching the sun rise. Watching the sun set. Each holds promise for a good life.

The sun lights our day, and goes to bed so we can do the same. One day isn't necessarily more important than another, but it is okay to make it special for any good reason or for no reason at all.

February 16

Keep me as the apple of your eye; hide me in the shadow of your wings. – Psalms 17: 8

Who and what are the wicked in our lives and how do they use violence against us?

In my case, I consider the intoxicants in my life to be the Wicked Witch of the West. It's a matter of self-criticism when I have to admit allowing these foreign substances or ideas into my body, into my mind.

Allowing me to be altered, changed, and at times corrupted by the damaging effects of what or who I have allowed into my life is my responsibility. I am my own gatekeeper.

People can be toxic. It took decades for me to figure that one out.

Part of that awareness opens us up to being hurt. We may be hurting ourselves emotionally or mentally when we allow others to push our hot buttons and take us where we ought not to go. It happens all the time, until one day we get it – that's not who we are or where we want to go. We are better than the behavior we get sucked into.

I can't blame anyone else if I am not being true to who I am and who I want to be. I have to take responsibility for my own growth and wellbeing.

February 17

The honesty of the upright guides them; the faithless are ruined by their duplicity. – Proverbs 11:3

To deliberately deceive someone constitutes lying. No matter what the words – duplicity or telling a lie, it's all the same. And, it happens all the time – in business, in political campaigns, in common, everyday life.

I have a difficult time telling a lie. It's hard to hide from myself. I may not always be totally honest with myself or others, but to deceive deliberately is harsh and uncomfortable – at this time. In my past lives – that's another story. A story I have already told, did the forgiveness exercises on, and hope to forget.

Today, my concept of honesty does guide my thoughts, words and actions. Just as a doctor takes an oath to do no harm, it seems appropriate for each of us to honor that same directive. If everyone lived according to the principles of honesty, fairness, or kindness there would be no movies, television series or books and magazines.

As a society, we thrive on knowing and passing along bad news, crime reports, natural disaster information and accidents. And, it isn't always the "faithless" that cause the problems. Faith has many meanings for many people. Whose faith, and how much?

February 18

We remember the fish we used to eat without cost in Egypt...But now we are famished; we see nothing before us but this manna. – Numbers 11:5-6

I guess the escape from slavery wasn't enough. Do we always remember the bad times as being better than they really were? Our reality apparently shifts with the passage of time. I always thought, or I was taught, that the manna that God rained down on the Israelites as they were crossing the desert was better received than this report indicates.

Poor Moses! He complains to God because the people are complaining to him. They all are tired of the manna that they gather daily; pound it and grind it and cook it in a pot and make loaves which "taste like cakes made with oil." I guess life in Egypt wasn't all that bad, and it left a good taste in their mouths – better than the manna.

Be careful what you ask God for. There will always be an answer, a change – because everything changes. Moses has a terrible time with this incredibly large group of people looking for better treatment from God.

What ever happened to the hard work and the plagues and deaths? Who are we to believe; maybe holding out the Promised Land as a carrot to the people didn't always work?

February 19

Rather it is your crimes that separate you from your God. – Isaiah 59:2

God doesn't move. We do. My God is everywhere. Hears everything. Sees all things.

We are the ones who turn our eyes from the goodness that surrounds us. It is our ears that close to the voice of God in the gentle tones meant to reach all mankind.

Our crimes may not be the kinds that get us in trouble with law enforcement but they are subtle distractions that take us away from our path to spiritual peace and contentment. Our connection is sometimes broken. Our need for God in our lives becomes lost in the rift and the shift.

Do we think of the hand of God as we do the long arm of the law? Or do we think of the hand of God as belonging to a parent reaching out to a child needing comfort and guidance? We are the ones who need to reach out and place our hand in the hand of one who waits for us to seek the warmth and safety available.

The ear of God is always listening for our inner or outer voice. And, just as a friend or loved one wants to hear words of gratitude and love – so, I assume, does my God.

February 20

And yet you are a man, and not a god, however you may think yourself like a god. – Ezekiel 28:2

We are frequently forced to return to our roots as fallible human beings. We are humbled once again to realize we have limitations – there is a God and we are not it. No matter how high we climb on the mountain, we are not the mountain. We remain human beings simply climbing a mountain – even though we feel godlike when we reach the mountain top.

God is awesome. The works of God expressed through nature lead us to the creator, but no matter how hard we pray – we cannot be gods. Now the question is would we want to be gods? The awesome responsibility would surely do us more harm than good.

If I were a god, then to whom would I pray? Where would I seek help and comfort outside of myself? If I were all there would or could be in my own life, how could I stand myself?

The problem with the concept that we could be gods is that that would apply to everyone, not just me. What a mess of egos that would create.

I think I prefer to have one God, for everyone. The same God. It helps to avoid confusion. I only wish that the one true God would pull his family together. Make them, us, all quit fighting, send them, us, to our rooms so that when we come out we would get along better.

February 21

How can it be that Pharaoh will listen to me,
poor speaker that I am! – Exodus 6:12

God seems to choose the unwilling more than the willing to do his work. There are very few volunteers to do the hard work of being a prophet or a spiritual leader. They have to be convinced.

Does that mean we can trust people more like us – the unwilling – to lead us out of our messes. Those who want to be leaders may not make the best leaders.

God gives Moses his marching orders but doesn't give him all the reassurances and hints about the miracles that will come if he simply trusts and moves forward.

Martin Luther King preached, "Let my people go," as did Gandhi, Nelson Mandela, and other world leaders who saw the inhumanity of slavery or second class citizenship. There is a bond between true leaders and our God – a bond of trust. We are asked to do so little, by comparison. Yet we falter, drag our feet, and eventually do the right thing.

It is odd that Moses felt he was a poor spokesman for the mission of rescuing his people from the tyranny of the Pharaoh. He lacked self-confidence. It seems that God likes that in people he chooses to do his work. We hear that the meek will inherit the earth – the poor speakers of the world who must be pushed and pulled to do, and to lead others to do.

February 22

A glad heart lights up the face, but by mental anguish the spirit is broken. – Proverbs 15:13

So much of our mental anguish is self-inflicted. We often are our own worst enemies – seeking all our answers within ourselves. So quickly do we break our own spirit – then look for someone and something outside ourselves to blame, or to fix us.

Keeping a glad heart can be a real challenge. We play mind games to keep our burden light, and our hearts glad. Talking to ourselves is not a sign of insanity; it helps us turn our focus away from the negative.

People who know us well notice the cloudy or dull look on our face.

"What's wrong? They may ask.

And, the response most often is, "Nothing. Everything is fine."

We cover up our dark moments and expressions. All is well! How fortunate to have a positive attitude. It should be a clue, that if we enjoy being around positive people, with hearts that light up their faces – we can do and be the same.

To attract rather than repel people is a worthy goal. Children notice. So often I smile at a child and he or she responds with a smile. There is a bond formed. A child knows a truly friendly adult.

A smile can't cover all the gloom and hardship in the world, but it is a beginning for attracting, rather than repelling others.

February 23

Father, into your hands I commend my spirit. – Luke 23:46

Death is a primary theme for most novels. It may be a violent death and the task of solving the crime. Or it may be the effect on friends or family members of the results surrounding a naturally occurring or pending death.

My first book was a fictionalized account of three days in my life when I was 10 years old, and my brother drowned. I added a section of resources for adults to help children deal with loss and grief.

Recently, I posted a children's story on Amazon as an eBook. It involves the ultimate death and cooking of a pet chicken during the Great Depression. My adult son couldn't see how I could do in the chicken in a children's story.

If adults can't help children deal with the loss of a pet – even for food – how can they possibly help children deal with the loss of a grandparent, a parent, a sibling, or a friend?

We hide death from children, thinking they are being shielded from something we are incapable of talking about.

And, yet, the little children are taught about the violent death of Jesus, because that is the only way to teach the little children about the Resurrection – the colored Easter eggs, bunnies, and baby chickens.

Dying is a huge part of life – best we learn how to talk about it – especially with children.

February 24

God is not man that he should be moved by threats, nor human, that he may be given an ultimatum. –Judith 8:16

There's a lot of hedging of bets when it comes to asking God to rescue us, save us and deliver us from evil enemies. We want to be sure our God understands our needs, and we make it perfectly clear.

We really have no comprehension of whom or what God is when we beg for favors, demand answers, give God an ultimatum. We want something to happen on our time.

The older I get the more I realize I don't have to give God my wish list. The God of my understanding already knows my every need. My job is to be grateful. Sometimes a task requires my hard work, other times it only demands my silence and willingness. I don't always recognize opportunity, but I am much better than I once was.

Two days ago I heard about the sudden death of a prominent member of our community. She had given her last measure of love to our community as an educator and leader in her field.

As a community, we all fell into line. We packed the church to overflowing at seven in the morning. We honored her by our presence. We honored her through music and prayer.

There was nothing to ask of our loving God but to comfort her family and friends in their time of great need. The love of God surrounds us.

February 25

How could I not look sad when the city where my ancestors are buried lies in ruins, and its gates have been eaten out by fire? – Nehemiah 2:3

During the Restoration and rebuilding of the walls of Jerusalem, our friend mentioned above begs the king to send him on this mission. An engineer of his day, Nehemiah sought the king's protection and safe passage, plus access to materials and laborers to repair the walls.

He is remembered for what he did because he kept records in a journal of some sort. He documented his work.

So many people pass through this life without leaving a record of their work or their accomplishments. I have kept a journal of some sort since I was in grade school. I had my girlfriends write in my journal when they stayed overnight or came to my parties. My friends were saddened when I destroyed my journals before I married at age 19.

There were reasons why I destroyed my history. But, I forgot what those reasons were. It seemed like the thing to do at that time. Now, I have again accumulated a box load of spiral notebooks – to which, I no doubt will add these working journals.

Some of us are meant to keep records, and most of us are not. Will I ever do anything with all these words? God only knows.

Because God is always looking over my shoulder when I write – I will follow the directions.

February 26

When a woman is in labor she is sad because her time has come. –John 16:21

Jesus used this example to let the followers know he would be physically absent from them, but ever present, and someday to meet again.

As a mother of eight children, I must admit that the pains of pregnancy and child birth were mostly forgotten once I had the fruits of my labor in my arms.

Pregnancy, however, is an extreme inconvenience and great discomfort, and health hazard for many of us women. Once the baby is born our attention is all about that child's wellbeing and continual maintenance – forever. We women tend to focus on others, often to our own neglect. There was little time to care about me when I was a 24-7 mother.

I was pregnant for 72 months, or a total of six years, or 2190 days. That says nothing about the pain involved in raising children or losing a grown daughter. Mothers want to be good mothers. We want to be loved and fondly cared for and kindly remembered. We don't (or try not to) complain to our children about the pain they cause us, because we want their love more than anything in the world.

Physical, mental, emotional pain hurts to our core. Some women can't, or choose not to, have children. That is their business. I know what it takes out of a woman to give up her body for procreation – it is bitter-sweet.

February 27

Trust in the LORD with all your heart. – Proverbs 3:5

During a low spot in my life as a young mother, a dear friend whom I consider my writing mentor and angel – wrote this passage on a small sheet of paper for me to reflect on and use frequently. Sometimes when I'm reading a book or going through a desk drawer, it pops up. It is never forgotten, she will always be remembered.

This is a passage that goes to the heart of my problems, and this is at the heart of all solutions. When I give up and give in, then I am at the beginning of my fork in the road. I am at the decision making place where I need advice, guidance, a loving hand in mine to lead me on a new path, through the dark forest or the barren desert.

When I have exhausted my own resources, I am at that place we call a turning point. Then, I am spiritually on my knees, dependent upon a power greater than myself to guide me.

Through the years, I have come to believe I can seek that guidance before I am driven to my knees. I can claim my birthright every day, at every turning.

February 28

Learn where prudence is, where strength, where understanding. – Baruch 3:14

That's a huge order. The implication is that there is no way we can achieve all that wisdom on our own. We can't learn it from a book, or an entire library. We only need stay in close contact with God our whole life.

Prudence is defined as "handling practical matters judicially." For me it meant raising eight children in a one-income household. That was the most challenging part of a large family.

I divorced when I still had six of my eight children at home – youngest age eight. Then, for the first time in 25 years, I returned to the full-time work force – with a master's degree and very limited child support. It's called survival, but also required prudence.

From that experience of survival, I gained strength and understanding, and learned the value of a long life with its ups and downs.

I made many mistakes during those 22 years between marriages, but came into the second marriage as a whole, complete, reborn human being. My eyes were opened regarding my personal vulnerability, and the ability to stray from my own spiritual path.

Of all the things I learned – ultimately experiencing the presence of a loving God who granted me forgiveness by allowing me to forgive myself and others was the best. There isn't any part of my life that I want to repeat.

February 29

As long as the Israelites did not sin in the sight of their God, they prospered. –Judith 5:17

I approach this day by noting that this is, indeed, that extra day that comes in February every four years. How could I have planned to do this daily writing knowing that? I didn't.

Judith, a pious widow, once more saved the Israelites from their enemies. This seems to be the same story repeating itself over and over again, throughout the history of the Old Testament. It seems to be a book about survival. Their goal in life was one of being left alone, and saved from the clutches of those who would do them harm.

It's always about doing good and avoiding evil, fighting off enemies and surviving. There is much talk about silver and gold, and natural resources, and good food and good health.

How much more complicated our lives are today. We have so many issues, so many ways to earn a living, so many ways to fail. The one constant would be the relationship with God. They, and we, are always trying or failing to stay on the right side of a God who hates wickedness.

Define wickedness!

How little or how much wickedness does it take to drive that God away? How much not-sinning does it take to prosper?

So many people prosper in this world. We have no way of knowing if their prosperity is the result of God acknowledging their lack of wickedness – or whether God loves them more, or less, than the poor.

March

Ancient Romans ceased wars
between old and new years.
March was the first month then.
March is named after
Mars, Roman god of war.

March 1

We have in our day no prince, prophet, or leader. – Daniel 3:38

The Jews living under the leadership of Daniel were suffering defeat at the hands of their captors, their enemies. They are begging Yahweh to free them from slavery in Babylon. They admit their transgressions and disobedience regarding the commandments of their God.

They blame God for handing them over to their enemies, for deserting them in their time of need. I'm struck by their utter feeling of emptiness – with nothing to offer this God of theirs. Nothing tangible to offer.

I know they were into sacrifices in those days, but I don't understand their complaint about having "no holocaust." According to Webster a holocaust is a "widespread or complete destruction, by fire." Also, the dictionary refers to "the genocide of European Jews and other groups by the Nazi's during World War II.

The question in my mind is why the genocide of thousands, if not millions of people, is referred to as the Holocaust. The reference in the above passage seems to think a "holocaust" is something to be offered to God to find favor.

What, indeed does our God ask of us besides acknowledging his or her existence, accepting guidance, and being grateful?

March 2

For the just man falls seven times and rises again, but the wicked stumble to ruin. – Proverbs 24:16

Seven means an indefinite number of falls or failures in this passage. So, if we consider ourselves "just" we can expect to have ups and mostly downs. It doesn't seem to matter how many times we fail at something, the important part is the getting back up. It would seem that no one can claim to be "just" or be self-righteous. For we all are humbled numerous times.

When we speak of enemies here it has less to do with sporting events and more with those people or countries with which we have sharp disagreement.

Recently, we, the United States government, met with the North Korean leaders in talking about providing them with food in exchange for their discontinuing their nuclear weapons testing. Rather than rejoice that they were starving, we are finding a way to ease the conflict and arms race.

We rejoice when our enemies come to the negotiating table to resolve conflicts. We prefer that to having war and destruction of life and property.

May we have more opportunities for rejoicing over solutions.

March 3

Seventy is the sum of our years… they pass quickly and we drift away. – Psalms 90:10

Agreed, time passes quickly. When we are young we are anxious to be older and have more freedom to do as we wish. But, it doesn't work in our favor for the most part. It takes many years before we learn to appreciate the present time.

Once we stop wishing we were either older or younger, then we can find some contentment – knowing this is as good as it gets – the now.

How sad to look back upon a lifetime and think of the years as "fruitless toil." If life is fruitless toil then it would be a good thing for the years to "pass quickly." Is this what we want to look forward to in our seventies, and eighties – a "drifting away?" That seems so dismal.

My mother use to say "you are as young as you feel" Some days I feel like I am 18 years old again, with a lifetime of learning, travel and enjoyment ahead of me. And then, my body reminds me of my true age.

Some days I bolt out of bed with no arthritis pain and the sun is shining and I have a great day ahead of me. Then, I am ageless. I go for a walk and have my conversation with God, and get inspiration.

Life is good. As good as I want it to be. I am grateful to be alive – the majority of the time.

March 4

O LORD, deliver me from lying lip, from treacherous tongue. – Psalms 120:2

The pilgrims journeying to the temple in Jerusalem sang songs to prepare them for their holy encounters. How often do we journey to a holy place, or a place that, should be holy, and do not prepare ourselves with kind thoughts and words.

When I call people these days I prepare myself to keep the discourse civil. Intense political issues and partisanship sometime get in the way of sharing a pleasant visit or phone conversation.

So many people are on edge and want to argue their point. Especially with adult children, other relatives or friends and neighbors – I want to keep the peace.

One person's opinion may appear as a lie to another. It seems that public discourse is now a "say anything you want" attitude. People can be so cruel. Then they try to laugh it off.

The tongue can be a terrible sharp weapon to cut others down.

If I consider every encounter a holy event, then it makes sense to prepare as best I can to be civil. To stop the conversation or walk away if I must, in order not to unleash painful words on those I care about.

March 5

Charm is deceptive and beauty fleeting; the woman who fears the LORD is to be praised. – Proverbs 31:30

What is a woman worth? The nature of the times and the prevailing culture seem to dictate her worth. Beauty and charm are requirements for attracting a mate, but the good book tells us they are nothing.

We women are foolish indeed to think there is any real value in trying to look our best to please ourselves or our mates.

Whose expectations are we trying to meet – our own or others?

Women are forced by culture to be competitive when it comes to attracting men. It does seem foolish to enter beauty contests – except when the prize may be a scholarship and educational opportunity. Why, indeed, do we women waste so much time and money in our attempt to please men? We bow down before the master.

We are slaves to our own vanity. It can be tiresome. Men don't seem to think they have to stay slim and dress well to please women. They show their vanity in other ways, by how much they spend or how many toys they acquire.

Women who live the good life and have a spiritual goal may be worthy of praise, but they don't receive much attention or praise.

March 6

Who, though it be to his loss, changes not his pledged word. – Psalms 15:5

In effect, a clear conscience helps to have a good night's sleep. An examination of our day's thoughts, words and actions is an assurance that we have not offended or abused our person, or our relationships with others. It is primarily the Golden Rule, to do onto others as we would have them do onto us.

Being true to our word is a learned art. Not going back on our promises to ourselves and others. When I started this daily writing on January 1, I made a commitment to myself – if I'm still alive, I will have written a minimum of 366 pages.

Sometimes I think I will run out of ideas – but that is where my trust in a power greater than myself teaches me and inspires me to trudge on.

Not everything I write will have significance and meaning if these words ever reach readers beyond me – and occasionally my husband. The value for me is in the process.

The lending of money, referred to following this passage, is a mysterious matter. So often I want to help others by loaning or giving money. It is a slippery slope – for, once you loan anything to a friend or relative the chain that binds can be painful for both borrower and lender.

Better to give it away.

March 7

How long will you vex my soul, grind me down with words? – Job 19:1

What a complainer. God is patient and Job's friends are patient. Even Job is patient to a degree. He is responding, or reacting, to the advice of his friends and the deaf ear of his God. We all have known times of utter despair, then our memories fade, and life continues.

Job is finally admitting he may have something to do with bringing misfortune down on himself – he cannot shake off the pain and guilt.

When I knew I was going to end my 25-year marriage, I prepared myself mentally, physically, spiritually – and still the pain of the loss of my dream weighed heavily on me. The days, weeks and months were dark, my whole life was upside down. But, I had to do it for my own sanity, and for the sake of my children – to free them from an atmosphere of conflict, worry and doubt.

Launching out on my own – to provide for the six children still at home – took everything in me to believe I was doing the right thing for the right reasons. I had to move forward – and, I became a different person.

March 8

Woe to those who enact unjust statutes and who write oppressive decrees. – Isaiah 10:1

Isaiah preached social justice and the care of the poor, children and widows. Jesus was raised in the tradition of the teachings of the prophets. The references in the New Testament of Jesus reading a passage from Isaiah certainly paved the way for his teaching in parables.

Jesus took the prophets a step further with his examples and stories. The care of the less fortunate was part of Isaiah and they shared the same history and heritage. Jesus taught nothing new or different from the prophets of the Old Testament. He simply gave traditional teachings a new perspective.

Isaiah preached against the oppressive decrees of the rulers within the Hebrew nation as well as outside their own community.

As in all things, there is more in common, fewer differences, more compatibility. The common thread between Isaiah and Jesus was broken by those who could not accept the way Jesus taught the people about traditional values.

March 9

Whatever is true, whatever is honorable, whatever is just, whatever is pure, whatever is lovely... think about these things. – Philippians 4:8

When the teenagers say "whatever" it usually means the discussion is over. They don't want to say any more, and they don't want to hear any more. Case closed. Far from what this version of St. Paul's message indicates. This is the beginning of discussion.

St. Paul goes deeper. We first need to ask ourselves a series of questions about what we truly believe. What is at the core of our value system? What, indeed, are we thinking?

For decades we have been trying to practice the "power of positive thinking," as though the concept is something new. But, it goes way, way back. The story of creation has imbedded into it the message described above – all is good.

If we are to believe the words and thoughts put into the mouth and mind of God by the ancient writers, then we know God was a positive thinker. And, hopefully still a positive thinker today.

Once God created everything, he surveyed all that we now enjoy, and said it was all good. And the world began to spin, and the sun has ever since shone. And, when God had created man, he, God, decided it was not good for man to be alone, so man and woman are both good.

The only requirement was not to eat of the fruit of the tree of good and evil, the tree of knowledge of good and bad. According to Bible writers, God did not want us to know about evil – the flip side of the good life.

March 10

Fear neither them nor their words when they contradict you and reject you. – Ezekiel 2:6

God called Ezekiel out of captivity in Babylon to speak to the Israelites on his behalf. The history of the Tribes of Israel is filled with God's repeated attempts to bring them into line by calling prophets into leadership. Not an easy task.

What stamina was required of the people who spoke for God? The people rejected one of their own repeatedly. God finally got the message, got it right – apparently – when Jesus came on the scene. According to scripture – God chose one of his own, not one of our own – to speak to us. Thus, he changed the face of the prophets.

Jesus took an entirely different approach to telling, or teaching, the people about a God who loves them – us. The prophets of the Old Testament had a rough time because the people were unwilling to accept one of their own to tell them what to do. They were a "rebellious house," a rebellious tribe of people.

Jesus was one among his own people as well. He was rejected by the leaders and accepted by the followers. The historical prophet preaches brimstone, fire, repentance and salvation.

Jesus taught love.

March 11

Whoever takes the life of any human being shall be put to death. – Leviticus 24:17

I can't imagine a God with nothing better to do than lay out in exact detail all that Leviticus prescribes for prayer, rest, sacrifice, holydays, redemption, rewards and punishments. The law defines such detail as how to bake twelve loaves of bread, as well as how and where it should be eaten – and by whom.

These hard laws exist today in the Middle East – the stoning continues. If an entire village throws stones at one person then they never know which stone actually killed the person, therefore, no one involved in the stoning will be put to death for taking the "life of any human being."

Are we to believe God gave all these instructions? There are many laws in the Old Testament books that are cruel, inhumane and unjust. Jesus wrote something in the sand that drove the men away who were intent on stoning a woman accused of adultery. He said that anyone without sin could cast the first stone. They all walked – or slinked – away.

The decision to allow or not allow capital punishment is constantly argued – a life for a life.

The discussion is not over – when does life take the form of a human being? Why does a person who is part of a stoning community or a firing squad get a free pass on the death of a human being?

Who has the final word? The final shot?

March 12

You have sown much, but have brought in little. – Haggai 1:6

Throughout Biblical history the prophets and the people are obsessed with structures, buildings, temples, and houses for the Lord. Once again we are dealing with the dismal condition of the temple of worship.

According to this particular prophet, the people are being criticized for maintaining their lovely homes to the neglect of the Lord's house. This is a God I don't know or understand. Fixation on a house of worship, rather than on kindness toward each other, doesn't sound like my God.

We see marvelous, glorious houses of worship built throughout the world, and then some of the leaders of these churches are human failures, corrupted by money and the desire for personal power. People become disenchanted by the wanderings and failings of their spiritual leaders – and they stop supporting them financially, and stop going to their buildings.

Once the purse strings are tightened, the leaders can no longer sell tithing to the people.

How are we fed by our spiritual leaders? Why must we keep giving more and more money to build bigger and more glorious temples or churches?

To praise God?

I wonder!

March 13

You have made your people feel hardships. – Psalms 60:5

If God had feelings like we have feelings, how would God feel about the accusations that he has caused them to lose in battle and be destroyed by their enemy?

These same people praise God for their victories. The sane, intelligent person must ask, "What about the other guy?"

Are we to assume, if there is only one true God that someone is playing favorites or switching sides in wars and in sporting events?

Recently, an NFL football player gained national media attention for kneeling in the end zone after making touchdowns, thanking God. Everyone is entitled to their prayerful expressions in public or in private. Personally, I prefer private.

Like public displays of affection between a man and a woman, a man and a man, or a woman and a woman – public display of affection between man or woman and their God makes me feel a little edgy – especially when we have a competitive situation.

We choose sides when it comes to war, elections, sporting events, and family arguments. Does God choose sides? Should we even ask or expect God to choose between us?

I want guidance to make wise choices.

March 14

We are all the work of your hands. – Isaiah 64:7

When God shows himself to the people they are filled with sunlight, warmth and joy. When God's glories go behind a cloud of difficulty, disorder and dismay his people lose heart and cry out about their pitiful state. They feel abandoned and begin to ask for forgiveness from whatever is haunting them.

Because God is not showing his presence and the people no longer feel his presence – they assume he is gone from their midst. They believe they drove God away, and they feel their guilt.

How difficult it is to remember God's eternal presence. Where on earth did God go? Does he board an airplane and flee to another country? Does he punish us by his lack of presence?

Or, are we so foolish that we lack the faith or belief in a loving, ever-present, supreme, comforting and guiding presence?

We are molded in the darkness as well as in the light. We are humbled by our own humanity and become as putty in the hands of the master potter.

We believe, therefore we are, and therefore we become.

March 15

May his children be fatherless, and his wife a widow. May his children be roaming vagrants and beggars; – Psalms 109:9

Ouch!

To curse your enemy is acceptable in most cultures. If you are going to fight and kill them, then why not wish the worst for them. There's always room to hate your enemies, and why not take down the entire family while you are at it.

I can't recall having that much hate in my heart. I've been angry, hurt and sometimes devastated – but not sure I'm capable of the kind of hate required to curse a person, and his wife or her husband, and their children, and their children's homes.

Jesus taught a different way of life, far from the battles he read about in the ancient scriptures. But, the world hasn't changed that much. War is still with us and killing continues. We have an arms race. Who can acquire the most devastating weapons of mass destruction, and how can they be delivered rapidly and at great distances? Are we talking about deterrents?

The radical Islamists bring down the Twin Towers in New York City; the United States bombs Iraq, and rebuilds their country – for the promise of access to oil. The U.S. supports a blockade to stop Iran from developing nuclear power to destroy Israel. Israel threatens to bomb Iran with nuclear missiles to destroy their capability to fire on them.

Where does the conflict end? When will we ever know peace?

March 16

Not on bread alone is man to live. – Matthew 4:4

Jesus quotes scripture. Reminding the tempting devil that the Israelites survived forty years in the desert not only because they were fed by God's manna, but because of God's love and care for them.

We are obsessed with food and drink. Especially drink. Most of the world has a food fetish. One thing that demands our attention is food, eating and drinking. Are we always hungry or do we always just want to eat? Putting food in our mouths – only in America – requires three settings a day. We go on a cruise and talk about the endless amounts of great food.

Yet people starve. They could live off our excesses. Food is everything in life. We schedule our events for friends and family around food. Pot lucks forever for everyone at every age. And always wash the food down with an alcoholic beverage. Good excuse for becoming an expert with wine or beer.

Food is necessary and should be enjoyable as well as nourishing.

What would happen to our bodies if we only ate when we were hungry, instead of eating several times a day because we can, or we are bored? What happens to us if we only think about our spiritual life when we are hungry for God's love? Nothing much!

Nothing would happen – because we have to have a reason, a desire, a need to feast at the banquet table of the Spirit.

March 17

Happy the man who meditates on wisdom, and reflects on knowledge. – Sirach 14:20

We read. We listen to sermons and lectures. We search for deeper meanings to life and our own pathway. We meditate by thinking to the point of non-thinking. It takes much practice to be able to quiet the mind and listen for the voice of God. We never know with certainty where the inner voice is coming from. We know, when we know, what is meant by quiet listening.

We hear the tick of a clock, the flow or drip of water, the soft musical tones, and the sounds of nature, birds, and wind through trees. Quiet has its own sounds. We learn something new in the quiet. We learn in the calm. Listen to the silence, the soft sounds in our own heads. Love is quiet. Wisdom, ideas, creative flow, they all bend in the wind – quietly.

We know what wisdom is when we hear it spoken, whether from the mouths of those around us or within the confines of our own silent, mental chambers. Learning is gentle, loving, and kind. Thoughts come together like pieces of a puzzle.

Wisdom sits quietly by our side, ready to share with us, any time, any place. We welcome wisdom into the quiet places in our souls.

Happiness and wisdom are quiet companions, and real teachers.

March 18

Tell me, you whom my heart loves, where you pasture your flock. – Song of Songs 1:7(B)

Song of Songs is the language of spiritual lovers or "pillow talk" with God. The soul is capable of deep and everlasting love and devotion. While the soul is engaged in this intense mystical union there is no room for anyone or anything else. To use physical terms – it is climactic. The soul knows no other greater joy.

The passage quoted above is followed by the letter "B," signifying the speaker of the passage to be the "bride." The soul has no sex – neither male nor female. Thus, there is difficulty in using human terms to describe a love experience between God and the soul. Even a man is a bride when wooed and won by God. Perhaps that is why women saints were more easily given to the ecstasy of Divine Love, although men saints use the same language.

Men are as capable as women in experiencing the rapture, but may have reluctance to speak of the experience in the same mystical terms as described in the Song of Songs.

So important to the soul is the question of where to "pasture" when not wrapped in the arms of a loving God. How does one trust the Divine Lover to always be there? How to always recognize the True Lover?

Trust, and more trust!

March 19

Be not jealous of the wife of your bosom, lest you teach her to do evil against you. – Sirach 9:1

Good advice for the man, but where is the good advice for the woman? Much of the Bible is written by men, for men, and against women. It is sad, but true – women seem to have one purpose in life – to obey and glorify their husbands.

When I was a much younger mother of many children, I formed a large group of women who gathered monthly to hear powerful speakers. Mostly political in nature. Mostly conservative in purpose. I even developed a speech that I presented on several occasions titled, "The Dignity of Women."

At that time of my life I believed woman's true worth was in childbearing and child raising – even though I spent a great deal of my "free" time volunteering in the community, attending church services, and promoting the candidate, political issue and party of my choice.

When falsely accused of being involved with other men. I stayed on my path through commitment to my own values.

Jealousy is a destructive and insulting weapon when used against someone you say you love.

March 20

If I saw one of my people who had died...I would bury him. – Tobit 1:17

What makes Tobit interesting is not the fact that he details his charitable works, but that he was punished for burying the dead, slain by the unfriendly King. Tobit lost all he had except his family.

Sometimes we believe we are doing the good and proper thing, only to be informed that our interference by charity is unacceptable to those who disagree with us. We don't think of it as being disagreeable but people don't always view situations alike.

When it comes to saying the correct thing at the correct time, we may run into misunderstandings and language problems. Out listener may be far more sensitive on a particular subject than we realize.

Some days it seems that I can't do anything right. I want to start all over again. I really didn't mean to offend anyone. I said the wrong thing, or said it in the wrong way. An "Oops!" doesn't calm the other person. No matter what I say, I'm only digging the hole deeper.

How sad to find out we are not perfect and that we are capable of saying or doing something offensive to another person.

March 21

I recall the dream I had about these very things, – Esther 10:2

The Jewish feast of Purim (lots) is celebrated in remembrance of Queen Ester, who saved her people from annihilation. Her uncle Mordecai spoke of her as he remembers his dream of a tiny spring growing into a river. She was the river.

How often do we dream and learn from a vision delivered by our psyche while we sleep? The question that baffles the experts is "where do dreams come from?"

Dreams teach us lessons about life, just as life has its lessons when we are awake. Everything has meaning, whether we are awake or asleep. The big difference is how we view these events. Some dreams wake us up in a sweat as we chase something or someone, and never catch them.

I've had dreams when I couldn't find something that was lost. I've had dreams where I was helping children pack their suitcases, and they forgot items. Sometimes it was real. I've had dreams where I go through one door after another, and never arrive at my destination.

Are these dreams reflecting some frustration in my life? Possibly!

Separating the reality from the dreaming is one of our Earth school exams.

March 22

What God promised our fathers he has fulfilled for us, their children, in raising up Jesus. – Acts 13:32

Paul, who never knew Jesus personally, became a follower and a disciple after the fact. He became a believer after being involved in the persecution of the friends and followers of Jesus. Paul was not only a Jew by birth, religious heritage, and training – but also a Roman citizen. He had it all.

Paul teaches us one thing about faith – that faith finds its own truth. Once we believe – we can't turn back. Once he accepted the Jesus he didn't know as the fulfillment of all his people's teachings he could only move forward – with a passion.

The passage above comes toward the end of Paul's preaching in the synagogue. He was allowed to preach among his own people about what the prophets had preached, and what those same leaders said about their God.

The strength of Paul wasn't enough to turn the tide – or bridge the separation being formed. The followers of Jesus were all followers of Abraham and all the prophets of the Old Testament. They were then forced out of their synagogues, and denied their heritage.

March 23

They betrayed you, outdid you, your good friends! – Jeremiah 38:22

Jeremiah warns his king what will happen if he refuses to surrender. Sometimes, surrender is a good thing. Fighting an unwinnable fight means we eventually get beat up. We give up frequently when someone or something proves to be beyond our reach.

Betrayal seems to be at the root of the passage. The loss of friendships happens because someone loses trust and respect for a person once held dear. Our insecurities make us vulnerable to the turning away from some people who no longer have a place in our lives. We outgrow friends just as we outgrow clothes or shoes or cars or houses or neighborhoods or clubs or churches.

We may think we are out-growing our friendships but our friends may be growing away from us, or we may be growing tired of each other.

Hard to know what holds most friendships together, but it usually is evident what causes a drifting apart. The bond breaks.

For no reason at all we move on – or, for a break in our hearts because of a break in our trust, in our love.

March 24

With each contribution show a cheerful countenance and pay your tithes in a spirit of joy. – Sirach 35:8

Today, I was downtown San Felipe, in Mexico, where we spend our winters. As I was standing by my car a young woman with a box of Skittles approached. It is common for the people in the government addiction/recovery programs to sell candy or gum to cover some of their expenses.

I asked to see her identification.

The young woman dug in her big cloth purse for her ID. I checked it and gave her $20 pesos. My friend, standing there with me said, "You're more generous than I would be!"

I said, "That's my daughter."

When a homeless woman has her hand out, I am honored to remember my daughter who died in 2004, homeless and deathly sick in Las Vegas. It's a small tithe to remember, and to help.

Jesus said, whenever you help one of these, least of all, you are helping me. I have a double reason. I help young women like my own daughter, and it is in the spirit of joy, the spirit of giving. I didn't take the woman's Skittles. So she could still sell them again.

And, I know, I will see my daughter again, on the streets or at the traffic stops – with her sign out – asking for money for food.

March 25

You need patience to do God's will and receive what he has promised. – Epistle to the Hebrews 10:36

Paul is the supposed author of the Epistle to the Hebrews, where he speaks to the people of his own heritage. He tries to encourage them to keep the faith of their fathers; which is the rule of the prophets and the fulfillment of their prophecies.

The word of Paul goes out to us all – once you believe, you will endure.

So often, in life's difficulties, we want to say, "This isn't what I bargained for.

First of all, when we make a commitment we don't bargain. We accept the terms of the commitment – whether a job or a marriage, a friendship, or buying a new car. If we think we should have had more information at the beginning then we look for the warranty, the license, and the small print.

Sometimes we have to disengage from a relationship or friendship. We must deviate from a career path, or take an item back to the store because it is defective or doesn't live up to the products promise.

With God it's different. I can't imagine how a true believer can become an unbeliever. Disenchantment, certainly! Out of every doubt springs knowledge and discovery – we find out who we are and where we fit in God's plan, or where God fits into ours.

March 26

The people who walked in darkness have seen a great light. – Isaiah 9:1

I find Isaiah one of the more positive prophets of the Old Testament. There is so much conflict, war, hunger, violence, mistrust of God, and misunderstanding of the people and their relationship with this God of theirs.

Isaiah is a man of hope and vision for people wandering around in darkness. There is light at the end of the tunnel. Instead of a train light coming at us, we better be on the train and heading out of the tunnel.

This passage is used by Christians to show how Jesus has fulfilled the prophet's vision of one who will lead them out of darkness and into the light.

When I have trouble sleeping at night my head takes me many places I would rather not go. So, I get up and go to the couch in the living room; turn on the light and read. I try to divert my attention away from the dark side of life and turn my thinking on to a different path.

Eventually, I tire of reading and close my eyes. I enter into a new dark – but safe – place. I think good thoughts and my inner world becomes a brighter place.

March 27

If you want to avoid judgment, stop passing judgment. – Matthew 7:1

If you want to really make a point in a debate you rephrase the statement and deliver it three times. Then the opponent, and the audience, is more likely to get the point. It may stop an opponent in his or her own tracks – or it may give them more information to rebut your argument.

Of course, in these days of rapid media information flow and the incivility that abounds in election cycles – which seems to be a constant condition – there is little time to put the words of Jesus into practice.

Someone recently told me that if I didn't want to be upset by the news then I should stop watching the 24-hour news shows. It makes perfect sense, except I would feel very deprived of information I need to make decisions about important issues.

The feedback I give in an empty room – reacting to a news report – gives me some satisfaction. I can exercise my judgment without directly confronting or hurting a real person. These are television images, not real, everyday people.

With real people, I'm much less judgmental. And, where I have been judgmental in the past, I exercise forgiveness. First, I forgive myself for being a flawed human – then I forgive the other person, for the same reason.

March 28

This is the day the LORD has made; let us be glad and rejoice in it. – Psalms 118:24

When I have the opportunity to walk in the desert in the morning I see the blue waters of the Sea of Cortez to the east and the San Pedro Mountains to the west in my Baja home. If I could sing, it would be the Psalm above. So often, I greet the day with this verse.

Every day is – this day. Every day is the day the Lord has made. Every day, I am glad and rejoice. How wonderful and glorious to be alive.

Every day, and every opportunity during each day to be glad, to be alive – is there waiting for me to connect. Even on a gloomy day, when things aren't going the way I want – I have the opportunity to release the song of my soul.

You may think I am in a great mood when I say these things – but the truth be known – I'm just getting over the 24-hour flu. I don't feel totally well – but my soul sings anyway, because I'm alive and filled with hope for the future.

The world news defies hope. But, does the world news really know about who we really are – and how high we have already climbed, how high we still can climb – how far we can fly?

March 29

We, on our part, have never ceased to remember you in the sacrifices and prayers. – 1 Maccabees 12:11

So many people touch our lives. The longer we live, the more often we hear of the loss of friends, relatives, school mates. Two months ago it was a dear friend – a woman who twice acted as a patient advocate on my behalf. A month ago word of a former business partner reached me. Yesterday, a high school chum emailed about the loss of his friend from second grade – he was my summer romance in 1950.

Great times, great friends! So often we drift apart, but the memories always stand vigil.

All we can do is pause to remember and appreciate the times we shared. Our holidays, and other special days always bring the past into our present. They are never forgotten. The great sacrifices we offer in this life consist of the letting go of people. We may want to keep them in our lives, but we can only keep them in our prayers.

I'm always amazed at the numbers and kinds of people who walk on my stage – and then walk off – to another stage. If all are actors, then it doesn't pay to memorize our parts – because we play so many roles that it is impossible to memorize and repeat our lines.

March 30

You shall love the Lord, your God with all your heart, with all your soul, with all your strength, and with all your mind; and your neighbor as yourself. – Luke 10:27

Jesus was recognized as a teacher among his many followers. Prior to telling the story of the Good Samarian, a lawyer stood up in the crowd and asked what he must do to gain everlasting life. Jesus asked the lawyer to tell the people "what is written in the law."

The law at that time was what was handed down from Moses, with interpretations by Isaiah and other prophets. The lawyer responded with the passage above.

It was only when the lawyer asked "who is my neighbor?" that Jesus told the story of the two men who passed by the man who had been robbed, beaten, and left to die along the road. The third man, who was from the looked-down-upon area of Samaria, took care of him. Then took him to an inn where he could be cared for. The good, compassionate Samaritan paid for the man's care, and offered more if needed on his return.

This is a story we all know well. I worked at a hospital named Good Samaritan. We once understood what it meant to care for our neighbor. But, so much has changed.

Hospitals no longer are owned and operated by faith-based organizations. In order to survive, institutions have turned their facilities over to the marketers. It's all about the bottom line.

March 31

He will guard the footsteps of his faithful ones. – 1 Samuel 2:9

God made promises throughout the history of the Israelites to protect them from their enemies and lead them through darkness and into the light. It appears that there were plenty of dark days.

I have a daughter who suffers from S.A.D. (Seasonal Adaptive Disorder) – a difficulty adapting to the dark days of winter. On the other hand, we live in perpetual sunlight, south of the border, down Mexico way.

I can't imagine that S.A.D. has anything to do with faithfulness to God – and the accusation about the wicked perishing in darkness.

Now, we are starting on the lengthening of days, and the shortening of nights. Are we more or less wicked in one season or the other? I think not.

I believe that I walk with God, but when I stumble, I can't blame God. I blame my clumsiness for not watching where I'm going. I could blame God for my stumbles, he has broad shoulders and he can handle it. But, I'm responsible for using my common sense and watching where I'm going.

When I get up during the night to make the short walk to the bathroom – I wait until my eyes are adjusted to the darkness, and make sure everything is working properly.

Dark or light – God is ever present.

April

Roman month Aprilis
Derived from asperire
Latin
To open buds and blossoms.
Or Aphrodite,
Original Greek name of Venus.

April 1

The LORD is good, a refuge on the day of distress. – Nahum 1:7

In a moment, we can turn our thoughts to a higher self – the God of creation – and the God who guides our spirit and our every thought, word and action. Do we sometimes get our signals crossed? You bet! We are human, even though our spirit is divine.

That one thought – God is good—can turn our life around on a dime – on a mere thought – a moment of surrender.

I have to assume that most of the people I interact with have their own connection with a God, and they pray as well. It doesn't have to be competitive all the time.

The spirit of cooperation lives in each of us, sometimes it is struggling to get out. If we go through life believing we have to be correct all the time, then we don't give others the opportunity to be all they can be.

I recently worked diligently on bringing a project to life. A couple of the times I let personalities get in the way – and very quickly realized that wasn't an obstacle I had to overcome. It was an opportunity to give way to a new and different way of moving forward.

April 2

A mild answer calms wrath, but a harsh word stirs up anger. – Proverbs 15:1

People tell me I have a calming demeanor. It works best when it doesn't always have to be about me or getting my way. Because I studied communications and publications, I think I expect more from me than I am capable of giving. If I keep my life goal in mind – to build peaceful relationships – or my personal relations goal – then I can stay on track.

I'm built for conflict resolution. I live for peace at all levels in my life. If I had a bumper sticker on my car it would read "Peace is Possible." I believe in the art of the possible, by putting one foot in front of the other and applauding the success of each person.

The words out of my mouth aren't nearly as well modulated and kind as my written word. I'm learning, but I'm not perfect with the mild answer that calms wrath. But, when it does happen, I am pleased and amazed that I didn't unleash the harsh word that stirs up anger.

Because I have a master's degree in communications, that doesn't make me a master of interpersonal communication, although I studied that as well.

Practice, practice, practice – and we learn as we grow. And grow as we learn.

April 3

Walk with wise men and you will become wise, but the companion of fools will fare badly. – Proverbs 13:20

Just like mother used to say "Pick your friends carefully, because you will be judged by the company you keep."

I did not have control over my children's choice of friends, nor would I want that responsibility. At one time in my youth – about the age of 11 or 12 – after the death of my brother by drowning – my best girlfriend's mother kept us apart for a time. She felt I was a bad influence on her daughter.

Patsy and I would arrange to meet away from our houses so we could be together. One time we went off to the zoo together – about three miles away.

We were friends. I never understood what there was about me that made me a bad influence – unless it was our different religions. That certainly wasn't anything that we cared about.

We were never in trouble. But for some reason, I was suspect. I think my mother finally had a talk with Patsy's mother, and we were able to resume our friendship openly.

As we are growing children, and living in an experimental world, we don't consider who is wise and who is a fool. We only do what feels right for us.

April 4

Your wealth shall be plundered, your merchandise pillaged. – Ezekiel 26:12

The prophet predicts the fall of the City of Tyre because of what words people of that city spoke against Jerusalem. The Lord, of course, always speaks through the prophets who record these sayings. There is always hell, fire and damnation to those who speak against the "chosen people" of the Old Testament. There is always an enemy, always destruction. There is never a mention of a God of anyone else. A narrow view – always attributed to God.

Reading about the visions and sayings of the prophets we always are reminded to beware of "false prophets." Who decides – and how does one decide who and what is false? There appear to be no certainties, and we see failing humans preaching and failing on a regular basis.

It seems the closer I get to following a human representative of the Divine Creator – the farther away I grow from that Divine Creator. The more organized, well-funded, and well-spoken a church leader becomes the more likely that person may eventually fail.

To thine own self be true. Wishing destruction on those who disagree with me seems self-destructive. Are we not all children of the same God?

If not, why not?

April 5

No prophet is without honor except in his native place. – Mark 6:4

The people we live with, grow up with, and grow old with, are so familiar we often can't see their glowing spirit. We know them in pieces – their faults and their successes. We don't have a God's eye view of the people closest to us. But, sometimes even those closest to us can wow us, and impress the hell out of us.

How many prophets are in our midst? We are told that what Jesus has done we can do – that includes the ability to see deep into souls and see their goodness. Sometimes we have to work harder to see past the disagreements and disagreeableness to see the prophet in our fellow, common man or woman.

We move too quickly through life and often see through a glass darkly. It's easy to see how Jesus could have been overlooked by his peers. Not all of them – but enough to cause his rejection, arrest and death. How can such a powerful personality touch some hearts and minds, and not others?

The heart that is open will recognize Jesus in others. The mind that is closed will be blinded to the light.

April 6

Fear God and keep his commandment, for this is man's all. – Ecclesiastes 12:13

"Man's all," according to St Jerome is "Unto this is every man born, that, knowing his Maker, and he may revere him in fear, honor, and the observance of his commandments." (The New American Bible, 1970, pg.742, footnote 12, 13)

One of the first questions in the catechism for children asks, "Who made you?" And, the answer of course is "God made me." How can anyone challenge this concept? Everyone has his own sense of what that means, because no one knows exactly who God is or what their God might look like. We only know God by the results of God's works.

Even the un-churched, unconverted, and primitive human being has a sense of a creator, someone or something that put the creative process into motion.

The United States Declaration of Independence proclaims that "all men are created equal." In the way of a creator, there is no distinction by race, creed or gender. Some civilizations are more advanced than others – but that hasn't saved them from extinction.

When does a society grow beyond its ability to sustain itself? When does an individual go beyond his own ability to survive, either alone, or as part of a society? We are only capable of living in the now. All our plans for the future are mere conjecture – the plan may or may not work.

April 7

I spoke to you when you were secure, but you answered, 'I will not listen.' – Jeremiah 22:21

The time we feel most confident, most powerful, and most healthy – these are the times we feel most secure; and most likely not to involve God in our lives. He may speak to us but our own chatter blocks the voice – the message. In our youth we are so taken with our sense of newness and freshness, which we believe is known only to us. We do not want to hear the voice of our parents, or any other voice. We are proud.

Sometime in our life, we shed that entire protective shield and become ready to listen. Hopefully, we don't have to be nearly destroyed to listen.

I just reached for a small crock of butter in the refrigerator – and it fell from my hand and broke all over the tile floor. The thing I have feared for a very long time happened. My hands have arthritis in the joints and fingers. I often ask my husband to take things off the shelves for me.

Once again, I must admit to my frailty. There are things I cannot do alone. A broken dish is different than a broken promise or a broken heart. I need to be careful while carrying things and people.

April 8

You shall love the Lord, your God, with your whole heart, with your whole soul, and with all your mind. – Matthew 22:37

When the lawyer asked Jesus what was the greatest commandment he referred back to Hebrew law, the commandments given to Moses. So, if we abide by these two commandments the other dictates become less urgent. Love is the basis for all we think, do, or say. Love, according to St. Paul is everything.

The words of Jesus as reported by Matthew, are similarly reported by Luke in chapter 10, verse 27. Apparently they bear repeating.

How we define love then becomes the issue. There isn't a singular interpretation for love. Individuals define it differently to suit their needs. The rest of the 10 commandments more clearly define what love is – with all its "shalt nots."

How do we know when we have reached that level of love of which Jesus speaks? How do we love with our whole heart, whole soul and whole mind? Is our intention and commitment to do enough or more than enough? We can only hope and trust that we have made the connection. But to doubt or worry about whether we are connected seems to negate that very connection.

I believe, with my whole heart, whole soul, and whole mind that I have turned everything over to God's care. My belief will have to be sufficient – for God has not spoken to me directly in words I can understand. I am. I believe.

April 9

Incline your ear to me, and save me. – Psalms 71-1

According to an interpretation of this passage, it is a "humble prayer in time of old age."

And, I have to admit I am old. 79 years old, as I write these comments.

My mother always said, "You are as old as you feel." Some days I feel my age. Other days I wonder who is inside my body. I look in the mirror and I see my mother. I don't see the young me in the mirror anymore. Yet I feel as though there is a lot more life in me. I have dreams for the future, and places to go before I die. Yet, there are so many of my friends, and relatives – and lifetime classmates – who have already gone.

They all have gone somewhere, but I know not where, and I suspect someday I will follow. Someday. Somewhere.

The older I get, the more I need the resources and comfort of a loving God. As we age, we tend to embarrass ourselves. We can't find the words we want. We can't do the steps in tennis or in dance we once did. We want to be rescued, delivered, saved from being less than we want to be.

Save me from myself O Lord, for, left to my own devices I will stumble and I will fall. Guide my footsteps, my wandering thoughts, and my love of life.

April 10

Toward the sincere you are sincere; but toward the crooked you are astute. – 2 Samuel 22: 27

Does God tire of our ramblings? Does a mother tire of the voice of her child? Probably yes on both counts. Certainly we are repetitive and certainly a child asks the same questions over and over again.

Sometimes I think God is saying to me, "Get some new material. I've heard that one before. Don't you remember my answer the last time you asked?"

How sad to think God might tire of my pleadings, but I think what God cares about is my sincerity. This is what I'm honestly thinking, asking, and listening for. I want to know how to do life better. I don't understand the "crooked" part. I suppose people can try to trick God, but I don't know how they expect to get away with it. The all-knowing God sees into my heart and soul. I don't even need to speak the words – because God already knows what I need.

Voicing my thoughts to God is for my own benefit – not God's. God can manage very well without ever hearing from me. But, I need to remind God that I am still here, still trying my best to be the best me I can be.

God already knows that. No news to God.

April 11

They struck me, but it pained me not, they beat me, but I felt it not; When shall I awake to seek wine once again? – Proverbs 23:35

It's hard to be indifferent where wine is concerned. Either love it or leave it. People who drink the wine are content with their reds and their whites. Tasting here and there, now and again. Lovely with dinner. Devine on tours, and with music.

Proverbs is harsh about wine, especially the reds. The last line of the diatribe against the drink implies a stupor of some kind where the imbiber can't feel pain when struck or beat up. But once the drinker has recovered from the effects of the drink then he or she is awake and ready to seek wine once again.

The pain is forgotten or never felt in the first place.

I drank early and often. My perfect right and any good or not so good reason would do. But, unlike our biblical character – I began to feel the pain – during and after. It wasn't as much fun as it once was. It messed with my head and with my gut.

When the pain of drinking became greater than the pain it was intended to dull – I said, "Goodbye dear friend, you make me sick, and I am tired of letting you have your way with me. Farewell old friend."

April 12

Hungry and thirsty, their life was wasting away within them. – Psalms 107:5

Tired of following the dream of a promised land, a better life, the desert was taking its toll on those wandering for decades. They were told by their elders, before they died, about the land of milk and honey, but it seemed to grow more distant by the day.

Was there a wrong turn somewhere? No maps to guide them. No wanderers coming toward them from the land they sought. So, it must be all they said it would be – since no one ever left there.

Moses kept the hopes alive and they continued their trudge to their happy destiny. Sometimes they wanted to give up. Some of them did. Some stayed back at the last oasis and made a home, a village. The Promised Land had been reached by some sooner than for others.

How often do we give up too soon? How often do we quit before the miracle happens? It's probably because we have forgotten that miracles are the rule rather than the exception. Waking up in the morning is the greatest miracle of each day. Enjoy!

April 13

For truth stumbles in the public square,
uprightness cannot enter. – Isaiah 59:14

Beauty is not the only thing in the eye of the beholder – truth is also a closely held commodity. Caught in the middle of a campaign season for the presidency of the United States, it becomes obvious that there is truth, and there are lies everywhere the truth indeed stumbles in the public square, and uprightness cannot enter.

Everyone believes what they say, no matter how reason and justice claim otherwise. It's a very confusing time in the public square. Everyone has his own version of the truth.

My mother used to say, "If you can't say something nice about a person then you should keep quiet." Quiet is not in my nature. Nor is quiet in the nature of most of the people I know. Quiet is not in the nature of our mass media, nor our politicians.

Conflict, name calling, hyperventilating, and raising your voice – that is the nature of the public square.

Before radio and television the preachers, doomsayers, and political hacks stood on their soap boxes in the public square and thumped on their bibles and handed out literature.

Now, they appear on FOX Cable News, CNN and MSNBC – and anywhere else they can hang out and voice their opinions.

Please God, more light and less heat.

April 14

The cities that were in ruins, laid waste, and destroyed are now re-peopled and fortified. – Ezekiel 36:35

So many civilizations have risen and fallen, and new civilizations rebuilt on top of the old. Everything seems capable of rebirth. This passage foreshadows the destruction and rebirth of the Hebrew nation, and their temple of worship.

The Israelite nation claims its heritage throughout history, in moving others off the land they claim belongs to them. All over the world the trespasser becomes the occupier. The Native Americans say that no one owns the land. Even the natives fought over territories.

The United States defeated Japan in World War II and rebuilt their country. We democratic countries that defeated Germany in two world wars rebuilt the bombed and destroyed areas.

When the United States is attacked it must rebuild its own land, as there is no other government we can force to rebuild the World Trade Center Towers.

We rebuild what has been destroyed because that's what we do – whether we caused the destruction or not. The world as we know it may someday be changed or destroyed, and no doubt will become something new and different.

April 15

They began to speak in tongues and to utter prophesies. – Acts 19:6

In Ephesus there were people who had been baptized by John, the cousin of Jesus. But Paul re-baptized them in the Holy Spirit, in the name of the Lord Jesus – by lying on of his hands. This raises questions about the symbols used by Christians, in that baptism using water – the symbol of life – is still used. The other thought is about the laying on of hands, used primarily by disciples of Jesus to bring the power of the Holy Spirit of God the Father and God the Son into the life of the convert.

Does rationing now occur among the Christian brotherhood, or sisterhood? Do we have levels of power imposed on all followers? Did Jesus not offer all the gifts of the Spirit to all believers?

Are not all people of God capable of receiving the gifts of the Holy Spirit? Most people today who have a problem with organized religion have more of a problem with the "organized" part that they do with the "religion" part. We live in societies that thrive on organizing – from the top down. So many people fancy themselves leaders. There are fewer all the time who wish to be followers. In the Christian world we **all** are followers.

April 16

May there be no one to do him a kindness, nor anyone to pity his orphans. – Psalms 109:12

And, what do you suppose your enemy is praying to his God about you? We assume that those of us who read the Bible are the only God fearing, God loving people on the planet. How foolish of us.

This bitter curse on the enemy tells us everything about the people of God and their dependence on God to destroy their opposition.

I suppose I am capable of such hatred, but I can't imagine how. I've had bad things happen in my life, and to those I love. I know I am capable of destroying anyone who would hurt or kill one of my children, but I have not been put in that position. There have been times when I was hurt to the core and given the choice of fight or flight – I must confess, I chose flight.

I'm a peacemaker at heart – but there are times I have to walk or I will do myself more harm than good.

My sympathy goes out to the afflicted or offended and my sense of justice can run rampant. I hope I never have to feel the kind of hatred described above.

April 17

You are my shelter. – Psalms 32:7

This is considered a penitential psalm where the psalmist pleads forgiveness for wrongs against God and fellow man.

He received God's blessing of forgiveness and direction for a new way of life, the psalmist is content to live life anew. Where do non-believers go for that kind of solace? Can a non-believer find it in his own heart to forgive himself for his wrongs?

In a world without God, as we people of an organized religion know our God – what then becomes the higher power? In the forests and jungles of the world, where people wander and hermit to survive; there must be some sense of divine guidance.

If we believe humans have free will and conscience – then that conscience is the guiding force. Even among the most primitive – that force moves and guides.

When I look deep inside myself to find my true self, I find that guiding force. In my dependence on that guiding force, I have freedom.

May the force be with you as well.

April 18

False swearing, lying, murder, stealing and adultery! – Hosea 4:1-2

Today I heard a woman speak from her heart that all she can feel about God is absence. He does not speak to her. It has nothing to do with knowledge of God – it's about feeling it in your heart and in your bones. And, yet, this woman has faith. She believes.

All of the false swearing, lying, murder, stealing and adultery mentioned above go on and on all around us. If it isn't happening locally it is happening and being reported all day, every day in the newspapers and on television. And, I say, not me, not now, and I hope not ever.

Remaining faithful to the truth of who we are at our very core is what our life is all about. Whatever goes on around us and in the world – we have a core belief as children of a loving God that we are loved, cared for, and guided every day of our lives.

Civilizations may come and go but the human spirit is constantly reborn. We grow and we thank God for every breath we take. Without God – I no longer exist.

April 19

Are you not aware that you are the temple of God, and that the Spirit of God dwells in you? – 1 Corinthians 3:16

Eastern religions have always advocated the divine, the spirit of life, and the holiness of the individual. There is some speculation that when Jesus was traveling during his hidden years he journeyed to parts of Asia where Buddhism was already practiced. As a result he may have incorporated some of their teachings into his stories and pronouncements.

Anyone's guess is as good as anyone else as no one seems to know with any certainty how Jesus emerged at age 30 as a recognized leader worthy of our attention. He taught that the Spirit of God dwells in us. Where there is life, there is God's Spirit.

Jesus was appealing to all people known to be living during his lifetime and beyond his time – he proved that God is truly everywhere.

It's a difficult concept to make into a reality. Yes! God's Spirit is in me. I believe that. But, to say God's Spirit is in each person on the planet – that's not so easy because our minds and hearts are clouded by what seems more real – the presence of evil in the world.

April 20

Honor your father and your mother, as the LORD, your God, has commanded you. – Deuteronomy 5:16

When I was young there was no misunderstanding the full intent of the fourth commandment. I didn't always obey my parents but I always respected and honored them. I didn't know about the long life and prosperity part of the commandment.

As a child I took risks, also dares. I had to prove I was daring and brave. I would fight off anyone who got physical with me. I would take off on my bike and ride miles into the countryside. I stole cigarettes out of my father's pack. I drank off the top of the pint of whiskey he kept in the refrigerator – for medicinal purposes. Then I would top it off with some tap water.

I never got confrontational with either parent. But, my mother and I would have heated discussions. My parents sent us to Catholic school – one and a half miles from our house – because we were being harassed by some of the kids in the public school. We had a lot of friends on our long walk to and from school.

We engaged in petty theft and my mother had to go to the police station to get my brother when he was taken there for stealing a candy bar from the drugstore. He couldn't play with Eldon any more. I guess my mother blamed Eldon. I learned from my brother's experience.

April 21

Mine are counsel and advice; mine is strength;
I am understanding. – Proverbs 8:14

The power of positive thinking has been around long before it became the fad it is today. Norman Vincent Peale probably was inspired by Proverbs and Psalms.

This passage is a reflection of what God is saying to the individual. Then the individual takes on the attributes of God by being wise and capable of giving good advice.

Mine is strength. What is more powerful than being able to say and to believe we are strength – no matter what? We have understanding. There is a message in everything that happens in and around us.

My mother had an eighth grade education, but she was an avid reader. She was wise beyond her years of formal education. She knew about the Power of Positive Thinking. She used a lot of what I call "Momisims." And, those momisims made a deep and lasting impression on me.

When Shakespeare's character says "To be or not to be, that is the question." I always thought "to be" was best. Just being is an awesome task. Being present for people. Being creative. Being a friend. Being well educated. Being thrifty. Being a caretaker of the land and its people.

Being is good.

April 22

For I know well the plans I have in mind for you, says the LORD. – Jeremiah 29:11

I know what my plan is. I know that God knows my plan as well. It would be great if God would give me a look see at his plan for me. I believe God has my wellbeing and prosperity on his list. I have to believe God has hope enough to go around for the future. We need a plan, because things are pretty much a mess in this world.

I'm writing this on my husband's 79th birthday. I had that same birthday six weeks ago. As we age we realize how good God's plan has been for us so far. Not everyone gets to live this long. My father died at 75, so I have him beat. My mother died at 84 – that's five years more for me. The old sayings go, "where there's life there's hope" and "hope springs eternal." There is a movie by that title addressed to older populations, where love tries to spring eternal.

Our neighbor here in Mexico, came down from California for a few days to close up their house for the summer. She goes home again to a husband dying of ALS – Lou Gehrig's disease. There's little room to make much of a plan when the time is running out that fast.

I have a motto on my Skype phone service page "Enjoy every day you wake up." Many people are having very dark days. Their prosperity flew out the window as the high rate of unemployment walked in the door.

April 23

Beat him with the rod and you will save him from the nether world. – Proverbs 23:14

Not all proverbs are good and worth following. This one, in particular, about not sparing the rod or spoiling the child, is abhorrent. The thought of beating a child with a rod sickens me. I raised eight children and couldn't bear to strike any one of them, no matter what they did. I sometimes flicked them on the arm or leg to get their attention, or swiped at them with a dish towel. Their father, however, would "take the belt to them," until I hid the belt.

I dealt with my problems frequently by not telling their father, because I couldn't stand having him punish them. My father spanked me once with a soft felt slipper. I think he cried more than I did. My mother's punishment usually meant reading something on a poster about what is expected of a good child. Or, I had to stay in the house for a time and was not allowed to go out and play.

I sometimes had to separate my children when they were arguing or fighting. I see nothing good about striking a child – or allowing them to strike each other.

April 24

My soul thirsts like the earth parched, lifeless and without water. – Psalms 63:2

Only the soul that has known the comforting presence of the love of God can know the depth of wanting and needing some evidence of that presence again. The soul thirsts most when it has drunk to satisfaction from the fountain of all life.

This prayer is so personal, as the soul seeks its lover. Only in human terms can we understand the utter desolation of being apart from the soul's only true love – the creator of that soul.

The feeling of lifelessness and the thirst for water ring true for me as I am recovering from food poisoning that totally depleted my body, and my soul. I was so dehydrated that I was on an IV drip for four hours to bring enough fluid back into my body. My mind was mushy and my mouth was so dry I had trouble speaking.

My soul knows that same thirst, that same hurt, that same longing for God to show his love and kindness to me. Then I must ask – do I withhold my love and kindness from anyone in my life? I hope not.

April 25

Some misfortunes bring success; some things gained are a man's loss. – Sirach 20:8

When we say that some people can't handle success, we never mean us. We think we could handle success just fine. After all, we have waited all our lives to succeed at something – our careers, our education, and our children.

The trick is not so much about our ability to handle success, but rather knowing when it happens. Recognizing our own accomplishments and our own success has something to do with acceptance and gratitude.

There were times when I was elected or appointed to a leadership position in an organization, and was immediately struck by the hard work ahead. It doesn't come easy, and when we lead we are immediately vulnerable, and open to criticism. I don't like being a leader. I'm content to do what needs to be done and sleep well at night.

There are gifts of a tangible nature and gifts that are meant to be used to help others, educate them, lead them out of darkness, show them kindness.

April 26

Hear this, you who trample upon the needy and destroy the poor of the land! – Amos 8:4

God speaks through Amos against greed. The poor are constantly defended in the Old and the New Testaments. Why do we not listen? Admittedly, there are many faith based organizations and individuals concerned with the plight of the poor.

The current status makes me wonder what we all would do if things were more equal. What if there was less poverty? What would we do with all that time and money we now spend on the less fortunate?

The United States Congress spends an incredible amount of time and material resources seeing to the needs of the less fortunate. It seems the wealthy have begun to feel neglected. Isn't their wealth enough?

Do the wealthy have to complain that we are spending too much time and money on the poor? The wealthy don't want to pay more taxes. Neither do the poor. To help someone who can't help him or herself isn't tax; it is one of the benefits from having enough, and a little bit more.

Is there an answer? How can we elevate the poor and also help those who are nearly poor and would be poor?

Many people are a pay check away from disaster. They are one meal away from starvation. They are one drink away from the gutter, and despair.

April 27

Forsake foolishness that you may live; advance in the way of understanding. – Proverbs 9:6

What is the most foolish thing we do? Believing we are all powerful, when we are not, is the height of foolishness. The voice of wisdom tells us that living is all about believing in a power greater that ourselves. Because so often we have tried to live successfully and been disappointed by our own actions.

To understand that we exist and are sustained by a power beyond our understanding – that is true understanding. We are humbled time and time again by our own foolishness, lack of understanding, and pride.

Days may seem long or short depending on how healthy our connection is with God. If we are empty, there is nothing or no one who can fill that emptiness but the God we are trying to love, serve and understand. When my mind is tired and dull, there is nothing but sleep to set me right.

The days drag on for the dull witted who wait for sleep to come. The years go fast when we are busy, and content. The days race by when we are happy.

April 28

Swear to me by the Lord that, sense I am showing kindness to you, you in turn will show kindness to my family. –Joshua 2:12

A woman's kindness to spies who were staying in her house is reflected in the passage above. Sometimes we have to ask for a favor for a favor given. She asked that the spies spare her entire family when they came back to invade her land.

Sometimes we are reluctant to ask a favor, so accustomed are we to giving to others. I know people who cannot bring themselves to inconvenience others, to the point they will attempt doing something alone where they really could have used help.

When we say, "God helps those who help themselves" we have to be sensible. God can sometimes help us by motivating others to help us. God isn't going to show up and hold the ladder while we climb up on the roof of our house.

Only when we recognize others as acting on God's behalf, for the good of others, will we be recognized as agents of good. Doing onto others as we would have them do onto us is still the Golden Rule. To give is divine, and to ask for help is also divine.

April 29

They therefore decided in favor of Alexander, for he had been the first to address them peaceably, and they remained his allies for the rest of his life. – 1 Maccabees 10:47

It's a mystery, how leaders are selected. What does it take to get a critical mass of people, being of like mind on an issue or topic, to choose a leader among them or bring in an outsider? Are there always people waiting in the wings; waiting to take the initiative, ready to step out and lead the charge. Or, does the critical mass all step backward and leave the poor unsuspecting future leader in fact – in charge?

Several times in my life I have looked around and everyone else has stepped back. I received encouragement and praise for work well done and found myself in a leadership position.

Many years ago, I had served two years as vice president of an organization of professional women. It was common practice for the vice president to step automatically into the presidency. But, there was a movement to have someone else run for the office. I took it as a sign that I wasn't the one for the job and didn't make a presentation. I basically dropped out. When I lost the race, another professional organization I belonged to grabbed me as president-elect. Everything worked out.

April 30

I will establish peace in the land that you may lie down to rest without anxiety. – Leviticus 26:6

If we spent an entire day without radio, television or newspaper then we might lie down at night and say there is peace in the land. I have nothing to fear. It's logical that many people ignore what is happening in the world, for we constantly expose ourselves to the wars, rumors of wars, killing in the streets and the injustices of man against fellow man.

There are men and women out of work who cannot provide for their families. They despair and panic and snap – and even murder the people they love the most – or they turn their weapons on themselves. What terrible things the human being is capable of doing. Does knowing about such tragedies help me to be a better person? It is doubtful.

There is very little I can do to bring peace to the world. I can only influence my small area of the universe. What have I done today to make the world a better place? Not much. I haven't had a positive influence on any one I know. Maybe some words of encouragement to a friend on the phone.

Maybe.

May

Maia
Roman goddess,
Mother of Mercury,
from Jupiter
Daughter of Atlas.

May 1

Then the LORD will guide you always and give you plenty even on the parched land. – Isaiah 58:11

How sad that in our day we lack such a direct contact with God. We pray, and offer alms, and do good works – but no one steps out of the shadows to offer us a kind word of encouragement.

We act on faith. We believe that we are going in the right direction – we are on the right path. Though we may not feel the presence and the assurance of God – we believe there is a God, ever present in our lives – and waiting to reward our efforts – when that day comes.

We have the words of the prophet, in the time before Jesus, who tells us that the reward for obedience to God's law will be fruitful land, strength in difficult times, guidance, and flowers in the spring.

On this first day of May, we rejoice in the lengthening of days and the fruitfulness of the land. The warmth of the sun upon our backs and upon the fruits of our labor brightens our days. Thank God for spring and summer.

May 2

Peace be with you, my brother, and with your family. – 1 Samuel 25:6

These words are easily said to one who is a friend or relative, someone we care about. The difficulty is saying these words to a person with whom we have issues, someone we don't like, or don't know very well. If we all could greet each person we meet with words of peace to them and all who belong to them – then there may truly be peace.

We all want peace and harmony in our lives and in our relationships. So much of what goes on in the world has a political tone. And then we ask, what does that means if it is political? I assume that means partisan. Politics is really the art of debate and discussion, and influence and movement – and sometimes lies and innuendoes. There is all manner of communication to force an opinion and make something happen.

There is nothing subtle about political opinion. There is a great sense of ownership. A sense of righteousness. Must we all think and act alike? How boring is that?

Can I wish you peace to your household, and at the same time disagree with you on some petty or important issue? I hope so.

May 3

He that offers praise as a sacrifice glorifies me. – Psalms 50:23

We are so firm in our original commitment to a project, and how difficult it is to maintain the necessary discipline to see it through. This daily writing meditation is an example. When it comes to the end of the day and I haven't written my thoughts, I feel blank. I can't even inspire myself.

All God asks is that we offer praise as a sacrifice, and to follow our conscience and go on the right path. Without the spirit of life inside each of us we could not even breathe. Thank God for every beat of my heart and every breath I take.

Each day that I write a page of praise I offer my discipline as my sacrifice. Once again, I remember my maker and offer my thanks for the ability to do such a minor and menial task. My God asks so little of me, and I have such a hard time remembering that little sacrifice.

I know if I ask each of my children to remember to think about me, call me on the phone, or send me an email – it would be asking more than they could possibly do. There are eight of them and one of me. I don't want or need that much attention. It would take too much of my time, and theirs.

Time is all I have to offer my creator. A few minutes of my time each day.

May 4

Remember this day on which you came out of Egypt, that place of slavery. – Exodus 13:3

There have been times in my life when I felt trapped or enslaved. During final editing I am revising what I previously wrote after reflecting on the above passage. Additional reflection caused me to change my approach to the relationship in my first marriage of 25 years. After more than 30 years, I have forgiven my husband for any grief he may have caused me, and I have forgiven myself for any grief I may have caused him and our children.

There were good times, of course, and eight children. Being pregnant and taking care of little ones for so many years could have caused me to feel trapped. Instead, I launched my newspaper and magazine freelance writing career. I pursued my bachelor's degree and completed a master in communications on a teaching fellowship. And then I divorced, sought full-time employment and finished raising six of the eight children.

On the surface, I was building a career, and had a full life. But, when the situation became intolerable, I took action. Not an easy choice, but it was the only way to get out of Egypt.

Egypt is not a place of slavery; it is a state of mind. To become free of the terror of the night and fear of the day took strength and courage.

May 5

In a word, you must be made perfect as your heavenly Father is perfect. – Mathew 5:48

Those who think they are perfect are not. Those who think they have done something perfectly have not. Those who think they have created a perfect work of art or writing have not. It's all about judgment. Either we compete or we have the best performance or the best product – but it is not perfect. We can't know perfection, nor can we achieve it without dying and becoming part of a whole new and different experience that is a mystery to the living.

Jesus challenges us to at least try to be made perfect as our heavenly Father is perfect. How can we possibly know what that means?

First we have to want to be that kind of perfect, and we may never know in this lifetime how much we have achieved. There must be something deep inside each of us that gives us life. When everything works perfectly in a watch that instrument keeps perfect time. Not a minute too fast or too slow.

We are not clocks or watches, even though we sometimes are too tightly wound and our spring breaks.

At this moment in time I have to believe I am the best me I can possibly be. Perfect – I am not! Working on being made perfect – that's God's job. I think I'll let Him take charge of that one.

May 6

Cursed be he who violates the rights of the alien, the orphan or the widow. – Deuteronomy 27:19

When I was a child the word alien meant someone from outer space. Currently, an alien means a person who comes into a country illegally. Aliens in the Old Testament, as I understand it, meant someone from another country, area, village or tribe.

But, the passage above indicates that the alien has rights that should not be violated, just as the orphan or widows have rights that should be respected. Each of these persons seems to find themselves in situations beyond their control. An orphan or a widow has lost the person or persons who cared for and cared about them, primarily financially.

All living creatures deserve respect and care. As a society, we may deny that we throw orphans and widows out on the street, but a person in a strange land, or strange situation, without means of support needs help.

From the beginning of time the human being has been imbued with the moral law. We are commanded by conscience to treat others with respect and kindness. Those who have lost the ability or the means to take care of themselves – the needy, need someone to come to their aid. The old, the frail and the pitiful people need our help.

May 7

May the LORD give strength to his people; may the LORD bless his people with peace. – Psalms 29:11

Our prayer should be for all the people on the earth since we are told we all are children of the same God. How can we say we love all people when we can justify killing any one of them – whether in the name of revenge or in the name of justice?

If all people are God's people, then all people worship the same God, and pray and gather their strength from the same source. I want the Lord to bless all people with peace – for until there is peace in each human heart and soul there will be no lasting peace in larger communities – or in the world.

Must there always have or be an enemy? What must we do to free ourselves of the need to fight an enemy? We hear that the enemy is within, true, but then how can we possibly reach those who would do us harm?

The more peaceful I am the less I am concerned with the problems of the world. The more I concern myself with the problems of the world the less peace I have.

I want peace for all – the peace that surpasses my understanding – but peace that can only be given and accepted through God's grace.

May 8

There are six things the LORD hates, yes; seven are an abomination to him. – Proverbs 6:16

Taking a personal inventory based on all of the above passage should make most of us feel pretty good about ourselves. How the author of Proverbs came up with such a limited number of things that the Lord hates is beyond me. And how can you possibly equate "haughty eyes: with "hands that shed innocent blood."

There is no equality of evil. Each fault or crime must be judged on its own demerit. All the actions described are, or could be criminal except the haughty eyes. I can't quite get with the criminal meaning there. A "lying tongue" can be vicious as well as criminal depending on the damage done.

There are those who sow discord among brothers, and sisters, and mothers and fathers, and a big section of society or community. They are political commentators, rabble rousers, and a variety of self-righteous or nearly evil persons.

Forcing our opinions on others can be offensive and can sow discord. Words can be far more vicious than haughty looks, or haughty eyes

May 9

Which of you by worrying can add a moment to his life-span? – Matthew 6:27

I need constant reminders about not worrying or being anxious or getting into a panic mode. As I write these notes we have just come out of our six months wintering in Mexico. My husband's house in Central Oregon sold last summer and our furniture is in storage. We are staying a few days with my daughter Teresa and her family. We will be spending next week in an extended stay motel. We go back for another week to see doctors and a dentist in Bend.

On that trip we will see if our RV is ready to bring out of repair after being broken into and vandalized during winter storage. We are waiting for the results of my husband's biopsies, hoping his prostate cancer has not progressed.

We have to start looking for a place to buy – a place to live in the Portland area. We are managing one day at a time. Trying not to worry or be anxious Realizing our problems are of the quality variety. I'm not ready to worry until I have something to worry about. So far we are managing not to destroy each other. We are aware of the problems of others, and wish them all better luck than they have had in the past.

Sometimes the days seem too short and I would love an extra hour. Other times, I just want to sleep.

May 10

The highways are desolate, travelers have quit the paths. – Isaiah 33:8

We all are on a journey, but we know not where we are going. Sometimes the road is smooth like a highway and we are clipping along with the cruise control on and there are no traffic lights to slow us down. Travelers who have had a flat tire or run out of gas are parked along the side of the road.

The trail of broken promises to ourselves and to others discourages our efforts. Nothing seems to work right, our ideas are rejected by our peers, and our friends betray us or go away and make new friends.

We only care when we are the ones who are in need. We can't connect with other travelers. Maybe we really want to outpace them and get ahead of everyone else. It's a race, and we feel we are losing at times, and other times we stop to pick up someone who ran out of gas. We're enjoying the company on the journey. At least for a while.

Once again, we care. We want to help others gain some traction. It may slow us down for a while to stop and help someone, but we do it anyway. It makes us feel better about ourselves.

How much reward or payment do we expect from those we have allowed to join us on our journey? Or are we rewarded by having fellowship for a time and doing a good turn?

May 11

I saw new heavens and a new earth. – Revelations 21:1

I read Eckhart Tolle's book *The New Earth,* and as I recall it was an optimistic view of the future of the planet, unlike the "end of the world" projections. I also read, *The Phenomenon of Man* many years ago. That author also took a less frightening approach to the end days. Basically, God is in charge, and if we are alive during those days we simply have to trust that we will be in the right place at the right time. It may be a disaster or it may be the beginning of something really wonderful.

The whole earth can certainly stand an overhaul. But, the drastic change we are all looking for has more to do with attitudes and actions of individuals toward each other than it has to do with the physical earth itself. However, with climate change at issue it makes a huge difference how we relate to our planet. Mother Nature is an innocent bystander when it comes to how we treat our environment.

When Jesus said he was the Alpha and the Omega, he was telling us his teachings reflect a continuum of development, a cycle of learning, and a cycle of living. Everything and everyone goes through a cycle of being. Everything and everyone goes through generation, gestation, and regeneration. All will be well if we only trust God's guidance, and learn a new way of trusting each other, and living together in peace.

May 12

O complacent ladies, rise up and hear my voice. – Isaiah 32:9

Complacency can be dangerous. I have seldom been in that place. I have six grown daughters and many women friends. Overconfidence is hard to find and difficult to judge. I've seldom felt over-confident. Just being confident sometimes is good enough for me.

If God is speaking through Isaiah to women then he should be clearer in his message. Complacent people don't make much progress in this modern world. And I doubt they will become overconfident.

It seems that someone who is satisfied with him or herself to the point of not caring about others, or not asking anyone for help or advice, doesn't need God until there is a problem they can't solve on their own. That doesn't make a person bad, it only makes them seem uncaring and aloof. If I forget to check in with God I doubt that is just a woman thing. Men and women can become complacent and over confident.

God must speak the same message to men and to women. Men and women both have to be silent and listen to what the spirit says. Being confident is a good thing. Most of us realize we are not alone in our efforts to be good human beings.

May 13

It is not good for the man to be alone. I will make a suitable partner for him. – Genesis 2:18

How strange that the writers of Genesis thought that God couldn't get it right the first time. Their God made all these animals and birds before getting the idea of creating a woman. That is not very creative.

It makes me wonder what kind of companionship God had in mind – or for that matter, what kind of companion this first man was looking for. It appears that somewhere in the process, sexual relations became part of the solution. Was it man or was it God who figured out something that suited his physical needs was what they were looking for?

Leave it to man to take some credit for the creation of woman. I can't imagine the all-powerful and all-knowing God could have possibly thought like the men who wrote about creation.

If the Bible is truly the word of God then we must admit that woman was more than an afterthought but really the completion of the creative process. Woman was the crowning glory of God's creation. Not just a companion for man, but a partner in all of creation.

Woman was created as an equal to man and filled with the same Spirit as man. Can we please re-think creation?

May 14

If you are ready to believe that you will receive whatever you ask for in prayer, it shall be done for you. – Mark 11:24

Although I ask God to help me make decisions, or bring about some particular order to my life, or assist a friend or relative with life's difficulties, I sometimes forget to say, "Thank you!" when prayers are answered and what I ask for is accomplished.

We just came through a difficult time when we left our winter home in Mexico to come north to look for a replacement for our summer home, our more permanent residence. My husband's house sold before we left for the winter and we were feeling "homeless." I kept saying that God would guide us. But when the wheels actually started turning I was so busy trying to keep up that I almost forgot to acknowledge the help we had received.

How wonderful to see God working in our lives all day, every day. It isn't accidental that people come together with such precision. One person returns a phone call and another doesn't. One real-estate agent takes the time to meet with us and another doesn't even return our call. One agent got the email address wrong and the mail wasn't delivered

Being in the right place at the right time is more than a mere accident. It is providential. God is providing – always guiding, always aware of my spoken and unspoken prayers and needs.

For all the times I forgot to thank you dear God, I thank you now.

May 15

Wealth quickly gotten dwindles away; but amassed little by little, it grows. – Proverbs 13:11

I can only imagine what it would feel like to gain wealth quickly. We all imagine what we would do if we won the lottery. I seldom buy lottery tickets, so my chances are slim to none that I would ever amass any great fortune from buying a lottery ticket. I support my husband's more frequent ticket purchases. I know he will be generous.

If I were to come into sudden wealth I know I would be very generous with my family. I would rather enjoy watching them share in my good fortune than to think they were waiting for an inheritance. My thirst for travel, culture, and charity would take a good part of the rest of sudden wealth. The older I get the less I need material goods. I try to simplify my life by ridding myself of excess trappings.

Anything I have at this stage of my life was amassed little by little. Except for the wealth of love and friendship that came into my life in 1999, when I married my dear Harry. He came with a nice retirement – but more than that he brought a kind and caring nature into our relationship. I am forever grateful to a loving God for bringing us together. My life is rich beyond measure because of Harry.

I only want to give the dear man a fair return on his investment in me. I don't even want to think of life without him – but age demands we must prepare for the unexpected and the unwelcome.

May 16

The simpleton believes everything, but the shrewd man measures his steps. – Proverbs 14:15

Our current political climate seems to have many people mesmerized and playing follow the leader, even though the leader or leaders seem to be leading in the wrong direction. Worst of all – either political party would be willing to agree with me, because, every individual has his or her own bias. Everyone believes he or she is correct – no matter what the evidence to the contrary.

The United States is in its year-long election buildup. The insanity of the millions of dollars going into the pockets of advertising agencies and broadcast media seems to escape the notice of sane people. No one wants to call a halt to the outrageous spending from all directions and sectors. Who are the simpletons? Who are the people making brainless utterings and leading or following the lie?

Who are the shrewd people – probably those who don't get involved, don't even try to convince anyone of anything, and don't want to get into the mix.

I've always admired the British for placing time limits and financial limits on candidates for public office. It's worse than what Christmas has become. Jingle bells and jingle cash register all year long.

May 17

Give up your anger, and forsake wrath; be not vexed, it will only harm you. – Psalms 37:8

We can give up anger once we figure out what causes it. For me, anger seems to be a result of disappointment, betrayal, or resentment – all of which can be emotionally deadly. It takes a lot of courage to deal with the cause of our anger. Sometimes it boils down to anger turned inside on ourselves, when we can't find a way to blame someone else for our misery.

It's so true that we are the ones harmed most by our own anger. No matter how justified our anger, it still erodes away at our good nature.

Yesterday, I put the wrong solution in my eye, instead of my contact lens rewetting drops. The solution I put in was citrus based water purifier. It was in a tiny bottle labeled Traveler's Friend. It was the same size bottle as my contact lens solution. The first reaction was anger. I was so angry with myself for doing such a stupid thing.

I experienced incredible pain as a result of my mistake. I expressed anger with myself because there was no one else to blame. I had to get over it because I was hurting twice as much. I finally had to give it up and get professional help quickly.

I don't handle anger or wrath very well. It hurts me too much. But, when I had young children at home I would fight like a tiger to defend any one of them from harm. Now, I sometimes get angry, but I have never learned how to be angry with my adult children.

May 18

Mistreat not a servant who faithfully serves, nor a laborer who devotes himself to his task. – Sirach 7:20

I've never had a servant, so it's difficult relating to the concept of mistreating one. There were times when one or more of my children accused me of treating them like servants, but I informed them they had free room and board, plus many other favors a servant wouldn't have. And, they had lots of time off as well.

Respect for all those who do work for us is a no brainer. When you hire someone to do work for you then they are expected to perform the task for which they have been hired – and to do it correctly. No one gets away with mistreating servants these days. At least not for long. When I read the book *The Help*, and saw the movie, I was outraged at the way colored help was treated in the South prior to the Civil Rights Act. I'm sure there are people who serve and are still mistreated.

In some respects, those who "serve" in the military can be considered servants. Currently, many of those who served faithfully are now home and looking for jobs so they can continue to support themselves and their families. They are being mistreated. They are not even given the opportunity to apply for a job or to be hired.

Many will consider reenlisting so they can get a regular paycheck. That is mistreatment of someone who has served faithfully.

May 19

He humbles those in high places. – Isaiah 26:5

We are living in a time when great countries are falling into near financial ruin. Those in high places can't seem to find solutions to the stability of their countries, states and cities. There is a tremendous outcry about the injustices, but nothing changes.

The lofty cities that are being brought down have been stomping on the less fortunate for decades. Now, there are so many poor that the scale is totally out of balance.

How many societies have been trampled by the numbers among the poor who eventually rise up and reverse the reign of power?

There is a saying about being careful not to step on people on the way up the ladder of success because you will meet those same people on your way down. There is always someone above and someone below us as we seek to make a comfortable life for ourselves.

Take and use, and consume only what you need, and use your surplus to help others reach a better level of comfort. The more we help each other the better society we build. To rise up communities where peace reigns – then, we need to hold hands and lend helping hands.

May 20

When they sow the wind, they shall reap the whirlwind. – Hosea 8:7

Confusion rules large parts of our lives. It would be wonderful if we could always act with certainty, but it doesn't happen that way. The phrases above have hidden meanings – much like our daily decisions. We don't know where words, acts or thoughts will lead. There are no guarantees. No certainties.

What we sow, we reap – Karma. If we live a life of loving and caring for others, we will have the love and respect of most people we meet and with whom we interact.

When a seed doesn't yield fruit or grain it is tossed aside. So much of what we attempt falls on deaf ears, or misses the mark entirely. We miss an opportunity by moments – seconds – days – hours. We don't have a clue why some days everything clicks along, on time, and is well done.

During the winter, I spent hours online looking for a furnished rental for our return to Oregon, a place to stay while we looked for a home to buy. Nothing materialized. God had a different plan. Within a few days after our arrival in Portland we found our future home – and everything fell into place.

May 21

It was no sin, either of this man or of his parents. – John 9:3

When the disciples asked Jesus about a man who had been blind since birth, he instructed them. It is difficult to imagine a time when it was dominant thinking that the sins or errors of the parent were passed on to a son. But then, how does that differ from the concept of an "original sin?"

Not much difference when you consider the story of Adam and Eve, the supposed first parents. Whatever they did to offend their maker supposedly doomed the rest of us to a lifetime of separation from God – unless of course we are born again and baptized with the water of salvation – earned for us by the life, death, suffering, and resurrection of Jesus Christ.

What would Jesus say today to those who ask why a person is blind or deaf or wracked by pain from one of a number of diseases? His answer to his disciples is so direct and so simple, even though his words were meant for those about to witness a miracle of healing. Jesus always talked about looking beyond the surface into the interior of the person.

All healing comes from within. Even with medication or surgery – the body must respond accordingly – the individual is ultimately the mechanism for healing.

May 22

They shook at the passing of insects and the hissing of reptiles. – Wisdom 17:9

The fear of God was cast upon the Egyptians when darkness came as a warning plague to let the Hebrews go. The people became conditioned to expect some terrible thing to happen next, because something terrible recently took place. They knew they were into something beyond their ability to control.

We also become conditioned to expect the worst when we have had a string of bad luck and financial misfortune. The shock waves are still reverberating; we still hear the thunder and are watching for the lightening to strike. And it may – or may not, strike. But, it doesn't matter, because we are already dealing with the fear of what could happen.

We spin our wheels, and worry too much about impending doom. A slight illness turns into a bout of pneumonia. It is so difficult to reign in the raging tiger – threatening us – and everyone around us. We hear the passing of insects and fear it is the tiger at our gate.

Living in the moment, in the now, and confronting reality is our only defense against the roar of the tiger, the collapse of stock market, or our own impending death.

Enjoy means inner peace. The practice of inner peace spares us from our imaginary demons.

May 23

We walk by faith, not by sight. – 2 Corinthians 5:7

Confusion rules large parts of our lives. It would be wonderful if we could always act with certainty, but it doesn't happen that way. The phrases above have hidden meanings – much like our daily decisions.

Confidence is more a matter of the intellect than the emotions. Feeling confident doesn't always make it so. I can speak the words and feel nothing. I don't know how to get the feeling except by doing the action. Faith isn't a feeling, but it can be strengthened by feeling. Sometimes God reaches into our lives and gives us a pat on the back or a hug. These moments are valued memories that support us when days grow dark. We only know what we did, and believe we can do it again.

Sometimes it's the blind leading the blind, the words are not always our own, but they come out of our mouths. We give what we never realized we had. We channel God's love and goodness. Sometimes giving words of wisdom when we have no idea we are giving someone something they need at that moment. The fact that we may not be practicing what we are preaching doesn't matter.

For, wherever two or more are gathered there God is – Jesus said so. We speak, and we touch each other. We share our experience, our strength, and our hope. We don't know where the words of comfort and faith come from – but we are bound to acknowledge that God is working in our lives, all day, every day.

May 24

Guilt lodges in the tents of the arrogant, but favor in the house of the just. – Proverbs 14:9

Most arrogant people I know seem incapable of either expressing feelings of guilt or ever admitting they are wrong. If guilt is there it appears to be under lock and key. If that is lodging, so be it. The just probably feel more guilt, even though guilt is uncalled for. The just are less sure of themselves than the arrogant.

Believing you are always right doesn't necessarily make it so. I'm more likely to trust and identify with people who admit to human error. The arrogant say they will not compromise values. Based on their principles they are always correct.

No one but God knows what takes place in the mind of an individual. No one can read the heart of another – only God.

I know I am capable of feeling guilt. Often the guilt is phony. It's not something I could have changed, avoided or can correct on my own. I have to be careful not to turn on myself. Everyone is methodically moving forward and attending to his own wishes, goals, accomplishments and failures.

We really share so very little, seldom really listening and caring. Our inner joy is seldom appreciated by others. Our inner life is our own responsibility, our own joy.

May 25

In a word, be strong. Do everything with love. – 1 Corinthians 16:13-14

Being strong sometimes means doing nothing when you want to do something. Restraint of pen or tongue sometimes takes tremendous strength.

Saying the hurtful thing, even though true, may be the wrong word at the wrong time.

Being strong can be as simple as skipping desert, not taking a drink, not smoking a cigarette. Some of us have great courage to overcome insurmountable obstacles, but lack the strength to pick up the phone and make that call that is nagging at us. Making a commitment of any kind takes strength and courage. Inviting someone to lunch so you can apologize for some wrong takes courage and strength.

Taking a class, taking an exam, writing a theme paper or a thesis – all take strength and courage. Admitting you were in error takes strength of character and intellectual courage.

Everything we do with good intention is done in the name of love. Using our strength and courage to help ourselves or to help others is an act of love. Jesus directed us to "pray always." He was saying to love always. Wherever God is, there is love.

May 26

He takes understanding from the leader of the land, till they grope in the darkness without light. –Job 12:24-25

Friends of Job tried to help him understand the purpose of his suffering. They tried to help him direct thoughts along more pristine lines. He was wallowing in his own misery and couldn't see his way out. He constantly proclaimed his innocence – that he was an honest and just man.

He complained bitterly that God had made some kind of mistake by causing him to suffer such great loss, such great mental and physical pain. He couldn't hear the voice of his friends or his God. He was enduring the kind of darkness in his soul that many before and after him experience.

Leaders of people and communities of people are also subject to misunderstanding, and darkness that clouds current decision making. Leaders are more at the mercy of their own lack of good judgment than those who follow.

Because leaders have greater responsibilities they may also be subject to letting their own egos get in the way of following a power greater than themselves. They can be drunk with power, self-absorbed, walking in darkness, staggering like drunken men.

The more we feel everything depends on us the more likely we are to fail. Lean on God.

May 27

Cease your cries of mourning; wipe the tears from your eyes. – Jeremiah 31:16

I met with a friend going through tough times – separation from a spouse, job instability, health issues – generally bad times. But, I was encouraged by the person's attitude; that trying to change it would cause more harm. We each move forward at our own speed and in our own way. Carrying sorrow, resentment or self-rejection will only add to the rejection we already feel.

There is a time for mourning, a time to take care of ourselves after deep hurt or loss. Sorrow may not seem like its own reward, but sorrow that resolves and ends and moves on is the only way to continue living.

Relationships die, and we mourn – whether the loss is from a death or a drastic falling away from the love and affection once shared. When I divorced my husband of 25 years, it made a huge hole in my life and in my future. My dreams were shattered. I would go running every morning and walking in the evening for weeks, if not months, to keep my head clear and my emotions in check.

My sanity depended on my holding myself together. Maintaining a home with six of my eight children was a goal and a challenge – plus, finding a job.

May 28

Joseph died at the age of a hundred and ten. – Genesis 50:26

Joseph survived the envy and cruelty of his many brothers to live a very long life. We learn from Joseph that anything is possible for those who trust in God, and remain faithful.

Living a long life can be a very good thing for those who remain productive, wise and healthy. A long life of misery is less desirable. Many live long lives in sickness and poverty. We have little choice in the matter. Old people are having their security swept out from under them every day. Lifetime investment and savings are dwindling down because of rising costs and reduction in payments and support.

When I took sociology in college in the 1970s, we saw a film about growing old and being poor. A terrible combination when we add chronic illness to the mix, along with the inability of family members to help out, and the inability of government to keep up with the cost of caring for the aging population growth.

To be sure our children are not burdened with our care in our failing and frail years, we have long-term care insurance. Costly though it may be we want to spare our loved ones the excessive cost of our care in our golden years. And, to ease the pain of our passing, we have pre-paid cremation and burial or distribution of our ashes.

May 29

Wait yet a little and I will instruct you, for there are still words to be said on God's behalf. – Job 36:2

Job had three friends who came to his comfort and aid, to instruct and encourage him – though much of their advice fell on deaf ears. He finally came around and accepted his misfortune and moved on to a ripe old age with restarted wealth and renewed values. He realized that as long as he was still alive then God must have a use for him. His work was not over when disaster fell upon him and made him a humble, down-on-his-knees broken man. He was instructed by his own misery and the kindness of his friends.

Job had a lot to say about what God did to him and how miserable he was. He later had a lot to say through the apparent authorship of the Book of Job. He tells of his misfortune in his own words. He speaks and writes God's words to him. This was a prelude to the *Conversations with God* book made popular in the new age of spiritual growth. Job quoted his three friends as well as bringing his entire story to a community of believers.

We assume one person wrote about all the experiences and all the words spoken to him by God and his friends. He ultimately had a purpose in life. He lived another day, another life that praised God by demonstrating how God worked in him and through his friends.

May 30

A torrent of rain descends; the ocean gives forth its roar. The sun forgets to rise, the moon remains in its shelter. – Habakkuk 3:10-11

Everyone goes through a period of time when it seems as though their world is ending. And, for some it actually does end. No one can know with certainty if there will be a tomorrow – yet we go on day to day expecting another sunrise and another sunset. We expect another good night and another good morning.

There are times when the weather draws the shade on our bright days. When a tornado is threatening and everything gets dark and quiet – the calm before the storm. That sort of calm is not soothing but rather eerie.

Once, when I was visiting my mother outside Detroit we saw the storm warnings ticker across the bottom of the television screen. My aunt, also visiting, and I went outside to sense what was happening. The dogs were not barking; the birds had ceased their songs; and stillness reigned. Fortunately, the tornado never materialized.

So much of our feeling of impending doom never matures into a full-blown storm – and we thank our God one more time for holding back the storm and destruction.

May 31

Do not yoke yourselves in a mismatch with unbelievers. – 2 Corinthians6:14

When we let go of people who are toxic in our lives we do both them and us a favor. Perhaps we are also toxic for them. We may not be doing them any tangible harm, but we probably are enabling them to keep being jerks in our lives and training them to do the same to others.

Believing we can change another person's attitude or actions is a disservice to that person, and we end up being disappointed and probably resentful. We make many choices in life, choices about people we draw close to us.

So many marriages fail because people don't really know themselves well enough to make wise choices. Many relationships are doomed from the beginning. How can we know another person well enough to live together for our entire adult life when we rarely know who we are, or what we want?

Our sexual drives are driving us when it comes to relationships. Intelligence is often clouded. Many end up yoking themselves in a mismatch with unbelievers. It may be more about not believing in oneself and not trusting the other person than it is about our belief in a God. Everyone has to believe in something, or at the very least believe in themselves.

June

Juno
Queen of the Roman gods
And patroness
of marriage and weddings.

June 1

Behold, sons are a gift from the LORD. – Psalms 127:3

I find it difficult not to take issue with Psalms in regard to the valuing of sons over daughters. So much of our world cultures do place a higher value on male babies.

When I was in Catholic grammar school we brought our pennies to school to contribute to the ransom of Chinese babies. This was in the '40s, long before Communism took hold in China.

When the chart on the wall reached $5, we had enough to send to the Maryknoll Fathers in China to ransom one baby from being drowned. At least, that's what we were told, and that's what we believed. We didn't know and didn't ask if we were ransoming boys or girls. It didn't matter. But history seems to be on the side of male babies being saved.

This preference for boy babies has been going on for centuries. Male babies are most often considered heirs to the throne or family fortune. Someone to carry on the family name – assuming girls marry and take the husband's family name.

Sons are indeed a gift from the Lord – as are daughters. I gave birth to six girls and to two boys. These gifts from God are equal in value in the eyes of God – and in my eyes as well.

June 2

Some seed, finally, landed on good soil and yielded grain that spring up. – Mark 4:8

Recently the film "Lincoln" received many honors. It was a story of a man who used riddles, parables, and humorous stories to first of all, gain the attention of his audience or friends in a gathering. Some who heard the story before left the room. That didn't stop Lincoln from finishing his story. Most of the time, he sent his listeners away trying to get the message in the story.

Jesus had a following of considerable numbers – enough to cause the religious leaders and politicians of his time concern that he was stealing their thunder and moving the people away from them. His stories and his healings got him in trouble with those who believed their way was the only way.

The passages preceding the one above detail the various ways the farmers' efforts to sow seed had failed.

When I was young, I visited my grandparents' farm during the summer – sometimes during harvest. I saw the results of their efforts, as well as the work they put in to preparing the soil and planting the seed – and praying for sunshine and rain.

It pays off to listen to the wise ones – to nature itself. There is a season – and timing for everything.

June 3

Go to sleep, and if you are called, reply, "Speak, LORD, for your servant is listening." – 1 Samuel 3:9

Samuel thought the voice he heard was that of his mentor Eli, when he woke and went to Eli three times. This calling was Samuel's first encounter with the Lord, and he did not recognize the voice as one calling him to a life of prophesies. Eli helped Samuel to realize who was calling him. Then Samuel finally answered, "Speak, Lord, for your servant is listening."

It can be so difficult hearing the voice of God in our cultured lives. That's why we take time away from the world to be quiet and listen to that voice within us that speaks with the voice of God.

How can we be certain?

We can only ask God, as did Samuel, to speak, for we are listening.

Being ready and willing to listen is the first step, but being ready and willing to follow the direction is an entirely different matter.

We may not like what we hear. We may not like what we are asked to do. We may not want to continue to listen to the voice that places new demands on our time and on our willing natures.

If we believe that prayer is our way of communicating with God, then we must be willing to listen to the response. Our free will allows us choices.

June 4

Come to terms with him to be at peace. – Job 22:21

Job's friend Eliphaz speaks to him for the third time, humbling Job by reminding him of the times he was less than kind to friend or neighbor, or worker. Job has been chastising God for not understanding his plight. So his friend rebukes Job to come to terms with God and be at peace.

It is in making peace with God that his friend tells him he will learn how to recover from all that has been bringing him down. Job is finally getting the message.

What a good friend it is who will give us good advice, and will not let us continue to live in denial. When we continue to wallow in self-pity nothing good can happen. A true friend knows this about us.

Job's friend has talked to him before, along with two of his other friends. They are getting ready to do an intervention on Job. Maybe this time he will listen.

How desperate we sometime become. How impossible it may seem to dig our way out of the pit of darkness. We feel so sorry for ourselves that we can't see any light at the end of the tunnel.

When all else fails, we give up, and, emotionally or physically drop to our knees and beg God to instruct us – to speak to our hearts.

June 5

Love the LORD, your God,… heed his charge; his statues, decrees and commandments. – Deuteronomy 11:1

The Lord brought the Israelites out of Egypt by protecting them from harm and opening the way promised them by their God. The Egyptians by all standards did not measure up with God. Why God loved and promised one race of people his protection over another is still a mystery. Apparently God did not believe in a level playing field – that all men are created equal.

We were led to believe we all are children of the same God. The God of the Old Testament, or Hebrew Bible, appears to have played favorites. This recorded favoritism gives sway to the competition among all religions.

I was raised in a tradition that believed in the conscience as God's direction in the lives of all people. That same tradition preaches there is no salvation unless you accept Jesus Christ as Lord. It is the same tradition that teaches that each individual is responsible to perform based on their knowledge of right and wrong.

Are all men really created equal? Do we divide them at birth or as they are growing? Can we ever see each other as God sees us?

Namaste! The God in me acknowledges the God in you.

June 6

Toward the faithful you are faithful; toward the wholehearted you are whole hearted. – Psalms 18-A: 26

David thanks the Lord for rescuing him from his enemies. In song, or psalm, David praises his Lord – a good way to keep the Lord on his side. No one likes to help someone out of a jam, to just have that person walk away, go look for new friends, or forget to say "thank you" and begin asking for another favor.

Thus, the old adage, "Do onto others as you would have them do onto you." Or the words of Jesus, "whatever you do to the least of your brethren, you do onto me."

Oops! It's not just about how God treats us and how we communicate with God. There is a multitude of other people in the equation. Maybe God won't notice if we mistreat – gossip about a friend, or slander a foe. Maybe God will be looking the other way.

But psalms tell us that God is astute when it comes to evaluating the ways of the crooked. Can't we just put a little twist on the lie?

One of my dictionaries says astute is an "adjective, having or showing an ability to accurately assess situations or people and turn this to one's advantage." I assume that only human beings are capable of acting contrary to their own best interests. Only God knows all, sees all.

June 7

Listen to your father who begot you, and despise not your mother when she is old. – Proverbs 23:22

Human behavior takes many twists and turns. Proverbs tells us how to behave. This particular section tells us how to behave at the table of the ruler, how children should behave in the presence of their parents and their elders. It tells us about "winebibbers" as well as drunkards and gluttons. Apparently even the ancients had trouble telling one from another

There are many proverbs and many rules and warnings.

Such a flood of reprimands and rules can be overwhelming. No matter what anyone says to us, their actions are louder than their words. Children, especially, are very observant. Their parents may tell them one thing, but a child observes the parent's behavior as a dead giveaway. They are not necessarily practicing what they are preaching.

The hypocrite always has the louder voice. The one who cannot hide the truth from us is the one we generally choose to ignore. Children learn very early about who they can trust, who tells the truth and who they choose to imitate or ignore.

We can't sell the truth, we can only give it away, for its value has no number – it is invaluable.

June 8

My sheep hear my voice. I know them, and they follow me. –John 10:27

Shortly after he became Pope, Francis, spoke to priests about bringing the "lost sheep" back to the church. He also made a reference to their needing to "smell like their sheep." Sounds odd, but the shepherds of old slept with the sheep, watching over them night and day, to protect them from wolves or thieves. Thus, Jesus speaks of knowing his sheep and they know him.

Most of the church elders in Jesus' time took offense at the reference to sheep and shepherds. They were too good to identify with the lowly sheep, or the lowly shepherd. They were looking for a "real" leader. One who would rescue them from the Roman rule.

When I was in Petra, Jordan, with a group of pilgrims, we all stopped to watch a Bedouin shepherd edge his way along the hillside to rescue a stray lamb that seemed unable to move from the spot he was in. Maybe his coat was caught on branches, or perhaps he was young, away from the rest of the flock, and unsure of his footing. He was in a strange place and waited to be rescued.

We cheered and applauded when the shepherd rescued the stray lamb. How appropriate is the message of Jesus – rescuing strays.

June 9

Why do you search for the Living One among the dead? – Luke 24:5

I had to stop the daily writing because we were heavily involved in moving and unpacking, and getting organized. I felt like I was in a cave. The living room of our new home had huge boxes stacked high and wide. We could barely move in the house. I was buried under boxes and having nightmares. It felt like a tomb. I felt claustrophobic.

There have been many times in my life where I felt the breath being sucked out of me: Following the death of my brother when I was 10; Then, during the divorce process ending a 25-year marriage; Then, the death of each of my parents; and, then the sudden death of my 46-year-old daughter.

Death of a loved one has a way of sucking the life out of us. But, we go on, because we must. There is no other option.

When I started back to writing on this particular page it was, or is, actually April 10, a little more than a week after Easter. The above quote was a random selection on June 9. So it was time to reflect on it now. I have posted these selections in advance, through the end of July.

On the televised broadcast of the Easter Vigil Mass from St. Peter's in Rome, the Pope read his homily about the death to the soul consumed with bitterness. He said not to look for the living (love) one among the dead – the negative, and the bitter people.

Ironically, that same homily was delivered word for word at the church here in San Felipe, Mexico. Point well taken.

June 10

The LORD will open up for you his rich treasure house of the heavens, blessing all your undertakings. – Deuteronomy 28:12

We are given to understand that the will of God was far better known to the people closer to the beginning of time. If the words of the prophets, story-tellers, and spiritual teachers of the "old testament" days, are truly inspired, then they were fortunate to have that certainty. Today, it is difficult to sort out the truth.

This particular chapter is dealing with the blessings of obedience. Obedience to what, and to whom? The treasure house of the heavens seems to refer to food and the good weather for everything to grow – the rain and the sun, in proper measure.

The blessing of all their understandings, again, refers to resources. What need did they have for gold and silver, what they needed most was sufficient bounty from the good earth. The good among us think of others. It's in the heart of all to share from our abundance. At least there was a time when it was so.

We are given abundance so we may lend or share with other people and nations. No one likes to be dependent upon the goodness of others or to have to borrow – but someone has to do it.

June 11

Beloved. Pray for us too. – 1 Thessalonians 5:25

During the heat of political campaigns for president of the United States it gives us pause to consider prayer for others. How do people really get better ideas and change their attitudes, and perspectives?

Must we always have arguments – especially when some consider compromise a bad word, worse still, they consider the meaning of the word compromise as a disastrous strategy. At that rate there never will be peace and accord, as long as there are two powerful people, leaders or political parties or movements with opposing points of view.

In our debate classes we learn the art of public discourse – how to disagree and still be respectful. Our societies are skilled at conflict but deficient in conflict resolution. We pray for the day when we can sit down with our brothers and sisters in this country and between countries, and enjoy the spirit of compromise and respect and agreement.

I pray, first for myself to hold others in respect and caring. We can certainly disagree but spare me from being so disagreeable that I'm forced to make amends – by my own conscience I pray for peace, for all peoples to find areas of agreement.

June 12

This will mean health for your flesh and vigor for your bones. – Proverbs 3:8

By doing well and avoiding evil we are promised healing of body and soul. When we are young we seldom think about the need for healing. As we age, we can barely think of anything else.

When we are young and enjoy good health we believe we are powerful and have all the energy we need. We seldom think about God, unless we need a date for a party, or help with a test.

Unfortunately, many young people suffer ill health and disabilities. But as long as we are functioning in our youth we don't think that much about others' health issues. It's a shame, but it isn't our problem. It takes time to learn compassion for the suffering of others. We now pray for their good health, because they ask, because we care. I wish it were as simple as the Proverb says. Not so.

Doing well sometimes has to be its own reward. If we do well because we think it will bring us good health we may be disappointed. The returns are not always what we expect. Helping others does offer healing for the heart and for the soul. Feeling good is often the best reward for helping other.

June 13

One God and Father of all. – Ephesians 4:6

St. Paul makes everything sound so simple, for a man who was writing letters to his followers during his time in a Roman prison. Paul was both a Roman and a Jew. He had been a persecutor of these same people before God's intervention. These people he now sends letters to, and encourages to stay firm in their faith in the risen Christ.

The one who calls himself a "prisoner for the Lord" speaks of love, humility, meekness and patience. He is encouraging the followers who are not yet calling themselves Christians. He still speaks of one God, one people, one purpose on earth – peace.

If this prisoner could see Christians today, what would he think or say? The divisions are greater than ever. All those who say they are following the Christ are harboring so much arrogance, hatred, and intolerance that St. Paul might not recognize them.

There always have been divisions. It's a matter of the intensity of these divisions – or whether we really are one people, with one God and Father of all. The early Christians were fewer, and perhaps it was easier to be one.

June 14

A lamp to my feet is your word, a light to my path. – Psalms 119:105

Some nights, actually most nights, I get up and find my way to the bathroom, as many times as it takes. There are small night lights plugged into several outlets along the way. Even the light showing "0" on the microwave in the kitchen and the green Wi-Fi light in the bedroom.

It seldom occurs to me to turn on a light, because there is enough light from the moon or the small night lights.

I have a friend with macular degeneration who depends on all the light she can get.

I realize the Psalm above is referring to the spiritual path and the need for guidance from the God we depend on for light – or enlightenment. The light that fills our hearts and souls with wisdom and understanding is the light that is the lamp to our feet. The word of God isn't always easy to hear or see in action. We have to make straight our own path, removing all the rocks and filling in all the holes.

God may provide the light for our path, but we are ultimately responsible for grading and paving our way. We have to keep our eyes open so we will recognize the obstacles on our path. We can't always blame others for the potholes.

June 15

Get rid of all bitterness, all passion and anger, harsh words, slander, and malice of every kind. – Ephesians 4:31

I have heard that nature abhors a vacuum. We try to break old habits without filling in the gaps – and we fail. I learned long ago, the hard way, about buying new clothes. I felt the urge to go shopping and try on clothes, and bring home the package, and hang it in the closet. I learned that I could do all that without removing the sales tags.

Since one of the things I hate to do is to go back to a store to return an item, I didn't want to exchange for something else, I wanted the cash credited back to my VISA card. It didn't take many trips like that to break the habit of seeking an immediate gratification by purchasing an item of clothing.

All other attitudes and behaviors can be easily and consistently altered – if we really want to make change in our lives. This passage deals with vices to be avoided. There is another word that sounds the same – vise – as in a grip, or holding things in place. A vice is also a habit that holds us in its grip. Our task is to release the grip and break the chains that bind us.

We can be free of whatever has us in its grip. We can be free of vice in life.

June 16

Of his fullness we have all had a share. –John 1:16

John, son of Zebedee, was a real person who lived in real times when Romans ruled his part of the world. He truly believed that the God of his people would send a real person to rescue him and his people from all that threatened them. He believed someone would show them the way.

That someone proved to be one from among his own people, someone John and his brothers and many others came to believe was sent by God, anointed by God, and the one who would fulfill the prophesies that had been carried down through the centuries.

At the beginning of this Gospel according to John, he seems to pick up on the same prologue from Genesis, the first book of the Old Testament. His opening words are even more poetic than Genesis. He says, "In the beginning was the Word; the Word was in God's presence, and the Word was God."

John's faith declares Jesus as the Word, and the Word and God as one.

John speaks of John (the Baptist), the cousin of Jesus who lived in the desert, as a member of a strict rule that waited for "the One" who would come after him. His followers became the followers of Jesus as well. They were all Jews who believed Jesus was the One promised by God, through the prophets, to lead them.

June 17

While from behind, a voice shall sound in your ears:
"This is the way; walk in it." – Isaiah 30:21

Isaiah was the most respected prophet of his time, and the distant times to come. He warned the Israelites against forming an alliance with the Pharaoh of Egypt. The life of the Egyptians, however, must have been attractive to the people Isaiah tried to guide. Perhaps some of those old warnings and fears never go away. Perhaps the people of that region will never fully trust and work and live in peace with each other.

The people are promised an inner voice to keep them on the path, and a Teacher they will see with their own eyes. Yet, with all that help, the people strayed. Are we any different? How often does that inner voice get drowned out by the constant din of news reports and commentators on television?

What a relief it is to turn on the mute, that wonderful little button that frees us from loud commercials. Blessed are the recording mechanisms that allow us to record now, save, and play later – using skip, fast forward, and mute.

Where is our mute button? Why can't we bring back that small, inner voice when we want it, on our time? Maybe we don't really want to hear it anyway.

June 18

When he prayed again, the sky burst forth with rain and the land produced its crop. – James 5:18

Sometimes when I select a passage randomly – just opening the Bible and pointing – I'm timid about writing my thoughts about the passage. I often sit in awe of the words and the original meaning – and I am humbled by the power of the words.

I read the above passage first as a blessing on the crops and the harvest, but upon reading the footnotes and other passages leading up to this one – I learned a new lesson. I learned about context in the Bible. I learned that the writers of the Bible had talent with words. I am a student of literature, and believe the old and new testaments are insightful writing, good literature, mostly interesting story telling.

It is perfectly alright to study these ancient words for all they have to offer – historically, spiritually, and for literary content.

In this passage, James is referencing Elijah and the power of prayer – and the power in asking others to join in prayer. James says, "The fervent petition of a holy man is powerful indeed. Elijah was only a man like us, yet he prayed earnestly that it would not rain. And, no rain fell on the land for three years, and six months."

Then, follows the passage above – he prayed for rain, and rain came. Dare we doubt the possibility of the truth here – somehow – prayer – works?

June 19

I have never stopped thanking God for you and recommending you in my prayers. – Ephesians 1:16

A few days ago a friend called because she was distressed about a friend of hers who has been undergoing treatment for cancer and was hospitalized from too much chemo therapy. His mouth and other parts of his body were burned. And he had a high fever. He is blind as well.

My friend, also legally blind, in tears, asked if I would pray for her friend. I said, "of course." She went on with more detail, and then asked if I would help her say the "Serenity Prayer," as she couldn't remember how it went, couldn't remember the words. Very slowly, word by word, I said a line and then she repeated: "God, grant me the serenity to accept the things I cannot change, the courage to change the things I can, and the wisdom to know the difference."

The following morning my friend told me she called the hospital, and her friend had been released. His fever broke. She was so hyper she asked God to make her humble, because she might think she was responsible for her friend's healing.

I assured her it was alright to feel a part of the healing. Why else pray, if you don't think it helps?

June 20

Teach me to do your will. – Psalms 143:10

Every day is different. When all goes well we forget about yesterday's troubles and struggles. We only want a level playing field where we have at least half a chance to succeed.

The old song about "Yesterday, when I was young," reminds us how good it was as well as how terrible it might have been. But, we survived the tragedies so far, and we have lived to play or fight again. Even the worst of times have moments of relief. As long as we stay connected with our higher vision of who we are and who we can become.

We each need our sense of values and goals to achieve. We seek guidance from human sources. From those who know more than we do about life. Those who have walked this path – and with their bumps and bruises, have reached a place we can admire and strive toward.

It is so difficult sometimes to know the will of God. I think sometimes we can only practice what our medical doctor practices, "to do no harm."

As long as we do the right thing for the right reason, we can only hope we will get the right results. May our God spirit guide us on our path.

June 21

Let tomorrow take care of itself. Today has trouble enough of its own. – Matthew 6:34

How will I know and understand the words of this passage. I know deep in my psyche that everything always works out like it is supposed to. I can only do my part and then wait impatiently for the results. All things come together in God's time.

My career as a writer was laced with deadlines. When I first wrote for community newspapers I worked off and on during the week, doing interviews and taking photos to accompanying the stories. I specialized in feature stories and profiles, as well as school and community news. All, while raising eight children, infant to age 16.

On Sunday afternoons I prepared a big family dinner. Then I went into my laundry room/office – and typed my column, my stories and photo captions – on my Corona electric typewriter, with carbon copies.

When finished, I drove downtown Portland about 10:00 PM at night, and dropped everything in the night delivery slot at the newspaper office – the first of many deadlines.

There is a time for doing what we need to do. There is a time for letting go, and trusting that all will be well. We like to do everything perfectly – but we can only do what we can do.

June 22

They publish the fame of your abundant goodness. – Psalms 145:7

One bible says “celebrate,” another says “publish the fame of your abundant goodness.” There was a time before printing presses and internet and television, when celebrate meant shouting from the rooftops or announcing from the pulpit, or some other platform. Far fewer people shared the good news of what God had done for them. Life was quieter, more mundane.

The idea of abundance has changed considerably as well. What once was considered sufficient, or fulfillment of our needs, has become an abundance of our wants and desires. We dream bigger, and we dream more often – almost instantly – of what will fill our lives with that abundance we seek.

Commercials for AT&T on television show a man sitting on the floor with a few young children, asking them, “What is better, more or less?”

Of course children repeat what they hear and see. Of course, more is better. Absolutely, more is better.

But, is it really better for us?

No one would think of answering “Less is better.” No one would think, or dare say, “Enough is best, and a bit more to share with others.”

We don’t really know what is enough, do we? “Enough” is far vaguer than “more or less.” Abundant goodness will have to be enough, whatever that may be.

June 23

Those who live according to the Spirit set their minds on the things of the spirit. – Romans 8:5

People raise their eyebrows when I say with some enthusiasm that "next to me, my husband is the most important person in my life."

The fact is, if I am not right in my spiritual life, my spiritual connection, then I am not good for me, for him, or for anyone else. I cannot be something I am not, or give something I do not have.

I took a long time growing up. Although I am the mother of eight grown children, I admit there were areas of neglect in my life. Like knowing who I really am, how I teach people to treat me, who deserves my respect and friendship, and how not to abuse or mistreat myself and others.

The Spirit lives in a positive, kind and understanding person, more than in a mess of negativity and discontent. I have to decide every day which side of that love-hate relationship I want to be on. It is so easy to go along, to get along.

But, that's not who I am now, or who I choose to be in the future. I live in peace. I come in peace. I am waving the white flag of surrender. I do not want to be the kind of person I once was capable of being. I want to grow in the Spirit.

June 24

Be glad in the LORD and rejoice, you just. – Psalms 32:11

We are well aware that we do not always think, say, and do the right thing. But most of us try – day after day – hour after hour.

If we came to believe we were without fault that would be the greatest fault of all. Our pride and arrogance would get the better of us. We sometimes see people who seem to have smooth sailing. Everything they try seems to work for them. We are in no position to speculate about anyone else – every human has something to overcome and deal with.

All the Psalms that call us to celebrate and rejoice and be glad tell us we are "just" and "upright of heart." The only thing we know is we have sought and received forgiveness. We have corrected course and we are back on the narrow path to a life of being of service to our fellow man.

We see others in a different light. The light we use to look inside our own lives is far dimmer than the light we use to view others.

The hardest thing we do is be glad and rejoice, and be grateful for the blessings in our own lives instead of trying to match the accomplishments of our friends, neighbors, or relatives.

I almost always want more – especially more time – one more day to do it right.

June 25

He who pursues justice and kindness will find life and honor. – Proverbs 21:21

The book of Proverbs is also referred to as the Book of Wisdom – although there is another Book of Wisdom that was written later, by someone other than Solomon. These books were often referred to by Jesus and his followers – who were raised on these traditions – these words. Thus there is a common thread throughout the history of the Hebrews and the early Christians.

It is hard to argue with the messages in the Proverbs. The phrase above comes from Solomon's words – and many of these short phrases have been rewritten over the centuries in more modern terms. Solomon was considered the wisest of men and so his words still carry great weight.

To pursue justice and kindness can be seen as contradictory, since most justice as we know it is delivered with very little kindness at all. There are places in this world – and in the United States of America as well – that have abolished the death penalty for crimes committed.

Where do we draw the line when it comes to killing in the name of justice? All wars are considered "just wars" and condone killing in great numbers. There is no tempering of justice with mercy in war.

June 26

Let us not grow weary of doing good. – Galatians 6:9

Paul had disagreements and arguments and discussions with the other followers of Jesus, whom they agreed was the Christ, the one sent by God to redeem and unite all mankind. They had disagreements about which parts of the ancient Hebrew laws and traditions to continue, and which ones to drop or set aside for a time.

Paul always argued for upholding and including the law of Moses, the commandments given by God to the people wandering in the desert forty years in search of the Promised Land. Paul considered the search to still be continuing – only the Promised Land was now something beyond the world as known at his time – it was less tangible and more mysterious.

The phrase above comes near the end of Paul's short letters to Galatians – pleading with them to keep all the history and intention of their ancient heritage and relationship with the God who gave them the Christ – to be firm in resolve and pursuit of doing good.

The harvest probably refers to the gathering of more followers as much as it refers to the ultimate goal of a heaven beyond this earthly life.

June 27

My mouth shall speak wisdom; prudence shall be the utterance of my heart. – Psalms 49:4

Prudence is just another name for doing the right thing. That thing we feel in our gut when we have struggled with the pros and cons of an issue is called resistance, worry, concern and doubt that holds us back from making a decision. Then we feel relief and release once the right decision is made. Then we feel wise.

The decision making comes slower as we age, and sometimes the decisions involve more serious consequences. Our heads become filled with options that may seem correct one time, but not another. We would hope that practice would at least make decision making easier, smarter.

The more functions that become automatic the better chance we have for concentration on the important decisions. This Psalm shows us the ideal.

When I turned 80, I said to my friends, "Isn't anyone going to ask me if I feel any older?"

They asked.

I said "I don't feel any older, I just feel a lot wiser."

I just hope I can fulfill my own prophesy.

June 28

Live as free men, but do not use your freedom as a cloak for vice. – 1 Peter 2:16

Freedom comes to us in degrees. Children have tremendous freedom because someone else is taking care of them, or should be. They go outside and play. They know they may not cross the street, but they still have plenty of space to move around in because they are young, carefree, and active. They don't know that much of the world outside their yard and their house. They have not yet been given responsibility for anyone or anything beyond their little world.

Most of us abhor the concept of slavery, ownership of another human being. Those whose history is one of having little freedom know all too well how it dampens the spirit, clouds the vision, and diminishes opportunity and prosperity.

Those of us who have always lived as free people can't possibly understand slavery or living under a dictatorship. We cherish our freedom to the point of not acknowledging how much freedom we have. We want more. Sometimes we take more than our share.

All peoples of the world are living with boundaries placed on them by government, family, employers – there are rules and more rules. That's what we do to have a more orderly existence.

June 29

My refuge and my fortress, my God, in whom I trust. – Psalms 91.2

It is easy to forget about or ignore God's presence in our lives when all is well, it's all going according to our plan. Out of sight, out of mind, just as we forget friends, family, and neighbors when we go away on vacation. They are still "back home," but we are off having a great new adventure.

God is different. When we move to a new location, God moves with us. When we go on vacation to Hawaii or on a safari in Africa – God goes with us. We don't even have to pack any extra clothing or leave room in our suitcases for God to squeeze in on our return. There is room for all the fun stuff we buy while away. God fits right in – no problem – duty-free.

The God we may choose to ignore during the good times has plenty to do while we are having fun – but we still register on God's radar. Somehow, God has time for us even when we don't have time for God. Amazing how that works.

The beauty of a belief in a God who is all powerful and ever present is that we know God exists in good times and bad.

June 30

"Let there be light, and there was light." – Genesis 1:3

Darn, I should have said that, or darn, I shouldn't have said that. I know better. I'm better than that. My tone of voice gave it away. I'm really not as sharp as I pretend to be. My thoughts seem slow and muddled. I can't remember that person's name. I recognize the face, and the name is on the tip of my tongue. I'll do my alphabet exercise, and when I get to the letter the name will pop into my head. Almost always.

I'm not perfect. I just keep trying and hope no one notices that I'm not always clear in my thoughts and in my expression. I used to be a lot smarter. If I keep quiet then no one will notice that I didn't understand what is being said. I have nothing to contribute. People will just assume I didn't hear the comment or question. I choose to listen more carefully at some times. And, sometimes it just doesn't matter.

When the world began, we assume there was a void, no light. Then, even if you believe in the "Big Bang" theory when all the neutrons in existence expanded into the sun that now lights and heats the universe – you must admit that was a fortunate accident of nature. Just as every spark of intelligence is a miracle.

July

❧

Named for Julius Caesar
In 44 BC because
he was born in the month of Quintilis,
Latin for fifth month,
the former name of July when the
Roman year began in March.

July 1

Justice will bring about peace; right will produce calm and security. – Isaiah 32:17

If I could choose just one bumper sticker for my car it would be "Peace is Possible." In spite of all the negative rhetoric assaulting my ears, I am stubborn in my belief in the goodness of God and the ultimate goodness in human beings to work together for the common good.

Call me crazy, but I still believe that anything is possible if we want it. My generation has known very little peace – the absence of war. The war industry lives on – producing the hardware for conflict. We sometimes wonder how we can redirect all that energy, production and employment that contribute to conflict – toward conflict resolution and conflict abandonment.

We have plenty of justice, at least the activity that calls itself the justice system, but how much peace does all that activity produce?

"Right will produce calm and security."

Is that my "right" or your "right?"

It all begs the question, are we capable of living at peace, without conflict, without war?

I will continue to believe in Isaiah's promise of a "peaceful country, secure dwelling and quiet resting places."

July 2

We who are receiving the unshakable kingdom should hold fast to God's grace. – Hebrews 12:28

If we consider the writings of the first followers of Christ on their individual merit, it is miraculous that someone wrote a letter that someone else saved. Today, we receive a letter in the mail, or an electronic mail message – and it is gone soon after it is read.

Because letters were so rare is the logical reason why they were saved. Letters not only took great effort to write on the parchment of its day, but the delivery time was problematic. I'm even less familiar with the speed and ease of getting letters from one city to another, even hundreds or thousands of miles apart, today.

Bible footnotes indicate that this letter to the Hebrews was probably written by someone other than Paul; a prolific and well educated follower of Paul, resourceful at getting his messages delivered, in words of Paul.

Paul is constantly asking his followers to stay the course, finish the race, and keep the faith in the belief that Jesus was indeed the fulfillment of God's promise to the Hebrews of old. Paul was communicating with people who heard second or third hand about this Jesus person.

We were led to believe that Jesus told his apostles they could heal the sick and raise the dead, as he had done. There had to have been proof to keep all these followers interested.

July 3

Take as a model of sound teaching what you have heard me say, in faith and love. – 2 Timothy 1:13

Almost everything written in the Bible, old or new testament, is wisdom or truth, as known to the writer at the time, and handed down through the ages, translated and rewritten, again and again. People were more trusting in those days. Now we need at least three reliable sources, with direct quotes as examined by a committee of our peers or a panel of experts to believe.

In other words, it becomes more difficult to know who is telling the truth. Few of us are secure in our own thinking to believe the first thing we hear without checking with three different cable news shows.

I saw an affirmation many years ago that serves me well, “I will know what I need to know when I need to know it.” When I remember to trust this affirmation, I can let go of the problem. Sometimes the right outcome presents itself, and I am free of the responsibility and the worry.

Love is the answer. To want good for myself and for everyone else in my area of influence – that is the goal – to believe in the best outcome.

July 4

And I will walk at liberty, because I seek your precepts. – Psalms 119:45

I have always been a goal setter, constantly reading and seeking. It has been this way since childhood learning and education, both formal and informal. Everything in life has a purpose and a goal.

Human beings have an incredible need to control time and space. We have clocks and watches and smart phones that tell us the day of the year and the time of day. This is our crude attempt to create order out of chaos.

When I retired, or as I honestly admit, I quit my day job, I asked a friend how she kept track of what day it was.

"I take a newspaper," was her response.

While in Mexico during the winter, we do not have a daily newspaper. We do, however, have a calendar, and a clock, and satellite TV with the day and time constantly noted and available.

We humans are capable of limited freedom to think and say and do what and when we want. We need a sense of order, routine, organization, and time management.

However we choose to get there, we do need a sense of purpose and meaning in our daily lives. We need our dreams for the future, no matter our age. It's a habit I cannot break. I am a planner, a dreamer, and sometimes a schemer. Even at 80, I dream big. I don't know what it means to act my age.

July 5

When the trumpet blows, listen! – Isaiah 18:3

The news of conflict on the African continent bombards our quiet and busy days. Do we hear the voice of God in the turmoil in Egypt or Syria or Libya? Isaiah refers to the land of Ethiopia in this section, and the land of Egypt. There are expectations that the people of the world, even then, would find a way to live in peace.

This God of Isaiah is always calling on prophets and their followers to listen to the words of peace and build communities of caring for one another.

It appears the people are always ready to fight off intruders and invaders. Protection of person, property and territory is as old as creation. The writers of the Bible seemed to be at war or near war constantly. There were fewer people, and even those few couldn't get along.

We are told we all come from the same roots, if we choose to believe the Adam and Eve story that implies incest for procreation. There were two brothers, and Cain slew his brother Abel. No mention of other couples or families, so we have to assume the survivor married his sister, or sisters, to continue the creative process. This premise seems rather unhealthy.

July 6

Not on bread alone shall man live. – Luke 4:4

We live in the midst of abundance and yet children go to bed hungry all around us. Families are displaced and have lost their homes, many living in their cars.

We were traveling on the interstate highway one time and stopped at the rest area. There was a man and his wife and three young children, probably under age eight. They had a sign asking for gas money for their old motor home. I gave the woman $20. I said it was for my daughter Carol, who died homeless in Las Vegas when she was 46. I can't stand to see women and children homeless. They were doing their best to stay together, doing odd jobs, home schooling, and begging.

I never had to beg. I never wanted for food or shelter. Times were tough, but somehow there was always a way out. More rope when I thought I had reached the end. We do not live on bread alone, but we do need food, and shelter, and the other basics.

Families in financial trouble must try to stay together. They need the love of each other to survive. They want to live.

Jesus said the poor will always be with us. They are everywhere. They are poor and hungry and homeless.

How can we pass them by without some offer of help? I guess we learn to turn the other cheek – away from them – because we can't bear to see them so poor.

July 7

Be silent while I teach you wisdom. –Job 33:33

Elihu, the youngest of Job's three friends who tried to talk sense with him has just rebuked Job that he should quit complaining and justifying himself.

A true friend will not enable the person who is totally off track. Elihu tells Job to shut up and listen, so he can teach him something. This friend begins to share his experience, strength and wisdom with Job, and his words begin to take root.

Though younger than Job, this young friend finds the courage to tell the very nay saying Job that it is time to quit blaming everything bad on God, and just accept the fact that suffering of one kind or another is, simply put – a part of life.

We are so like Job. We always look for someone or something to blame for the hurt and sorrow we encounter. We waste so much healing time engaging in blaming and resisting the guidance and support of those who see more clearly into our suffering.

I have many friends who will speak the truth to me in my times of trouble, doubt, and self-loathing. There is a way out of misery – it's called accepting, forgiving, and moving on.

July 8

I am the Alpha and the Omega. – Revelation 1:8

This passage repeats again toward the end of Revelations. Our finite minds can only accept the words, without fully knowing all the mysterious meaning behind the words.

When I was taking a class in Philosophy during my undergraduate final year, I wrote a paper about our human circle of alpha connecting with omega. If we believe that nothing can be totally destroyed, but only changes form, then that applies to us humans a well.

We come from somewhere and when we die we go somewhere. That part of us that lives and breathes and thinks and moves the various systems in our bodies – that part of us lives on somewhere and somehow.

What is true for God, for Christ, for all the prophets, and all people who ever lived – is true for each one of us.

When the door opened to allow us into this life, we were already mapping our course through to the next life, following the demise of these human bodies.

If God is everywhere, in all things, and God is Spirit, and Spirit is indestructible – then we will all know the circle of life.

July 9

Let it be "yes" if you mean yes and "no" if you mean no. –James 5:12

Say what you mean, and mean what you say. It all sounds good, and possible, but there are many slips between the lip and the tongue. We spend so much of our lives trying to please others, to be loved and accepted.

To say what we honestly think and feel can have consequences we may be unprepared to deal with. The slip frequently occurs between the tongue and the other person's ear. Just because I have a master's degree in communications doesn't mean I can always get it right. It's what we call "misunderstanding." I didn't mean for it to sound like it sounded. I didn't mean to insult, demean, or confuse you.

We do the best we can to get our message out. Maybe the younger generations have it right about brevity. There may be less opportunity for misunderstanding in 140 characters, including spaces and punctuation, than in spontaneous face to face communication, or even phone conversations.

Sometimes the less said the better. My mother said, "If you can't say something nice about a person, then maybe it is best to say nothing at all."

Our mothers often knew best. Not always, but enough times to listen and remember what we once heard and learned.

July 10

You have blessed the work of his hands, and his livestock are spread over the land. –Job 1:10

This passage is early in the Book of Job, when everything is going well. He has his family, property and status intact. Satan is the one speaking to God about all the good things God has provided Job.

Does Satan really exist? Does God really favor one person over another by paving the way to wealth? Is this book a novel or the reporting of facts by a person trying to make sense out of the good and bad happenings in his life?

In our modern times, how must a man or woman think and feel when a tornado or hurricane totally destroys their property, the animals on their farm, and the loss of children or other family members? Too often we blame God, as in "Act of God," or the devil, as in "the devil made me do it," for what happens in our lives. I don't know who is harder at work, God or the devil. It doesn't seem realistic that an all-powerful God would fall for the game that Satan plays here – challenging God, as in "I dare you." It seems more like a human being trying to place blame – somewhere – anywhere – to explain the terrible losses, for which there is no rational answer.

The Rabbi, who wrote the book about, when bad things happen to good people, seems to counter the argument in

Job's account of the pact that the devil makes with God. For some things there is no reasonable answer, no one thing or person to blame. Pain of loss cries out for answers – and answers do not come. God is silent – we can only accept and move on.

July 11

We are truly his handiwork, created in Christ Jesus to lead the life of good deeds. – Ephesians 2:10

St. Paul insures us that we can take no credit for the good we are or the good we do. All that good is a gift from God. In that we are his handiwork and his creation we are living in his debt. However, it seems to me we are responsible for maintaining all that good with subsequent good deeds. And, what about the person who has nothing but trouble and woe – who is the handy man in that case?

I can be grateful, and thank God for all the good in my life. What do I do about things that go wrong? I know God wants me to be happy, joyous and free from illness and worry – but, that is not the way day to day life works. There are good days and not so good days. Who is to blame there? Does God get all the credit and none of the blamc? Do we have to accept all the blame and get none of the credit?

I know life isn't fair, but when we hurt, we hurt. God doesn't hurt. God is immune to pain, suffering and death.

If Jesus hadn't suffered we would not be able to accept that part of him that is God. Jesus taught us how to be compassionate – and how to share happiness, through kindness and forgiveness.

July 12

Look about and see, they are all gathering and coming to you. – Isaiah 49:18

Is Isaiah begging or bragging? Does he take some credit for the way people are repenting and returning to the worship of their God?

If Isaiah is referring to all the people of God, as they are known at that time – then what can we single out as the accomplishments of God's people today?

We are all one – all children of the same God. Our accomplishments as a community, country or world community can only be viewed as the almighty power in the universe views us all – as either cooperating or in conflict. Together, we have a mighty power – but as soon as we kick those behind us climbing the ladder of what we consider success, we weaken the entire fabric of society.

If it is really "all about me" then I have lost my way to success, and peace of soul. This is all about one act at a time. Are we moving forward as a civilization, or are we on the decline? We are each responsible for our own thoughts and actions – and our own omissions.

When could we have been a better person, but made a different choice? If we ask for divine guidance then we are responsible for acting spontaneously on the inspired guidance we receive.

July 13

Daughter, it is your faith that has cured you.
Now go in peace. – Luke 8:48

This is not the date or the anniversary of my daughter Carol's death. It is a day I have chosen to write about her, and to heal my soul.

She, of course, is in a better place – and I truly do – and must believe this or I could not go on living. She had 46 years on this planet – and many of those days were troublesome for me – and absolute terror for her.

We look on the lives of those we have loved and lost without judgment, but not without some regret. For a mother there always will be the question of what I could have done different. Where did I fail her? But, my faith tells me I must let it all go. I must believe she – my daughter – has touched the hem of his garment and she now knows peacc.

Will this feeling of loss and regret ever leave me? Probably. Temporarily. But, on birthdays and anniversaries of a death the pain once again washes all over me – and I hope it cleans out all the cobwebs on its journey through my soul.

My mother always said "life is for the living." That was after losing her only son, my brother – when he was only half past eleven.

July 14

Forty years in the desert you sustained them. – Nehemiah 9:21

Trying to fit a passage of the Old Testament into its historical perspective can be a daunting task. At some point, all the prophets and those recording the history of the Hebrew people begin to sound alike. History continually repeats the errors of the past, the people of the past. Why do we insist on recording the past when we learn so little from it?

We can argue whether every word in these sacred books is inspired by God, or whether people simply tried to give an account of what they knew of the time in which they lived.

Nehemiah is one more person sounding the alarm on his people, the people of God. He reminds his people that they, and those who came before them, were given the instruction of God's spirit in their lives. It's the parent reminding the child, "I worked and slaved for you – and now look at how you act, how you ignore me."

Sure, they were cared for during their wanderings for forty years in the wilderness – they survived.

What happens to us, today, when we are surviving our wanderings in our desolate spiritual wilderness? Do we take comfort knowing others, before us, have survived?

July 15

Listen to counsel and receive instruction, that you may eventually become wise. – Proverbs 19:20

Proverbs always sound like my mother. She only went to the eighth grade as a girl living on a Pennsylvania farm. Her father had black lung disease from working in the coal mines. Her brothers worked the farm during the day and the coal mine afternoons and evenings. Her older sister left the farm around age 16, and found employment in a laundry in Detroit. About age 16, my mother left the farm and joined her sister at the laundry.

My mother ended her formal education but never stopped learning. She probably was as well educated as some high school graduates in my day. At least she thought so – and told you so.

I don't know how she became so wise. But I thought she was wise. I didn't always agree with her and often snuck around under the radar of her direction. She always had a saying – which I suspect came mostly from proverbs. I heard them often enough that some of them stuck with me, and I sometimes repeated them to my own children.

Did my children hear any of my mother's wisdom coming out of my mouth? I can only hope it is so.

As I now near the age my mother was before she passed from this life – it isn't so important what she said, but more important that I acknowledge her wisdom.

July 16

The LORD will guard your coming and your going, both now and forever. – Psalms 121:8

We are constantly reminded that we live in an unsafe world. We have been to places in this world where I knew while I was there it probably was the only time I would be in that place because of the security risk.

All the places in the Holy Land that are sacred to people of all faiths have been increasingly unsafe for decades. I hope there might be some respect for holy places – places important to millions of people. But there are no guarantees.

When we were in Egypt, the year before the Arab Spring peaceful rebellion, we had an armed guard on board our tour bus. We trusted the people who guided us to also protect us. We probably travel – or have traveled – considerably more than the average American. We are trusting souls.

We don't consciously place our trust in the Lord of all, but like little children we go our merry way, expecting to be protected. When we return, however, we consciously express our gratitude to the powers that be for a safe journey. I hope the Psalm is true – that we are protected now and forever.

July 17

Draw close to God, and he will draw close to you. – James 4:8

Since God is everywhere, he or she never moves. We move closer or farther away.

God is only a thought away – a second in time. So, what is our excuse? Are we too busy or not interested in maintaining a healthy connection? We manage to do the same thing with our friends and relatives – no time – out of sight and out of mind.

So pull up a chair, have a seat, re-connect with the only power in the universe. The power from where all other power and energy and ideas get their bearings.

When a sailor is adrift at sea, he looks to the sky at night and the sun during the day for direction. When we feel lost or adrift, it can be as easy as stepping out of our crazy pace, our racing brain, and ask that power to lend a little light, heat, energy, and ideas.

We don't have to look over our shoulders to see who is following us, we only have to slow our rapid pace and wait for God to catch up. Sounds easy – right – all we have to do is think like a child – God will wait for us to catch up, or find us if we are lost.

July 18

Let me hear the sounds of joy and gladness. – Psalm 51:10

There was a period of my life when I felt that I was doomed to misery forever. Even when the sun was shining, the days seemed dark. I knew there was a way out. I knew if I waited it out, my days would get brighter. There was no joy.

I bought a book of Psalms. The title had "joy" in large print. I wondered what joy felt like. Something magic happened. Joy started seeping in, a little at a time. I read verses that made little sense to me, but for some reason I believed if I continued to read these passages joy would become more familiar to me.

I don't know why some things work for me when my overriding thought is doubt. I'll do it, even though I doubt it will work. I guess that's called faith, and a bit of hope.

Sometime, somewhere, I have had success with reading something – and the wheels turned, and then I kicked into gear. Suddenly you hear the laughter of little children again; now, music sooths restlessness, and the sound of your own voice is less irritating.

Joy returns, and it stays, and it grows, and there is no more need to wallow in your own darkness and gloom. It's a miracle. Light comes through the cracks in our consciousness. We are alive, again.

July 19

He made my feet swift as those of hinds, and set me on the heights. – 2 Samuel 22:34

The Hebrew Bible is an historical account of many battles, told from the perspective of their fault, strength, and guidance from God – and that is all we know. I believe, somewhere it is said, that the victorious get to write the history. There are many versions of history of the war in Viet Nam – and the Korean conflict, as well as World War I and WWII.

What are we to believe about God? Whose side is God on anyway?

My God is on my side. And, that's the only truth I know. When the Buddhist says Namaste, he or she is acknowledging the God or spirit in both political parties. With that belief, how could a Buddhist ever enter into conflict? How could anyone enter into battle believing the enemy is truly another expression of the same God?

Life has become all about winning, all about conquering and success. The battle that the people of peace wage is one of conquering our own demons, our own enemies. The enemy truly is within each of us when we refuse to acknowledge the humanity of every other person alive.

Unfortunately, for most people, life is all about self-defense, standing our ground, being right, and killing.

July 20

He has made everything appropriate to its time. – Ecclesiastes 3:11

We think we know the truth about many things and many people – but we do not know the many truths we claim to know. We constantly discover new insights that allow us to change our opinions – which we consider our truths.

Most of us were schooled and raised to believe there are infallible truths – never changing rights and wrongs. We were taught to defend our closely held principles. A pragmatic approach to life's happenings was frowned upon – "compromise" was considered evil.

We continue to act out of our own stupidity and ignorance and stubbornness. Why are we always right and someone else always wrong?

Welcoming change and discovering new ways of solving problems and living and forgiving is our only salvation.

July 21

No one makes a fool of God! A man will reap only what he sows. – Galatians 6:7

According to the American Heritage Dictionary, Karma, a Hindu and Buddhist teaching, is "the sum and consequences of a person's actions during the successive phases of his existence, is regarded as determining his destiny."

We know from the writings of Paul that he traveled extensively throughout the known world of his time. Perhaps the Asian thoughts regarding the sum of our actions and Paul's comments regarding reaping only what we sow merge at some point.

The destiny of the Buddhist and the destiny of the Christ follower seem to mean the same thing, whether life after death or life before death.

Why do we debate such small differences in the meanings of spiritual teachings, and lose appreciation for the common good?

All people of good will mean well. All good people who do good deeds are well-meaning. Shall we listen more to what people say and observe what they do, and let the judgment fall upon others, not us?

It's an awesome responsibility to make judgment on others, a job given to those who are trained and skilled as judges.

Our responsibility is to assess our own thoughts, words and actions.

Neither God nor the devil makes us do anything we are not willing to do. Neither can be made the fool of our actions.

July 22

There are in the end three things that last: faith, hope, and love, and greatest of these is love. – 1 Corinthians 13:13

Many years ago one of my daughters asked me to read the well-known passage of St. Paul quoted above, at her wedding ceremony. This passage is generally associated with conjugal love – the joining together of two people in marriage. But, I suspect that the meaning of love or charity goes much deeper.

I, who write on this passage, and those of you who read what I write, we pride ourselves on our intelligence, and our ability to read and write. That ability does not necessarily give us the true meaning of the words we speak, or hear, or write or read.

If God is life, and God is love, then every living thing, every living person is an expression of God's life, and God's love. The native in the jungle cannot read or write, or speak or understand English language, or other formal, "civilized" languages. Yet, we must certainly agree that that human being has a soul, a body, a mind – and can love.

Just because an unschooled human being has never read the words above, and knows nothing about Jesus, Moses, Buddha, or any other avatar, prophet, or spiritual teacher or leader – does not mean that person is godless or devoid of godlike qualities.

Intellectually knowing about God, or the love of God, isn't the same as the ability to love, and the practice of loving.

July 23

May he who is the Lord of peace give you continued peace in every possible way. – 2 Thessalonians 3:16

During an 11-day stay in Rome, I took a side trip to Assisi, Italy. While our group was exploring the Cathedral in the valley, I took a few minutes to pray in the small chapel that was enclosed inside the huge building. The small chapel and adjoining infirmary where St. Francis lived and died were preserved in this cocoon.

The small voice that came from deep inside my heart and soul said, "Lord, make me an instrument of your peace."

That peace of St. Francis is the absence of hatred, injury, doubt, despair, darkness and sadness. Once we overcome those negative traits, and replace them with love, pardon, faith, hope, light and joy – we will know peace – the peace that our benevolent God intends for us to experience.

There is work to be done for each individual to know that kind of peace. Each of us is responsible for doing what it takes to know the kind of peace that reaches out to others with consolation, understanding, love, giving and forgiving.

Wanting serenity, peace, security, comfort and love in our lives requires the willingness to ask, listen – and act accordingly.

July 24

Your adornment is rather the hidden character of the heart, expressed in the unfading beauty of a calm and gentle disposition. – 1 Peter 3:4

Unfortunately, this lovely passage is one that instructs "wives to be subject to their husbands." We don't often hear that direction coupled with the other admonitions, such as, "you husbands, too, must show consideration for those who share your lives."

Because women have been "subject to their husbands" without the consideration by them in return, many women rebel and reject the rule of their husbands over them, their children, and the entire household.

In a more perfect world, everything would be love and kisses and mutual respect and total honesty, and acceptance of the minor faults of each other, and forgiveness, and, oh, my, god, it all sounds so much like *Alice in Wonderland* – where everyone lives happily ever after.

I am past 80. I was married for 25 years to the father of our eight children. Then, I divorced and still had six of those children at home. I lived the life of a single, working, woman for 22 years, and completed the raising of our children. I had no intention of bringing a replacement father into my home while our children were still there.

Then, miracle of miracles, once my children were grown and gone and I was a whole, complete woman – a good man, like the one St. Peter describes – came into my life.

July 25

With me are riches and honor, enduring wealth and prosperity. – Proverbs 8:18

As a writer, I am always aware of words and meanings of words. I am aware of how the meaning can change when the words are spoken, and how those same words are being received. In an auditorium filled with people, each set of ears hears the speaker, or views the lecture, play or film in their own way.

Babies have no prior experiential knowledge of words. They listen and they repeat, and eventually discover meaning by putting the pieces and inflections together.

How and what each of us reads into the passage above is individualistic. What we bring to the reading determines what we will take away from the reflection on the words. For me "riches and honor" can mean so many different thoughts and things. Things I may never experience or need in my life.

Riches are plentiful, even though I live what I consider a simple life. Riches in old or new biblical terms usually refer to spiritual matter, our relationship with our God, loved ones, and the universe – not necessarily material goods.

Honor, for me, is the recognition and appreciation and acceptance for the life I have, and for the lives of others. I value and honor you, as I value and honor myself.

July 26

This is my commandment: love one another as I have loved you. –John 15:12

In the commentary leading to John's writings there is much said about who actually did the recording and the writings. John was the "one whom Jesus loved." He is most often portrayed next to Jesus at the Last Supper, and at the foot of the cross until the end. It is told that John cared for the mother of Jesus following the death, resurrection, and ascension of Jesus.

Much of John's writing records the final words of Jesus. John lived in a time when followers of Jesus were considered "fallen away Jews." Even though John and the other followers tried to maintain peace with their fellow Jews, they were mostly unsuccessful. So, when the words of Jesus – written by John – refer to his "commandment" he is not necessarily introducing an eleventh commandment.

From all we have read, Jesus seems to be summing up all the commandments and teachings into the one concept of "loving one another as God has loved us."

We can only assume Jesus was not just speaking to his followers alone, but to all who would come after them. It is said that John lived out his life on one of the Grecian

Isles and his writings reflect Greek tradition and style of writing.

Love to all followers of Jesus means to pray for one another, encourage success and cooperation, and diminish disagreement.

July 27

In him we live and move and have our being. – Acts 17:28

On days when I frequently turn my thoughts to the fact that there is a force at work in this universe that put everything into motion and keeps us all alive – then, I am in tune with that power.

Because we all come from the same source, we feel at peace when we are tuned in to that source. Just as the computer needs an energy source, we do as well. Whether on alternating or direct current, we are more fully functioning when we are charged up and ready to go.

The reference to poets in the phrase that follows is perhaps referring to those who see beyond the obvious, those who express feelings we all are capable of but can't bring ourselves to express. The beauty of a quiet inner life is that we each and all can be poets – without words. We see and hear and feel at a deeper, and often incomprehensible and inexpressible level. Far deeper than we believed we could go.

The poet in us needs no words, we sense the wonder and our only response is to enjoy whatever connection we make or feel. We truly feel the Spirit moving within us – and we would share, if we only knew how. A smile or expression of love and joy – that is plenty for us – if we will only accept the gift.

July 28

"Lord," they told him, "open our eye!" – Matthew 20:33

The dynamic working of miracles during the time Jesus was recruiting followers often becomes lost among the events of his life – the birth, death and 40 days on earth after his resurrection and before his ascension.

The particular incident above is just one of many. Jesus was leaving Jericho, with a large group of people following him. Two blind men sitting by the side of the road began shouting for him to take pity on them. He asked what they wanted, and they said "open our eyes."

The blind men had heard the rumors about the miracle worker, and they believed enough to ask. And, they could see again.

How much proof do we need to know that miracles are possible in our own lives, and in the lives of those we love? Do we have to see a miracle unfold before our blind eyes to believe? Do we only need to acknowledge that the strange coincidences that occur in our daily lives are actually little miracles that happen when no one else is looking?

How do we decide there is something magical working in our lives? I have seen with the eyes of my soul – enough to convince me that life itself is a miracle, and if I think about it, there are miracles happening every day, all around, and inside me.

July 29

Not that I am referring to being in need; for I have learned to be content with whatever I have. – Philippians 4:11

If I was courageous, I would adopt this phrase as my new mantra. However, I know there will be moments when I do not believe I have everything I need, and fewer times when I can say I have everything I want. Life has taught me the difference between wants and needs.

Time has become a commodity. There never seems to be enough of it. A day ends and I have not crossed anything off my "to do" list. Truth be known, I can't always find the list, it is buried under the day's "in basket" additions.

Although not overly ambitious, I seek more time because I love my life, I am a researcher, and explorer – always interested in something new or different.

One of my books is titled *Snowbirds Unlimited: Tales from the Restless Traveler.* Admittedly, that restlessness is mostly good and productive. It is a restlessness that seeks to squeeze every bit of joy out of life. My life is full, perhaps too full. My glass may be half full, and never half empty, but my cup runs over most of the time.

I am grateful to have lived as long as I have, and content with what I have today.

July 30

Do not neglect to show hospitality, for by that means some have entertained angels without knowing it. – Hebrews 13:1-2

Jesus taught loving everyone always, not just His followers. But, Paul has a concern that the Jews who rejected Jesus as the fulfillment of Jewish prophesies were still clinging to their rituals and observances to the neglect of their fellow "Christian." Paul wants Christians to focus on Jesus, knowing it meant separating themselves from family and friends who disagree.

Paul is developing a tight knit group of followers. A difficult task. This chapter is Paul's last, and he reminds his followers of their sacred duty to love one another, and to take friends into their homes, because many were rejected by their families because of their differences regarding Jesus.

Kindness in thought, word and deed becomes the way Christians recognize each other and the traits by which they still should be recognizing and treating each other. Unfortunately, there are many brands of Christianity today, and people may be as far apart as the early Christians were from their Jewish fellowship.

It would seem that all Christians would be well served by honoring the spirit of Jesus' teachings, to love one another as the heavenly father has loved all.

July 31

God called the light Day, and the darkness he called Night. And there was evening and there was morning, the first day. – Genesis 1:5

The people who first wrote about creation came light years after the actual events that separated light from darkness and it was called day. The writers of Genesis who lived centuries before us may have had an entirely different perspective regarding creation. If the creation story has holes and lapses of time then isn't it possible that the theologians of those early days lacked sufficient knowledge to explain this grand phenomenon?

Discovery based on logic and proof may have something to offer those who take these bible passages literally. The languages that separated nations during the biblical account of the building of the Tower of Babel –still separate people and nations.

Genesis credits God with naming the light Day and the darkness Night. Well, really, isn't it human beings who use language, and human beings who name everything – in their own language.

Does God speak to you in Hebrew, Greek or English? When God created humans, they were given dominion over land, sea, and air – and all that grows, and swims, and flies, and roams the earth – and God gave man the right to name everything – according to the Bible.

August

Named for
Augustus Caesar
in 8 BC.
August, formerly Sextilis,
sixth month in the
Roman calendar.

August 1

I have come down from heaven, not to do my own will, but the will of him who set me. – John 6:38

John continues to quote Jesus, who says clearly that he is doing the bidding of someone else – the entity he calls The Father. When Jesus tells us that he and the Father are one it confuses the issue. Because Jesus also tells his followers they are all one with him.

Theologians struggle with separating the human nature of Jesus from his divine nature – and then they struggle with combining both natures. They insist that Jesus was totally God and totally man, yet they often deny Jesus the choice of one nature over the other.

I cannot understand how we can insist that Jesus is totally man – and yet insist that he did not know a woman in marriage, or father children. Why do we draw lines in even suggesting the possibility?

My questioning will not set well with the fathers of the church. But, I ask in good faith – if God created man and woman to bond together to create children – and this is a holy act, a human act – why not Jesus?

If Jesus was doing the will of Him who sent him – what are we to make of "free will" or knowing God's will for us? Are we human, or are we divine, or are we – like Jesus – both?

August 2

In his mind a man plans his course, but the LORD directs the steps. – Proverbs 16:9

I am a planner, organizer and goal setter by nature. In my youth I believed everyone was just like me – they planned organized and set goals. How soon I discovered different.

There never seemed to be a path to success, unless I paved the path and then walked it. I didn't fully appreciate the universal power I choose to call God. I always asked, prayed and thanked that God power for things and events, great and small.

Somewhere along the way, as a mature adult struggling with dodging life's curve balls, I began to believe the truth of it all. Something, I could not explain, was helping me get through tough times, and making tough decisions.

The proverbial light bulb was finally turned on. I was not alonc and struggling. The universe was listening to my pain and pleading. The way opened up – and I couldn't take all the credit anymore. Sure, there were people encouraging me, and I was doing the footwork – but something beyond my understanding was guiding my way. I may trip over the cobblestones occasionally – but I do not fall or sink into the mud.

August 3

For you shall go out in joy, in peace you shall be brought back;
mountains and hills shall break out in song before you. – Isaiah 55:12

One morning while walking in the Mexican desert I asked my higher power for proof of his or her existence, and the mantra that came back to me was, "Out of gratitude springs joy."

The mountains to the west did not break out in song, but I did feel some sense of wellbeing and happiness – for no apparent reason except my inner voice speaking to me, and I listened.

It's different trying to explain that good feeling that sometimes washes over us, but it could be God's grace, love and joy.

When we hug our children, or kiss our spouse, there is a feeling of love, appreciation and happiness. Why should it be any different when God reaches out and hugs us? We may talk to our friends, family, loved ones and say "I need a hug!" They answer with an embrace – arms wrapped around us – and we feel so much better.

Whether the spirit we call God is our father, our mother, our brother, our sister, or our lover – a hug feels like the right thing to ask for at the right time – and it feels so good to be home.

August 4

I will heal them, and reveal to them an abundance of lasting peace. – Jeremiah 33:6

Jeremiah was one of many prophets in the centuries before Jesus came on the scene. God's comforting words above got him through one crisis – the fall of Jerusalem – but fell short of saving him from exile, and in the end murder at the hands of his own countrymen.

There appears to be nothing permanent about healing. In the end we all die. The prophet may serve as a channel for the messages God sends to his people, but, there is no guarantee the good that comes from the promise will benefit the messenger.

We are told there was a time of healing and a time of peace after the fall of Jerusalem. There were, however, other falls – or destructions of the temple. It would seem that God does not hold our temples, churches and other places of worship in as high a regard as we do.

Buildings fall from earthquakes, forests burn from lightning strikes and fires; land and properties are washed away by tsunamis, hurricanes, and floods.

Wind, water, fire, all need to be harnessed to be of use to humans. Everything under the sun needs to be controlled to be useful.

August 5

Mend your ways. Encourage one another. Live in harmony and peace. – 2 Corinthians 13:11

Paul bids farewell to the people of the church he founded in Corinth with the above passage as he moves on. He reminds them that the only way they can survive as followers of Christ is to bond together with encouragement and harmony.

That bonding continues today, as it always has, when groups of people who are of like mind gather together under one roof or in one place, and express their common beliefs and aspirations. They believe in the power of numbers. But, what of those hermits who have little or no contact with their fellow man or woman?

Henry David Thoreau lived alone, a mile from any neighbor, on Walden Pond in Concord, Massachusetts, for two years and two months. However, Thoreau was not really a hermit because he did come out of his solitude when it suited him. And, in his own way he was in touch with events of his time. His church was his cabin and his woods. He was a man of great learning and tremendous intellect.

His writings still inspire individuals who want to learn to live more simply and less dependent on society and governments for existence. Not an easy task, but creating less of a footprint on the earth is a worthy goal.

August 6

For I am about to create new heavens and a new earth. – Isaiah 65:17

Over and over again, those who speak for God predict punishment, and promise redemption. New civilizations open up all the time. Each new civilization seems to lack sustainability. The one we are currently part of, continues to have built-in, self-destruction.

When will human beings get it right?

It doesn't seem to matter if some do and most don't. There is little agreement about the correct path to sustaining our current version of civilization. We literally can't agree on the time of day or the day of the week. Is it just because part of the world is on the opposite side of the globe, only facing into the sun half the time, as are we?

Are we all like siblings, struggling for attention? Some of us act out in negative ways to get that attention. Others of us think we have the formula for successful living all figured out, and we certainly want to tell all those other people they have it wrong – in creating their own hell on earth – and we – the chosen ones – are right-eous.

August 7

Remove the sandals from your feet, for the place where you stand is holy ground. – Exodus 3:5

Although human beings continue to put a human face on God, with a human voice, and all the other human attributes – verses, such as the one above tell us that God puts man in his place. It is God who says, "Come no closer!" to Moses. God sets boundaries. How close is too close?

When Moses saw the burning bush he moved closer out of curiosity. Had Moses put his hand into the fire would he have been burned? God got Moses' attention with the burning bush, but also let Moses know he was limited, though attracted by the fire.

No living person has ever reported seeing the face of God – perhaps that is because God has no face – nothing that we mortals could recognize or identify.

Do we know what electricity looks like?

Do we know what an atom looks like?

Do we know what wind looks like?

Do we know what a soul looks like?

What difference does it make what we see anyway? We see results. We want to see what fire can do, what happens when the wind blows, when a baby draws its first breath outside the womb – suddenly independent of the mother – a person. What we can't see still exists – in its own form – in its own time. Do we need to see the face or hear the voice to answer the call?

August 8

One nation shall not raise the sword against another,
nor shall they train for war again. – Isaiah 2:4

We don't have an Isaiah speaking to us on behalf of God. Everyone who speaks of peace to us today speaks only of ending war. We Americans can quickly mobilize our industries and populations to go into battle, but we are so slow in ending conflicts.

The United States has been involved in a war in Iraq and Afghanistan for more than twelve years. Thousands of people from all sides of these conflicts have died, and hundreds of thousands have been wounded or left homeless. We can't seem to run our country without an enemy with whom to do battle.

Just like Israel of old, we Americans assume we are always on the right side, and our God is always looking upon us with favor, and promising peace and prosperity.

We no longer raise swords against each other, because we now have more powerful weapons. No more hand-to-hand combat. We are no longer looking the enemy in the eye; no longer acknowledging the humanity of the enemy; no more regard for other families and homes, or the existence of body, mind and soul.

August 9

The LORD is my strength and my shield. – Psalms 28:7

Two days ago I had unbearable pain in my groin. Every step I took caused terrible pain. I got through one day gritting my teeth, taking Aleve, putting ice packs in my lap. Crying, praying, and begging it to end.

The next morning, I called my doctor's office and talked with the nurse. She got back to me after talking with the doctor. I was advised to go to the emergency room at the hospital.

At the same time, I called Silent Unity's 24/7 prayer line – my good friends for over 30 years. I told my story and the nice woman prayed with and for me. The prayers continued for 30 days.

My husband drove me to the hospital. I spent more than two hours being evaluated and having X-rays. When they finished and there were no fractures, lumps, bumps or any evidence of injury – I got on my feet – and the pain had diminished dramatically.

God does, indeed, work in mysterious ways. God works through the doctors, the nurses, the radiology technicians, and the people praying for me. I asked for a miracle – and I got one. I believe my faith healed me – with the caring attention of many people.

August 10

Rejoice in hope, be patient under trial,
persevere in prayer. – Romans 12:12

Paul, who was both Roman and a Jew, wrote a long letter or epistle to the followers of Christ, no doubt former practicing Jews, now living in Rome. He was conflicted in his loyalties to his own heritage.

This man, who had been seeking the Christ followers and exposing them as rebels against the Roman Empire, then dramatically converted to follow the man, Christ, he never knew. Whatever Paul did, he did with enthusiasm. He was powerful as a convert, as a speaker, as a writer.

There is no one more zealous than the converted. And, for Paul it was a total turn around. In this part of his letter he tells his friends in Christ to be strong to love one another as brothers, to be patient under trial. Paul, himself, is staying out of the line of fire from the Roman army and rulers whom he now rejects and speaks against.

It is difficult to know the first intent of these early followers of the one they believe will free them from the domination of the godless Romans.

There doesn't seem to be a plan, or any real sense of organization, they are only told to persevere – not knowing for what purpose.

August 11

When they ceased, they ceased. And they are as though they had not lived, they and their children after them. – Sirach 44:9

This particular chapter of the book, sometimes called Ecclesiasticus, refers back to the greats among their ancestors – such as Noah, Abraham and Jacob. These are the names of men who left a memory of "praiseworthy deeds."

In some ways this passage sounds like one of the curses from a previous reading. Especially the part about there is no memory of them, because when they died they were forgotten – "as though they never had lived, they and their children after them."

Human history holds many people in their memories; families hold loved ones in their hearts and thoughts with photos and mementos.

We all want to be remembered, to be thought well of. My daughter Carol passed at age 46, years ago, but her memory lives on in the lives of her two daughters. Even though we are not in touch often, there is always Facebook. I catch up with family members online.

History may name those who meant something during their time on earth. I would hope that every human being who lived has someone who remembers them. My promise to my own daughter is "I will not forget you."

August 12

May peace be within your walls, prosperity in your buildings. – Psalms 122:7

We have many greetings, all over the world, when people meet for the first time or when they welcome a friend or family member into their home, and, again, when they are meeting over business transactions.

These icebreakers are courteous and friendly. The parting comments may not always end on a friendly note.

It is a good sign that we as a civilized nation or family of nations at least come into our encounters with a sign of respect and confidence. The Buddhist says, "Namaste" on coming or going. They recognize the good in each other before and after their encounters.

We, in America, say good morning, afternoon and evening, as the time of day dictates. We are offering the best wishes to each person we meet in this way – although the habit of doing so may most often escape us.

We say "Good bye" and wish our friends, family and business encounters a pleasant remainder of the day, the week or any period of time we want – until we meet again and exchange the same expression. Whether thoughtful or habitual, the hello greeting and the farewell are good.

August 13

And you shall be secure, because there is hope. –Job 11:18

Job's friend Zophar of Naamathite speaks to Job for the first time, trying to get him to face the reality that he may be at fault regarding his misfortunes. It may not all be blamed on God. There may be a lesson to learn in accepting, understanding and surviving all the tribulation. His life's work may yet be ahead of him.

How often have I been at the end of my rope with some situation, and I have been pulled back from the brink of total despair by the kind words of a friend or mentor? I cannot count or remember the days or the ways.

Hope is more than a word. Hope is an action or movement of the mind toward the possible – away from utter hopelessness. Without the troubles in our lives, we would not need, nor have known, hope. We learn by living, that all is not lost, there is hope. When I was a child, I heard my mother say, "Where there is life there is hope."

I also heard that the only sin for which there is no forgiveness is despair, or total loss of hope. That is something known only to the Creator. When Judas hung himself in total despair it seems to me that he met his God, his Lord and Savior, his forgiving friend, Jesus.

Judas was first of all a victim of history. If all things happen the way they are meant to happen – even Judas deserves benefit of the doubt.

August 14

The prophet turned and saw them, and he cursed them in the name of the LORD. – 2 Kings 2:24

Elijah, well known and well respected prophet during the 587 BC period around the destruction of Jerusalem, apparently trained followers, referred to as "guild prophets." One of his prophets, perhaps his son, was the direct successor named Elisha.

Elisha was present when Elijah went up to heaven in a flaming chariot drawn by flaming horses. The new prophet donned Elijah's cloak and started challenging the population and performing miraculous and wondrous works.

At this point, I began to question the inspired word of God in this great book – holy, or historical. Elisha was going to Bethel when "some small boys came out of the city and jeered him." They shouted, "Go up, baldhead." That's when the prophet took offense and issued the curse above.

Now, really, is this how we expect a holy man of God to behave? It seems he over reacted.

"Then two she-bears came out of the woods and tore forty-two of the children to pieces." Without further comment, the prophet continued on his journey.

Is this a lesson for children not to call people insulting or silly names, or bullying? Or is this a warning to would-be prophets to "lighten up?"

The old "sticks and stones" argument doesn't seem to work on this prophet. As we see, names do kill, some people just can't take a little name calling, and others may be warned not to call names.

August 15

If a land is rebellious, its princes will be many; but with a prudent man it knows security. – Proverbs 28:2

Rebellion in the land appears to be the work of a poor leader. I doubt it is ever that simple. The many princes means the top guy has no control over the people and their rebellion. Prudence is the art of making right decisions.

A leader can only lead if the people let him or her. The age we live in now does not seem to favor leaders of any stripe. I believe if Jesus came back as a Democrat or a Republican, he would be ushered out of the Senate or the House of Representatives. He would not have the money to run for election in the first place. And neither party, nor any other party not yet devised, would think that Jesus has what it takes to be a leader – much too compromising in nature.

All our Christian brothers and sisters probably wouldn't recognize Jesus in a three-piece suit. Who thinks Jesus would come down out of the clouds in his flowing robes, looking just like the pictures we see of the white skinned middle-eastern man with the golden hair and beard?

I doubt we would recognize a prudent leader – except by the atmosphere he or she creates. Do you really think Jesus would have the charisma to attract both the political right and the progressive left – and the centrists?

August 16

Who do you say that I am? – Matthew 16:15

Do we not all ask this question about ourselves? Who are we and what do you think I am? We feel authentic, true to ourselves and our goals, but so often we feel misunderstood.

I am a wife, I am a mother and a grandmother and a great-grandmother. I was a sister until my brother died – but I was still the same person. I was a daughter until my parents both passed – many years apart. I am a cousin and a mother-in-law, and a step-mother, and at one time a daughter-in-law.

How is it I can be all these different people and still feel like the same person? If I was acting I would be all the characters all the time, in every act and every scene.

Jesus was fishing for an answer to his question to see if his followers were paying attention to anything they had heard him say, or had seen any of the miracles he performed. I suppose we all ask ourselves on occasion "who do people think I am?"

Of course, it matters what people think of me. When I question my own behavior in a specific circumstance, I wonder what on earth I was thinking. I'm not that kind of person. What would my mother think of me now?

Only God sees the real me.

August 17

Pray for the peace of Jerusalem! May those who love you prosper. – Psalms 122:6

I was in Israel and Jordan for two weeks in 1996. We simulated our baptism in the Jordan River with the complete dunking. Although we were in a Palestinian facility, we had to hurry our ceremony to close by 5 pm – when the Jewish Sabbath began. We had our feet – actually, our entire bodies – in all three religious territories.

It happened many times on the pilgrimage – we were Christians, sometimes in Islamic territory and sometimes in Jewish territory. The old Jerusalem is divided into four sectors – and we could take a few steps and be in one, or one of the other sectors.

We were in an area of northern Israel and could not go further north because there was bombing going on in the area where our group was scheduled to go. One morning outside the old city of Jerusalem, four of our tour group pilgrims just missed being involved in a bombing after walking by a building. At Carmel, there were armed soldiers guarding a school bus while children toured the holy site.

As we left our hotel to board the bus to the airport for our return to the United States, I bought a gold chain for my mother's gold cross – and a black T-shirt with the phrase from Psalms – "Pray for the peace of Jerusalem."

August 18

The sun must not go down on your wrath. – Ephesians 4:26

When I was a child, my mother frequently quoted this passage; only she said “anger.” I guess anger meant more to children than wrath. Wrath seems much, much worse, like≈– ready to hurt or kill.

I have felt anger, and I have felt wrath. Even though I prefer to forget that I ever felt angry – irritated enough to want to strike out in hatred and seek revenge – I have to admit, I have felt that way. I have let the sun go down on that kind of emotion. And, I was the only one hurt by my own anger.

I can’t air my memories of my anger because I prefer not to hurt anyone any more – even with recounting the events, the memories. Today is what matters. Today, I have no room in my heart for anger or wrath. I will have to leave that to others, those who have the stomach for it. I am now a peace seeker.

I don’t know if there is really a devil or not. Devil spelled backward is “lived,” and evil spelled backward is “live.” Live and let live – another phrase my mother frequently used. Anger goes away when I choose to live, enjoy life, and love myself and others.

August 19

Then you may securely go your way; your foot will never stumble. – Proverbs 3:23

Actually, I read this quote the day after the April 15, Boston Marathon finish-line bomb explosions that killed three, and caused numerous lower extremities to be damaged or amputated. Nearly 200 people were injured and hospitalized and treated.

How can we possibly know when and where to go to be safe? How can we live free and be safe in an increasingly unsafe world?

Certainly, many of the injured were God loving, people loving, and good people. Through no fault of their own they were in a dangerous place at the precise moment a bomb went off. It's impossible to always know when we are in harm's way.

There are times when I believe I have been held back from going somewhere and being in the wrong place at the wrong time. Even God has limits. Even guardian angels have limits.

When I feel like I am falling asleep at the wheel while driving, and suddenly I jerk the steering wheel back in line, I have no idea what saves me from harm.

I've not had any broken bones, though I have stumbled and fallen many times. Even as I get older, and am more careful of my footing there is no guarantee of safety.

August 20

So be assured, daughter, I will do for you whatever you say. – Ruth 3:11

Naomi, wife of Elimelech of Bethlehem, went with him to Moab with their two sons. The two sons married women in Moab – and when he and their two sons passed away Naomi was left with the two widowed daughters-in-law.

Naomi planned to return to Bethlehem and told the two widows to go back to Moab. Ruth refused to go, instead insisted on staying with her mother-in-law.

Once in Bethlehem, Ruth gathered food in the fields and from the table of Boaz, a relative of Naomi. To make a short story even shorter – Ruth became the wife of Boaz when he purchased the land that belonged to Naomi's deceased husband. Ruth became the mother of Obed, the father of Jesse, and the grandfather of David.

It's all about who you know, who you were related to, and how land was passed down from one generation to the next. A woman's value was pinned to the property of her husband or her father. Ruth has a short book in the Hebrew Bible named for her. But her only claim to fame was who she married and the heir she bore.

Are we women worthy of recognition for being more than who our father or our mate may be? Ruth was a very brave and caring daughter-in-law. The passage above is spoken by Boaz to Ruth when she slept at his feet to show loyalty – pre-nuptial.

August 21

Let us discern for ourselves what is right; let us learn between us what is good. –Job 34:4

One of Job's friends, Elihu, in conversation with another friend, tries to make sense out of Job's ranting about how good he is and how unfair God is to him. The friends are trying to help Job, but Job is so negative that he doesn't hear what they have to say, or see any way out of his misery.

It is so difficult when a person we want to help negates every single suggestion we make. They want to wallow in their own misery, and we have to let them go until they are ready, until they reach the bottom of their pit. Job is already dismissing God, feeling deserted and alone. Sometimes friends have to walk away and let their friend wallow a while longer.

Turning from a totally negative attitude to one that feels some optimism is a big stretch. Grief takes its own time. Each person has his own way of grieving a loss. Some want to talk, some do not. It's hard to know when enough is enough.

We can listen as a friend shares grief and misery, without absorbing the negativity and carrying the pain.

Time heals all wounds, it has been said, but there are no guarantees regarding the length of time it takes. Sometimes we have to move out of the way of the train wreck.

August 22

So David went up there accompanied by his two wives. – 2 Samuel 2:2

I realize customs were different in ancient times, when having two wives was simply a statement of fact. However, having two husbands is seldom mentioned. When a man has two or more wives, the additional woman is usually a harlot, the widowed wife of a dead brother, or a servant woman to bear a son in the event wives number one or two have proven incapable of achieving such a feat.

This event takes place when David is about to be anointed King, following the death of Saul.

Apparently, the multiple wives situation takes place when there is a shortage of men and an abundance of women. And frequently it is, or was, a matter of economics. Today, extra women, and their children as well become a problem for the welfare department.

I certainly don't advocate multiple spouses, but there must be a way for women to maintain some sense of dignity and purpose when the man who fathered her children has left the scene. The responsibility for carrying on usually falls upon the woman – although, in our modern age, more fathers are being left to raise the children when the mother is on military duty, or just moved on. Not a pretty picture either way.

August 23

Incline your ear, O LORD; answer me, for
I am afflicted and poor. – Psalms 86:1

This is the first line of David's prayer in time of distress, apparently following the destruction of the temple in Jerusalem, which is lamented with some frequency in Hebrew history.

I doubt that David is "poor" in our sense of the word. I would guess these are the words of a man in great pain of soul. He suffered, as we all do, deep psychological and emotional pain – with no apparent way out of that pain. He was "poor" in spirit.

We call it depression, and treat it with medication. We, as a society, have lost our ability to heal our own deep soul wounds. Our soul pain then spreads throughout our bodies – and manifest in a variety of ways.

Shouting out to God to get the attention and inclining of God's ear, does not of itself heal our pain. It does, however, pave the way to finding a solution. It's easy to get the "ear" of God, since this all-powerful entity is always listening, to everyone, everywhere.

How awesome, that this God can sort out all these millions of cries of pain coming from everywhere on the planet. How often do we cry out – then pause – then listen – then find a way out of our pain? Who really made the pain go away?

August 24

I saw a white horse; its rider had a bow, and he was given a crown. – Revelations 6:2

Revelations, or Apocalypse, is the last chapter, or book, of the New Testament, or the Christian version of what has, or will, come to pass. Wrapped in mysterious symbolism and allegory, this book is treated as a "what if" and a "maybe" picture of what may or may not happen during the times in which it was written or in the projected "end of times."

The writer's identity is uncertain, and its validity sometimes questioned. Many prophets of doom use this book to put the fear of God into their followers. The people living in the times when these words were written were still living in fear of the powerful Roman army and its rulers.

The white horse mentioned here is cut from the thundering herd of the four horsemen of the Apocalypse, and is said to represent the Parthians on the eastern border of the Roman Empire. People, including the writer of Revelations, still hoped that the Romans could be stopped in their quest for world domination.

Hope springs eternal – that good will overcome evil. When we see movies related to the Apocalypse – we assume it means the end of bad times.

August 25

Remember that the days of darkness will be many. All that is to come is vanity. – Ecclesiastes 11:8

Some days I select a passage at random and study the words for a day, or several days – waiting for inspiration and meaning, to light up my page.

Light is indeed sweet. I can't improve on the meaning here. And it is pleasant for the eyes to see the sun, but not stare upon it. I have a friend who is legally blind with macular degeneration. She says the sun is her best friend. Those of us who have better eyesight say "yes" that is so true. We dare not take this blessing of light for granted. It is indeed a gift.

Those days of darkness are not just because the sun is hidden by clouds. Darkness sometimes penetrates our souls and we wait for the light to free us from the gloom of whatever holds our joy hostage.

I looked up several meanings of the word "vanity," and the best I can come up with is the lack of gratitude. Being so self-sufficient we don't need anyone, or anything they can do for us. Our pride is overwhelming. "Thanks, but no thanks," we say – and, "no thanks" is what we get in return.

August 26

I have provided in it a place for the ark in which is the covenant. – 1 Kings 8:21

Promises! I have to be careful about making promises to God, to myself, or other people. Promises kept are wonderful. Promises broken can haunt me.

I promised to love, honor, and at that time it was obey my first love, the father of my children. It was a crushing blow to my pride to admit failure and have to break that promise. No matter what the circumstances, or where the blame falls; breaking up is hard to do.

Everyone has a breaking point. There is a time to hold fast, and a time to let go. You can give a person your hand to lift them up, or they can take your hand and pull you down. When you start sinking, then it is time to let go – and, hopefully, let God.

I've probably made a promise or two to God to get me or someone I love out of a hole in the ground. Now, I don't recall those promises. I don't even recall what I was asking for. So soon we forget yesterday's problems, yesterday's broken hearts, and broken promises.

August 27

"Father, forgive them; they do not know what they are doing." – Luke 23:34

No matter what time of the liturgical year we read these words they send the same message. No matter how often or how we are offended, or persecuted or misunderstood – we can benefit from an attitude of forgiveness; even though it is the most difficult action we are called upon to perform.

That doesn't mean the person who hurts us can continue to do so, or that a person who breaks the law in hurting us should go without judgment or retribution.

I think Jesus was addressing broader issues than what was happening to him specifically. I think he was saddened that the people he was here to help, and to lead out of their Roman domination – ignored him. His father, the God of us all, is addressed to forgive those who, by their own actions, are rejecting the person and the message, and the messenger.

The only real cure for resentment is forgiveness. If I wallow in my own self-pity because of "them," I suffer. If I forgive "them" because of their ignorance or ill-will, then my suffering is diminished.

August 28

God has been generous toward me, and I have abundance. – Genesis 33:11

Some of us have had a problem accepting the goodness and generosity of others. Until, we learned differently. We once thought we needed to do everything for everyone, all the time.

Once we learned to accept a complement then we could become better receivers. Once we learned gratitude for what others did for us, then we could accept with gratitude what God had freely given us – our very life and breath.

One of the first things we teach our children is how to say "please" and "thank you." Our children and grandchildren can't always remember that bit of politeness. I send checks to grandchildren for birthdays and Christmas. If I don't see them, then they may forget to acknowledge the gift. Everyone has my Email address. When my bank statement arrives, and I see the check number noted, then I can rest assured that the checks were cashed by the right people.

I assume the check and card got to the right place. Once, I had to cancel a check because, after three months of not showing up on the bank statement, I asked the question, and wrote another check, and paid to cancel the wayward check. Darn!

August 29

Even though I walk in the dark valley, I fear no evil. – Psalms 23:4

We see and hear this passage frequently at funerals. What exactly is the "dark valley" of which we speak? Is death a "dark valley" or a light onto our path? I prefer to think when I die I am going into the light, a far better place. It may take great courage to pass over to the next life, but now, really, is when I need the courage – facing the difficulties each day has to offer – along with the fear of the unknown future.

This 23rd Psalm refers to God as the Good Shepherd, and we are the sheep. This is the same image Jesus uses for his followers. This is one of the many common threads between the old and the new testaments. There have been times when I have felt like a poor little lamb that has lost its way.

Grown men don't seem to mind referring to themselves as "poor little lambs who have lost our way," so why feel strange about admitting we have "gone astray." It's all part of being human beings without knowledge of the future. We don't always have a light on our path – so we do occasionally get lost.

August 30

Remember not the events of the past, the things of long ago consider not. – Isaiah 43:18-19

I've lost count of how many times I have reinvented myself – and started over. Life is full of new starts. Every day is an opportunity to be born again.

With new starts comes the shaking off of disappointments and regrets, and unachieved goals. Why is it we dwell on our failures rather than our successes? We are told we learn more from our mistakes and failures than we learn from our success. That sounds phony to me. I want to learn from success.

I completed most of the work toward my bachelor's degree when I realized I could start work on my master's for the same undergraduate fees. I gained nine post-graduate credits before I received my Bachelor of Science degree in arts and letters. This put me in a favorable position to not only apply and be admitted to a master's program, but to actually be recruited for a teaching assistantship with full tuition, books, and stipend.

I learned from my achievements that I was capable of much, much more.

August 31

I will state directly what is in my mind; my lips shall utter knowledge sincerely. –Job 33:3

I learned to speak my mind, by simply doing it, over and over again. Through most of my lower education, I sat in the middle or back of the room. I noticed my classmates getting the higher grades sat toward the front, and frequently volunteered. They spoke with confidence and were usually correct with their responses and rewarded accordingly.

It wasn't until I was married, had several children, and returned to the classroom that I received renewed courage to speak my mind. I was attending one evening class each term, and it took two decades to complete my bachelor's degree. Once I transferred to the four-year college for my final year, I was in my forties, with seven of my eight children at home.

I know the "college aged" students didn't appreciate this "older" student sitting up front and knowing most of the answers. I was serious about my studies. I am still serious about my studies and continue learning, whether in or out of the classroom. I am a glutton at the buffet of knowledge.

Since I am compelled to speak my mind, I want to be as educated as possible, so as not to be an embarrassment to myself.

September

September
Septem
Latin for 7,
the seventh month in the
Julian or Roman calendar.

September 1

How long will you set upon a man and all together beat him down as though he were a sagging fence, a battered wall? – Psalms 62:4

We do tend to kick a man when he's down. Make him feel responsible for his own misfortune. We drive through the "bad" parts of town as fast as we can – concern that it might be catching – or that we may be in danger.

We make snap judgments about people based on the color of their skin, the clothes they wear, the cars they drive, and anything else we can imagine so we can get away from "them."

I was laid off from a middle-management job. They called it "downsizing" or "eliminating my job." I still felt the pain of losing a job and drawing unemployment.

Later, I started a business with a friend, and after nearly six years we had to close the doors. I had been in bed for ten days with pneumonia and had plenty of time to think about the financial hole we were digging – so, we closed up shop.

I went on unemployment again. It's hard to feel good about yourself when you are scraping to make ends meet. I came back once again, and today I remember well – how it could be again.

September 2

Then the LORD God planted a garden in Eden, in the east, and he placed there the man whom he had formed. – Genesis 2:8

This passage comes from a section titled "Second Story of Creation." Why on earth are there two versions of creation? Why would a third version be found unacceptable?

In this version, God creates man before all the other creatures, supposing these other creatures and the Garden of Eden are for man's use. The first version of creation seems to leave the process of evolution as a possibility more than this version.

Why can't God get it right the first time? Or on the other hand, why did the writers of Genesis have two versions of the creation story? Perhaps the thought of man evolving from another form of creation simply was beyond their imagination. Are there perhaps other versions of creation that are still beyond the imagination of man?

Perhaps man and woman as well, are still evolving.

Nothing goes backward. We don't un-evolve. We don't return to a former expression of being. All we know is what we have had, and what we are today. Our imagination and intelligence seem to know no bounds, except for individuals who regress or digress about the origin of human form.

September 3

The beginning of wisdom is: get wisdom; at the cost of all you have, get understanding. – Proverbs 4:7

As I am now past 80, I feel obligated to act as though I am wise, because of my length of time and worldly experiences. Sometimes I marvel at the thoughts I think and the words I speak, but, not that often. No one is wise all the time. When I write these words I do not feel wise. When I read them later I will feel as though someone else may have written them

So frequently, I have my most insightful thoughts in the shower. But my shower may take place an hour after I am awake. My husband goes into the kitchen to make his first cup of coffee and bring in the newspaper.

I take my time stretching and meditating and getting focused on a new day. There is nothing unusual in doing all that. But, there is almost always a thought during my shower that I feel is worth sharing with my husband. He looks puzzled when I say, "I was just thinking."

He doesn't say, "Oh, no, not again," but I sometimes feel it. He's far too kind to tell me I'm being strange again. Nonetheless, it's wonderful to have someone who loves me, and lets me share my great and small thoughts.

September 4

Your sons and daughters shall prophesy, your old men shall dream dreams, your young men shall see visions. –Joel 3:1

We all have dreams. Most, we don't remember. Some we do remember, and they may haunt us, or they may provide us with greater goals than we might imagine while awake. People who have lived and died may come back to us in dreams, with messages of love, acceptance, encouragement or missions regarding their unfinished business.

Science has a variety of viewpoints about dreams. They are real images in the minds and memories that host them. It's one of these questions, such as; do people blind from birth see anything when they dream? Then there are those things we see when we are fully awake, and they are called visions. There are doubters, those who may not have memory of their dreams or who may not admit to having visions.

And yet, believers and doubters alike can be called visionaries, because they have some sense about how something that is not, can someday be. We only need look around us to see what the human being has discovered, invented, written, produced, or built. We know that dreams and visions, no matter their form, do come true.

September 5

It was I who made the earth and created mankind upon it. – Isaiah 45:12

God reminds Cyrus, the liberator of Israel that he is still in control. We can't take too much credit for anything given to us. All that we create is merely putting something together in a new way from one or several somethings that already exist. We become re-arrangers.

When we meditate we generally close our eyes and re-imagine some beautiful scenery or event that reminds us we are not alone. We didn't have anything to do with making the water fall down from the cliff side, several stories high.

We may reach the mountain top and gaze out in awesome wonder at all that lies below. All we did was change our perspective. Instead of looking up at the peak, we look down at the valley below.

Because this is the only life we know, we can't imagine anything after this. I recently heard it said that we don't have to die to be in heaven. We can begin to appreciate all that is beautiful in this life – a little bit of heaven.

September 6

I remember the days of old... my soul thirsts for you like parched land. – Psalms 143:5-6

We remember the days of old, when sometimes everything was going our way – the comfortable way – with longing for repetition.

But, then, we remember the times when nothing went our way, it was endless misery, rejection, loss of love, financial failure or ruin. It seemed the dark cloud would be with us forever. We were doomed.

God didn't change. God didn't move. God – the all-powerful, all knowing – was with us – through joy and sorrow. The variable is me – the human in the story; the lack of understanding, acceptance, faith – my inability to pause and reflect, and appreciate who and what I am.

The soul seems to have a life of its own, almost apart from that which we imagine we are. Does our soul sometimes have its own "out of body" experience? Is that what we might call meditation?

Why bother to meditate, unless it achieves that total freedom from the world as we know it, and gradually move into another time and space?

Meditation can take us wherever we want to go, places we didn't know we wanted to go, and beyond the prison of self.

September 7

We are children of God...heirs of God. – Romans 8:16-17

Historically, the writer of this passage, presumed to be Paul, was a Jew and a Roman citizen. When he talks about being children of God he speaks as a Jew, who believes that Jesus is the promised one who came to free his people.

Although seldom mentioned, Paul, being Roman, was persecuting followers of Jesus who were perceived to be against Roman rule. There were dissident factions among the population of Jews as well as non-Jews, or gentiles. It took a stunning revelation to bring Paul around to becoming a follower of Jesus, instead of a persecutor of his followers.

So, the connection Paul refers to is from all that history. He considered himself a child of God the father of all creation, and an heir to all his God of Moses and the tribes of Israel intended for his people.

If the Hebrew bible writers believe as stated, that there is but one God, and that God created the first human being, then that God is the creator and father of all humanity. Therefore, all humanity are children of the same God and entitled to inherit equally all the good that God has created. Makes sense to me.

September 8

My servant Moses is dead. So prepare to cross the Jordan here. –Joshua 1:2

The Lord spoke the above words to Joshua, the successor of Moses, the one who would do battle at Jericho, across the Jordan River.

When I went on pilgrimage to the Holy Land, we visited the place where Moses passed his final days, watching his people head toward the Promised Land. I gained a perspective regarding the journey that had come up from Egypt on the Jordanian side of the Dead Sea.

I realized when I looked at maps how far Moses went out of his way to reach the land promised his people. They truly wandered around the desert for forty years. They were so close at the beginning and yet so far away as they wandered.

Moses never reached the "Promised Land."

How much farther do we have to go out of our way to reach the heaven that is so close, already inside of us? When we have moments, or longer periods of serenity we realize the Promised Land was inside of us from the very beginning of our exodus.

We are born to seek our place and purpose in the world, and we know when we have arrived, when we are truly home, when we can now say, "to thine own self be true."

September 9

I have become the sport of my neighbors... the just, the perfect man, is a laughing stock. – Job 12:4

Poor Job! Poor me! Poor everyone!

We are all victims of the judgment of our fellow man and woman. What they think of us may or may not matter. It may or may not change the way we think or act. But we waste our time, waste our sanity over what people may think of us, and how little respect and appreciation we get for all our good works.

If I was a perfect human being, and everyone respected my wisdom, and gave me praise, I would be sick in my head and lacking in any true humility. I am true to who I believe I am – today. But I don't expect everyone to agree with me. I would be bored silly, lacking any challenge. It is only by testing my thoughts that I find out what I really believe.

Being open-minded invites a wealth of information and opinion into my life, and I can take what suits me and mix it with other information I already have, and weigh it and sift it and take it or leave it. And you, my dear friends, may do the same with what I have to offer.

September 10

My comfort in my affliction is that your promise gives me life. – Psalms 119:50

This Psalm is in praise of God's law and is subtitled "Zayin" – apparently a way of numbering various songs, hymns or psalms. The Psalms are still recited or sung daily by monks, nuns, priests, other religious, and by Jews at prayer.

There is no melody, no music, except when we hear them chanted in response at prayer times. These songs or psalms themselves give melody to daily life. They bring joy or express sorrow, or praise and thanksgiving. Sometimes words fall away and the language of the heart and of the soul breaks through.

How seldom we simply celebrate life and breath, and joy – where words pave the way to reach the God of our understanding, who is the same as the God of our lack of understanding. How content we can be in simply knowing there is a power in the universe that knows we exist, knows us better than will ever know or understand ourselves.

And, wonder of all wonders, we know that that power we call God loves us, cares about us, and guides us on our path.

September 11

Peace, peace to the far and near, says the LORD. – Isaiah 57:19

This day each year reminds Americans of that horrific 9-11-2001, when more than 3,000 people from different countries and of different ages, died in New York City, Washington, DC, and in three planes that crashed – two into the World Trade Center towers, one into the Pentagon, and one downed in a field in Pennsylvania.

My husband and I arrived at the Portland, Oregon terminal about 6 am for our flight to Detroit for the celebration of my fifty-year high school class reunion.

When we reached our gate with boarding passes in hand, there were crowds of people glued to the television sets. Just past 9 am in New York City, a plane crashed into a tower. I asked what was happening. No one knew. The first plane crash looked as though it might be accidental, but now another, a few minutes later was obviously not an accident.

What was a minor nightmare for us, cancelling our trip turned into a national nightmare that haunts us to this day.

Where was our God that day? We have looked, to place the blame on a race of people, a nation, a religious faction. We cannot blame God for the acts of human beings, but we do depend on God's help in healing our wounds.

September 12

Let us make man in our image, after our own likeness. – Genesis 1:26

What strikes me here is the use of the plural "our" when this God of creation refers to making man in "our image" and likeness. We humans, who barely see past our noses, get hung up on the physical rather than the spiritual meaning of creation. We are not physically created in the image of God, since no one has seen God and continued living on this earth.

If we are so fortunate to have the Spirit of the Creator within our human being, then we have unlimited potential for being and doing good. We have dominion over all of creation and its living properties. We can't create something out of nothing, as the Creator has done, but we have responsibility for managing what we have been given.

In our human lives, we can make unbelievable things happen through discovery and invention. Nothing that God created or that we discover or invent is necessarily "less good." But, how our discoveries and inventions are used can cause tremendous trouble and pain if left outside our control or dominion. Here – we need help and guidance from the Creator.

September 13

The earth has yielded its fruits. – Psalms 67:7

It is that time of year when we look to the sky for the big harvest moon. The time when hot apple cider and football games go together. The end of the summer and the beginning of the cold, dark winter months give us pause to reflect on the bounty of the good weather, and the good times of harvest.

So much abundance from hands full of seed cast upon the soil, nurtured by sun and by water. It's all so natural, and all so special. We forget to give thanks throughout the summer, but as the growing season draws to a close, we remember to thank the powers that be for all the blessings of food that sustain us throughout the winter.

Most of our newer generations lack the close relationship with food that our grandparents or parents had. They planted seed, watered the fragile growth or waited for rain, plucked crowded plants to allow room to grow, and picked fruit or vegetable when ready to eat. Nothing was wasted on my grandparents' farm. Remnants from the harvest became food for animals or mulch for plant protection during the winter cold.

We are so blessed, for the gifts that are brought to our table.

September 14

All wives will honor their husbands, from the greatest to the least. – Esther 1:20

This passage is all about virgins, harems, eunuchs, kings and queens, and sexual favors they grant or deny each other.

When the queen didn't come when she was called by the king through the eunuch messenger, she lost favor. So Queen Vashti is out, and Esther is in. Esther, who has been prepared with all manner of cosmetics and fine clothing, becomes the faithful, adoring and obedient new queen.

If the Bible is the inspired word of God, then I have a problem with some of the goings on of that day. I suppose that Paul, in the New Testament got some of his ideas about "wives, be subject to your husbands" from episodes such as these in the "old" testament. This is more about the behavior of the wife than about the controlling nature of the king.

Where is the love?

Life is more about love than a command that "all wives will honor their husbands." The decree the king issued, because his wife did not come to him when commanded through his messenger, was made to cover every woman in his vast realm – rich and poor alike.

Can we please rethink that one?

September 15

The waves subsided and it grew calm. – Luke 8:24

Jesus was asleep in the fishing boat when his followers woke him during a storm. He was a calming influence on the wind, the waves and the rain.

Our storms are generally internal. We need calming, and turn to all kinds of relaxation tools and techniques. We do Yoga, Tai Chi, prayer, meditation, and take walks, read books, watch television programs, or write in our journals. Sometimes we even ask Jesus to show us how to calm our storms. Once we get results we believe, and, believing is healing, and calming.

When I was in Israel, our group boarded a fishing boat similar to the one referred to here. It was a very large vessel, accommodating nearly 50 people. The water was calm, but grew gray and threatened rain. They cut the motors when we were in the middle of the Sea of Galilee. The silence was almost deafening. But, it felt so very calming.

How seldom do we shut out all noise and disturbances?

Not nearly often enough.

September 16

But with you is forgiveness. – Psalms 130:4

When we talk about forgiveness we are very perceptive about the harm we have done to others, but not always ready to admit the harm we have done to ourselves.

It's so much easier to forgive others for the grief and misery they have caused than it is for us to acknowledge that we may have had a part in the harm done to us. Most often our part has to do with how we have taught people to treat us, and allowed abusive or disrespectful behavior to become a habit, or standard for treatment.

We stand up for our children, the poor, elderly and defenseless, but where have we failed in speaking up or standing up for our own human rights? As a mother of many children, I have wept bitter tears for the way I have treated them and the treatment or perceived disrespect I have received in return.

Sometimes I have to admit they learned some of the behavior I object to, from me – or my relationship with them. But, I have to be careful not to exaggerate my failings and totally forgive others for harm done to me. And, I have to always remember to forgive myself – a flawed human being.

September 17

The quiet words of the wise are better heeded than the shout of a ruler of fools. – Ecclesiastes 9:17

I've heard it said that poets and artists more accurately reflect the mood of the people than the politicians or rulers of their day. Poets and artists are quieter in the expression of their views by far than those who grab the headlines and pulpits to project their views with thunder and lightning.

We tend to ignore the noise in search of quiet truth, but it becomes more difficult all the time. So much of what we get today is heavy handed commentary. We grow weary of being shouted at, and told what to think. Say it once. Say it twice. Say it again and again. Maybe we hear it the first time.

Repetition works well with children, when they are learning something new, and they need our constant reminders, encouragement and praise.

But, adults who have years of education, learning, and ability to put their own thoughts together with new information, may not require badgering.

Repetition works well in advertising and indoctrination.

No matter how many times a lie is repeated, repetition does not make it true. Mature humans know when to tune out and turn off noise.

September 18

Do not worry about your livelihood. – Matthew 6:25

During a time when I was worrying about my livelihood and how to pay my bills and take care of my children, living pay check to pay check – I joined Debtors Anonymous. I read the book *How to Get Out of Debt, Stay Out of Debt and Live Prosperously* by Jerrold Mundis.

I studied the book. I practiced the principles of the program. I posted the following affirmation inside the cover of my checkbook, "You are now filled with the rich bounty of God who supplies my every need now." Slowly, over a period of debt recovery and new sources of income, I overcame my worry with the practical relationship with money.

Life is more than food or clothes. Life is values – values and priorities and decisions based on the wisdom we gain by relating to money realistically and respectfully.

As a young girl, I watched my mother take the cash from my father's pay and divide it into envelopes she clipped together with a large safety pin. Each envelope was labeled to pay bills, or for food, or clothes, or birthdays, or holidays, or travel, or entertainment.

My father worked six days a week as a baker – we frequently went to dinner and a movie on Saturdays. My mother always budgeted for fun.

September 19

Sing joyfully to the LORD, all you lands. – Psalms 98:4

During tryouts for a solo part in our Christmas play when I was in seventh grade, I tried to project my voice, but couldn't – so I ended up back in the chorus. The song was about a doll that had a "pain in my sawdust." I wasn't marked for life as a failure, but I did suffer some loss of confidence in my ability to sing solo – and contented myself to be one of several voices.

Most of life is learning to be part of a chorus, whether singing love songs, sad songs, or songs of joy and thanksgiving. I love music. I'll never be solo in singing or making joyful sounds, but I can feel it in my heart and in my soul. We each have those moments when we wish we could shout out our joyful sound – our thanksgiving for what life has given us.

When each of my eight babies was born and I heard that joyful first cry I felt the song in my heart and I felt the solo throughout my body.

I delivered a new life. I finished my job. All was in God's hands now.

As the song goes, "He holds the whole world in his hands…little bitty baby in his hands." And, me, too!

September 20

They covet fields, and seize them; houses, and they take them; they cheat an owner of his house, a man of his inheritance. – Micah 2:2

Land ownership battles have been going on for a very long time. This land monopoly was denounced by Isaiah, and supported by God, speaking through Micah. The rich were exploiting the poor in the land of Judah.

For some people who acquire wealth, they never have enough; they always want more.

There is nothing evil about the acquisition of wealth and property. The evil exists in the methods of acquiring wealth and property, and the lack of ethical behavior. Total lack of consideration for the damage to individuals and their property is the moral issue.

The poor – the powerless and less ambitious – become the pawns of the rich and powerful. They become more powerless as the rich become more powerful.

The United States is currently feeling the effects of greed. The "haves" want more, and they are willing to walk on the backs of the "have nots" to advance their own cause. So many struggling lower and middle class families have lost their homes and their land and their jobs because they listened to the advice of the greedy, who directed them down a path to financial failure.

Nothing changes. Human nature gets out of control, the poor suffer – and they are blamed for causing their own suffering.

September 21

How did you receive the Spirit? Was it through observance of the law or through faith in what you heard? How could you be so stupid? – Galatians 3:2

Paul makes his argument to Jews and Gentiles alike that their faith in the Spirit of God, rained down on them by the life and death of Jesus, is their truth – not the promise in the law passed down from Abraham.

He has called them "senseless Galatians," implying there is an evil spell cast over them. He wants them to be clear that the Spirit comes from their belief in the Christ and not in the observance of the Hebrew law. There is a conflict between the observance of the law and the spirit of the law.

Are not most of our problems today based on the interpretation of the law, and the observance of the law as determined by our justice and legal systems? Laws are agreed upon by a body of people who may have a variety of differences regarding the wording of the law – and vast differences of opinion about the implementation and observance of the law – and, what constitutes a violation of the law.

Laws are man's attempt to create order out of chaos – but, in truth, every law creates a new area of contention and confusing tasks for the legal and justice systems.

September 22

I will give you a new heart and place a new spirit within you. – Ezekiel 36:26

Ezekiel, another of the great prophets, spoke for God to the people captive in Babylon that their salvation is at hand by changing their hearts of stone, to the recognition and appreciation of their God.

Early in 2007, I experienced sudden pain and discomfort that sent me to the emergency room in San Felipe, Mexico, where we have our winter residence. That was the first dramatic incident with an irregular heartbeat. The next two years took me to emergency care nine times, for one reason or another, and surgeries related to bowel obstruction, gastro problems, and eventually for the surgical implant of a pacemaker to regulate my heartbeat.

Although the emergencies and surgeries were separate issues, they all happened to this one body – this same heart.

The heart is frequently referred to as the place where emotions and attitudes grow or fester. Once I had the pacemaker regulating my heartbeat I began to feel the "natural heart."

I was cognizant of how the heart as well as the gut can take control of the entire body. Once I restored the "natural" heart rhythm I gave thanks to the great power in the universe that set me on the correct and steady beat.

My gratitude is boundless.

September 23

Guide me in your truth and teach me. – Psalms 25:5

When I wake I am a blank slate, doubting I will have a thought worth thinking, and words worth writing. If I relied on the contents of my own brain to get me started and keep me going, I would not have the courage to put pen to paper.

My first thoughts upon waking direct my foot on the path for the day. I turn my life and my will over to the care of the God of my understanding. I am an empty vessel asking my higher self, my higher power to guide me in seeking truth, in seeking the correct words, the wisest thoughts and actions.

This is the guide for my right actions And, I know I have not been abandoned. Any time during the day, when I feel lost for words or direction I can pause and re-think my way. I don't consciously wait for God's guidance, but I know when I need it.

When I think of God as my savior, I only know that having that connection saves me from acting or thinking on a much lower level. My connection with God truly lifts me up to a higher state of consciousness. And, it is all good.

September 24

Your word is truth! As you have sent me into the world, so I have sent them into the world. –John 17:17-18

I can only speak my truth as I know it at the time I speak it. We take a lifetime to determine for ourselves – what is our truth? God seldom speaks directly to each of us, so that we will know God's truth. For far too long we have trusted our spiritual, governmental and financial leaders to speak God's truth to us. We are adrift in the sand that blows in the wind.

Thus, we are responsible for discerning our truth, on our own, trusting the Spirit of Truth that Jesus promised us would be here for us in times of joy and times of sorrow, and disasters of all kinds.

Certainty is momentary and fleeting, only the fool believes he/she is infallible in conveying truth all the time. Like love, truth can only be defined in its actions. We can feel we have love in our hearts, but it is constantly tested according to our relationship with other humans.

Truth expressed is truth judged. We may have certainty regarding the truth we speak or the truth we write – however, truth, like love, is an activity by which our fellow travelers judge us.

September 25

"I will write upon the tablets the commandments that were on the former tablets that you broke, and you shall place them in the ark." – Deuteronomy 10:1-2

How striking, the detail to which God gets involved in the re-writing of the commandments that were written by God on tablets of stone. Moses must have felt some guilt after throwing down the first set of tablets when he became angry with the desert tribes with whom he had traveled for many years in the desert coming out of slavery in Egypt.

Deuteronomy is the last writings, or memoirs, for Moses. Apparently his mental faculties are still intact. He isn't adlibbing any of the account. This time he makes it all clear to the people. He elaborated on the original "ten commandments," and gave considerable direction regarding their duties as citizens of their new found promised land.

The law, as written by Moses, with considerable help from the Lord, lives on through the ages in the hearts and souls of the Hebrew people. Most religions respect the spirit of that law. There is nothing mysterious about the commandments – only the interpretation of those commands as societies become more and more complex.

September 26

Your light shall break forth like the dawn. – Isaiah 58:8

Early in the morning when we are in Mexico, the daybreak lights up the bedroom and I am awake. If I get up early enough to watch the day break, I am usually treated to the awesome sight of the sun rising out of the calm, blue Sea of Cortez. The world brightens up and the world is cleansed and healed and fresh for the day ahead. Yesterday's pain and wounds are forgotten.

Our wounds are so often of an emotional or spiritual nature. When it is dark outside, I feel the weight of the day. When the new day breaks, I am refreshed. I stretch like a waking kitten, and feel optimistic.

Why do we feel like we have to fight our way through each day? Now that I'm retired from a day job, I can reinvent myself every day. Although there is no need to rush or worry, it seems my past always catches up with me. I want to do it right, whatever "it" is, I want it done as perfectly as possible – for my own pleasure.

God has my back. I make sure of that before I start my day. I turn my will and my life over by letting go and letting God direct my path – and, I move forward.

September 27

When the grass is taken away and the after growth appears, and the mountain greens are gathered in, the lambs will provide you with clothing. – Proverbs 27:25-26

Proverbs reminds us that Palestine once was a land of abundance for all who inhabited and cared for the land and its yield.

The environment is good to us if we are good caretakers of the land.

In search of ways to prosper from the land we may at times squeeze it to death. Only common sense is required to know the growing and harvesting seasons, and to know how many times we can milk a cow or a goat before the animal can give no more.

We can milk the cow or the goat, or we can kill it for food. Then all is done for the animal – its usefulness to us is over. The land can only give so much as well. We can shear the wool off the sheep to make clothing to keep us warm and protected from the elements – or, we can kill the lamb for food – and the service of the animal is ended. We can gather eggs from the chickens for multiple uses for food. Or, we can have baked or fried chicken for dinner – and the service for the chicken is ended.

We do not have unlimited resources – everything comes to an end. To sustain our lives we must sustain the land for food.

September 28

It is the LORD who marches before you. – Deuteronomy 31:8

Fear can be paralyzing. Show me a person who has never known fear and I will show you a child, a saint, or a liar. We like to think we are fearless, and in control of our own lives, but all that can change in an instant when you see the train bearing down on you when your car is stalled on the tracks; or you run off the road, over the cliff and into the water.

It doesn't take a real threat to raise our fight or flight levels, it can be a perceived threat. Voices from the land of television news are constantly telling us how dangerous our world is, and how helpless we are – and that our own government is our worst enemy.

I don't like feeling fear. I have had periods of anxiety from vague or unknown causes; it is a terrible way to live. I can only believe, in the face of the unbelievable, that somehow, someday, it will all be different. It will get better.

I looked in the dictionary for the active verb for optimism. The only verb I found was "optimize." We are all called to "1. Improve to the greatest extent possible."

So, every day in every way we are getting better and better, or making the world a better place by optimizing ourselves into better human beings.

September 29

Shelter me against the council of malefactors. – Psalms 64:3-4

Somewhere in my early Catholic education the nun said, "The tongue can be a sharp and dangerous weapon, which is why God created you with teeth and lips to stand guard over the tongue."

It's hardly ever that serious, but there are times I should have been reminded, and wish others had known about that little message as well. This passage is clear about the malefactors, or evil doers, who do use their tongues as weapons.

In this day and age of rapid fire words on radio, television, Internet, Facebook and Twitter – many people act in haste and repent in leisure. What may seem like harmless fun at the expense of another person soon becomes an act of bullying and an invasion of privacy. The civil guidelines do not seem to come with each new piece of electronic equipment.

There are no limits to the amount of sharp-tongue-sword activity and bitter-word arrows that some people find out too late have done damage – beyond repair.

September 30

The earth brought forth every kind of plant. – Genesis 1:12-13

The argument about evolution or creation seems so futile. God or Spirit or energy forces may be all the same life force of nature. We debate about the unknown and unknowable actions of nature. Most religious folks prefer the easy, mythical, mysterious answer to a very complex system. Creationism is a nice manageable story or explanation about our very existence.

As long as there is no need to come up with a different story, the literal creation story will do. As long as a child continues to believe that Santa Claus brought all the gifts his parents paid for, that magically appear under the Christmas tree, then the parents continue the game. Even though the child long ago discovered the hiding places for the gifts – and, that child acts in his or her best interest and lets the parents continue the Santa saga.

Tradition has its good points. But, continuing to believe and do something because it is the way it has always been done doesn't make sense in the adult world. We have all given up the Tooth Fairy and Santa Clause story when the time came.

October

Octo
Latin for 8
Eighth month in Julian (Roman) calendar.
Gregorian calendar
instituted by Pope Gregory XIII
established January as first month,
making October the 10th month.

October 1

Things that are impossible for men are possible for God. – Luke 18:27

For God all things are possible. – Matthew 19:26

The followers of Jesus repeat words they heard him say. They didn't compare notes, and the translators didn't select one over another or edit out duplications. Jesus was, in effect, the local "street preacher." He told stories when asked questions, and gathered crowds.

The crowd in Judea was peppering him with questions about salvation and heaven, and who would find favor with God. Peter asked about the rich man, and Jesus said it would be more difficult for the rich man to enter the kingdom – but not impossible.

Unlike most people today, the people of Jesus' time were concerned about their afterlife. So, to speak these words today would be falling on mostly deaf ears.

Can you imagine Jesus going to a college campus and speaking about heaven and hell as it relates to the afterlife? Today, people want their heaven now, and they are doing all they can to avoid their current hell. We remember the simple minded Forrest Gump saying, "I know what love is."

There are many who already know what hell is; many who experience touches of paradise; many more who can't possibly think in such abstract terms as heaven or hell after this life.

October 2

From now on I announce new things to you. – Isaiah 48:6

When a new thought comes to me – from somewhere deep inside my heart and soul – I say, "thank you, God!"

Does it really matter where the thought originates? If it is a good thought; isn't that sufficient? If I just happen to generate this great idea from accidently putting several of the previous thoughts already stored in my brain; or if my spirit within guided me on that path; I am grateful for the idea – and I say, "Thank you, God!"

If something works for me, then I don't have to defend it. The philosophers made a habit of questioning their own thoughts and assumptions, and theories. Scientists test their thoughts against empirical evidence through repeatable experiments. Doctors, lawyers, and many other professionals are in the "practice" of their particular discipline, or art.

We say, "Practice makes perfect." We do not say that practice **is** perfect, since we don't really know what perfect is. We know when we have finished; when something is as perfect as we can make it. We know that someone may come along and improve on our work of art, literary masterpiece, world-altering discovery, or life-changing invention.

Our current technological growth cycle convinces us there is no end in sight for building a better mousetrap.

October 3

Men with seared consciences who forbid marriage and require abstinence from foods… which God created… Everything God created is good. – 1 Timothy 4:2-5

The early followers of Jesus continued to discuss, debate, and bring together the teachings of their holy prophets, and their new learning after experiencing the presence of Jesus in their lives. They are dealing with Hebrew scripture and warnings, and rules regarding food and life style.

In this passage, Paul is opening up the faith in Jesus the Christ to both Jew and non-Jew. He recommends to Timothy that he not become overly concerned with the regulations regarding food combinations – and that the matter of whether a man is married or not married has little relevance in following Christ Jesus.

The message that "Everything God created is good" applies to the abstinence from foods as well as marital abstinence. Most of the followers of Jesus were married. We know this specifically about Peter, who had a mother-in-law. Jesus was not necessarily advocating abandonment of family; even though some chose to leave their families to follow him.

October 4

Hear, my son and receive my words, and the years of your life shall be many. – Proverbs 4:10

We all are children at heart. Our needs are childlike. When we are troubled we seek guidance from our inner parent, just as we may have looked to our own parents for support, guidance, comfort, and security. I suppose that is why the man with the white beard became the symbol for God the Father. Since we don't know what God looks like, we accept what God can do for us, as the answer to "who is God?"

Instead of trying to understand God, we spend a lifetime trying to understand ourselves, and our relationship with others, and that God of our misunderstanding.

Are we looking for a long life, or for a meaningful life, a quality life? A long life can be miserable; there are no guarantees. My hope is that I will have just enough years to accomplish what it is I am here to do. I have several writing projects. Sometimes I think I have to work faster, because time may be running out.

It only matters to me. I want to finish what I start. But then, I may be starting so many projects because I want to be around to finish them.

October 5

He sent them forth to proclaim the reign of God and heal the afflicted. – Luke 9:2

God's power, Jesus' power, the disciples' power, did not end when that era ended. That power and authority to overcome our inner and outer demons; and to heal ourselves and each other, goes on today.

There are many ways to practice the power of healing. When we know our own strengths and weaknesses we can begin to heal our own afflictions through utilizing our strengths.

If we learn to love ourselves we can learn to love others. If we can forgive ourselves we can learn to forgive others. If we can change our way of thinking and doing, then we can accept the right and the ability of others to change their attitudes, words and actions. As the saying goes, we first need to get the speck out of our own eye so we can see more clearly and help others adjust and change.

No one has all the answers – no matter how arrogant and insistent. Understanding takes time, and patience, and true love.

October 6

Love your enemies, pray for your persecutors. – Matthew 5:44

Once I discovered that I am my own worst enemy, this whole process of forgiveness and loving my enemies began to make some kind of sense. We sometimes grow old believing we are fighting the same old enemies we have always fought. And, it's really not about "them" as much as it is about me.

As I grow older, I sometimes think the enemy is the passage of time and the fear of not having enough resources to see me through to the end. The enemy, however, is my lack of faith, lack of trust in the ability of my own human nature to live each day, one day at a time, with gratitude toward the universe, and all it has given me.

Every breath is a gift. Every day is a gift. Every sunrise and every sunset, and all that goes between, provide me with the resources to live a better life.

Even the bad days have something good about them. Just do the squint test. Close your eyes almost tight and see what you can see. Put your ear to the ground and hear plants growing. Just simply be a part of something great – our whole universe.

October 7

It is good to give thanks to the LORD. – Psalms 92:2

When I woke in the middle of the night to a full moon I looked out the window to a landscape nearly bright as daylight. I knew it would be brighter in the morning, and the sun would shine brightly – somewhere.

On dull days when I walk in the Mexican desert, the sun shines on select areas of the San Pedro Mountains, I stop and stare at the beauty of shadows and light.

Whether in the middle of the night, or the morning with or without its bright daylight, I give thanks to my God.

It becomes easier to see God in everything and everyone when I remember to give thanks. I am never alone; I am totally dependent on some kind of power that sets all things in motion, morning, noon, and night.

There are hurricanes, tornados, floods, famine, droughts, and battles of every kind imaginable. How does my peace of mind contribute to harmony in the entire world? It may not. But it is the best I can do for me, for those I love, and for the world at large.

October 8

Build up, build up, prepare the way, remove the stumbling blocks from my people's path. – Isaiah 57:14

Human nature demands progress. No matter what area we are defining, forward movement rules. Once we waged a civil war that involved the abolition of slavery as a way of life, we cannot go back to allowing one person to enslave or own another human being.

So many stumbling blocks had to be removed, so many views held by people who believed they were entitled to hold others in slavery – to harvest cotton, tobacco, and other crops – and continually perform, menial jobs under sub-human conditions.

We must build up, because that's who we are. We must pave the way, smooth the way – but, for what end purpose?

The means used for building up may not always be justified. The end result may be a worthy goal, but we do not build on the backs of the workers, the underprivileged, the poor and the defenseless.

Our values regarding human rights and privileges are on the line every single day – as individuals and as nations of people who claim to practice the principles taught by Buddha, Moses, Abraham and Jesus.

October 9

This widow is wearing me out. I am going to settle in her favor, or she will end by doing me violence. – Luke 18:4-5

Jesus told many stories about the kingdom of God. This one is about a corrupt judge, and a widow who repeatedly confronted him, demanding her rights. No doubt, she was persistent regarding her property and livelihood.

The widow's persistence paid off. The judge could no longer endure her pestering, threatening and perhaps some cursing as well.

So, she wore him down, and he claimed he was concerned she would do him violence. I can't imagine what kind of violence a poor widow could do, except to the judge's ears, and to his reputation. He finally was motivated to do the right thing.

The point of the story is that we not give up when asking God to help us, guide us, and save us from our own failings and weaknesses. Jesus tells us that God is much more responsive to our petitions than the corrupt judge who does not believe in God; does not concern himself with threats of God or man – but can't stand the verbal bombardment of a lone widowed woman.

Patience and persistence can, eventually, pay off for us.

October 10

Let the little children come to me. Do not shut them off. – Luke 18:16

When I was in Jerusalem at St. George's College with a group of Episcopalians, we attended mass in their chapel. When I returned from receiving communion and knelt to pray, the above passage came to mind. For some reason I felt like the little child of whom Jesus spoke. I have never had that feeling before or sense.

For that short time I knew exactly what was meant about "accepting the kingdom of God as a little child."

We can't always feel that acceptance because we may not be in a safe place. But, how glorious to feel that loving, and that trusting – and to remember how wonderful it feels.

I had always been taught that Jesus loved the little children, and I appreciated being loved. His followers objected to the mothers crowding Jesus and asking him to touch and bless their children. Jesus rebuked his disciples, and they allowed the children to come near their master.

The little child within us is always seeking love and acceptance. Now, we know where we can find it.

October 11

Through it all the seed sprouts and grows without his knowing how it happens. – Mark 4:27

Whatever is hidden and mysterious is what makes the world turn and seeds grow. Rain and sunlight are obvious, but the process is only discovered by watching, waiting, and seeing the results.

The evidence of a singular power setting the whole process into motion is hidden from our view. That power, that many of us choose to call God, planted the first seed, breathed the first breath of air onto the soil, and provided the first moisture to start the whole world blooming and growing, and producing more seed.

*Believing in some*thing we cannot see, but can only observe as it grows is called faith. Believing in a power greater than myself, that brings people together to nurture a common cause is called compassion.

Like the man in the story, we go to bed at night and rise to a new day, unravelling the events as we go, believing in what we cannot see, what we cannot hear or touch. We assume that everything we need will become part of our day, part of our lives.

There is plenty of room for doubt about whom or what keeps the world growing and being – but little room for denial. Something started life on our planet – something, not us.

October 12

Let us go early to the vineyards, and see if the vines are in bloom. – Song of Songs 7:13

The Song of Solomon, as the Song of Songs is sometimes called, followed the end of the Babylonian Exile (538 BC) era, when the writer expressed the pure joy of freedom. The seventh chapter, from which the above excerpt comes, is titled "The Beauty of the Bride."

In both Old and New Testament tradition, the Lord God is considered the bridegroom, or the lover of his beloved followers, his people, his church, and Israel.

The love between bride and groom, described in the most sensual language possible for its time, brings blush and some doubt to the soul that never has known such spiritual delight.

Even doubters search for the experience of pure love and joy described in Songs. Most people find that feeling in the sexual relationship that sends electricity surging through the body, mind and soul during sexual fulfillment. No wonder the most common expression at climax is, "Oh, God!"

Even the atheist forgets he has no faith, and utters God's name when at the height of joy or during the depths of sorrow. We all pray, sometime, to something, and sometimes to nothing.

October 13

For six days you may work, but on the seventh day you shall rest. – Exodus 34:21

Human nature teaches us that we must rest and sleep at the end of each day. The harder we work the more rest and sleep our bodies require. As we age, our bodies aren't doing the same physical labor we once did, but the aging process alone takes its toll of wear and tear on the mental and physical systems that run our lives. Then, we may require even more rest because it takes longer to get things done, more stress and more strain on our systems.

When we are young we can do anything, any time, all the time. We abuse our bodies with poor eating habits, the wrong kind of physical activity, and less sleep. When I was raising eight children, ages one (or less) to 16 (or more), I could get by on short nights, interrupted sleep. But, frequently, I napped when the young ones napped.

Rest is as important for the brain as it is for the body. Our thinking sometimes wears us out, gets us down, and needs renewal. When I was raising all those children, I was finishing my undergraduate education, and then pursuing a master's degree in Communications. I had a one-year teaching assistantship during the last two years of my marriage, with one married daughter, and one son in college – but six children still at home. It was a daunting, but obviously not an impossible task.

October 14

The flowers appear on the earth, the time of pruning the vines has come. – Song of Songs 2:12

Although I am responding to this passage in the fall of the year, when leaves are falling off trees, and there is a chill in the air, I still look forward to the springtime. There still is a promise of new life, new ideas, and new beginnings. We don't have to wait for the calendar and the weather to tell us that we can rejoice and rejuvenate.

This is the time of year we come to Mexico. This is the time when the desert is blooming from a heavy late summer rain. Yes, the roof leaked, again, but, it still is a roof over our heads, and we are not sleeping in an old trailer with the wind whistling through the cracks and crevices. There are families in the barrio living day to day on rice, beans and tortillas – with leaky roofs.

For some, here in San Felipe, public education is a dream for a better life. Those of us, who live a more fortunate life, in retirement, help the children by raising money to provide them with tuition and uniforms. The mothers find a way to keep the children in clean white shirts, and sometimes white pants or skirts. Parents love their children here as much as parents in Oregon or Pennsylvania or Alaska love their children.

Of all the things that grow on this earth or out of this earth, the growing children are the most important of all. Children deserve the hope and beauty that comes with springtime – all the time.

October 15

Reprove not an arrogant man, lest he hate you; reprove a wise man, and he will love you. – Proverbs 9:8

There are people who are willing to learn from their own mistakes, and the mistakes of others. And then, there are people who never will admit they made a mistake, and never intend to offer an apology or correct the error of their ways.

So, why bother trying to even talk with the arrogant; they already hate you, hate themselves, and hate everyone who thinks differently than they do. The only way to argue with an arrogant person is to lower your own values. You must go to the lower value and use the same arrogance with them. Is it worth the effort? I think not.

Being self-satisfied may have to be enough. There is no value in trying to tell others how good and righteous I am. I no longer have the energy or the desire to prove my point, to prove I am right. There are always more points of view than I can imagine.

If I have to argue with friend or foe to the point of surrender, I take little satisfaction in victory. I haven't really changed anyone's mind; only reduced myself to a lower level. I have been dishonored.

October 16

When I came among you it was in weakness and fear, and with much trepidation. – Corinthians 2:3

My entire career and education has been about words, their combinations, and their meanings. I have a master's degree in communications, but I do not consider myself a master communicator.

Paul, the most often quoted follower of Jesus, humbles himself in this passage, in this letter to his friends in Corinth. He admits his fear and trepidation when he began to explore who Jesus was and who the followers of Jesus were.

When Paul was on his way to search out these so called "Christians," with the order to disrupt and destroy them, he was struck by something that knocked him off his horse and to the ground.

Paul, so the story goes, was blinded, and instructed to search out the man he came to know as Peter. The rest is history. Paul became teachable. There is no record of how long it took him to receive his instruction. But by his own words, he now admits, they gained their strength and "convincing power" because of the Spirit that Jesus told his followers would be with them – and us – until the end of time.

What a powerful heritage we share in the Spirit.

October 17

He shall wipe away every tear from their eyes. – Revelation 21:4

Old and New Testament prophets speak of a more perfect world. They ask why a creator would set a world in motion without a rescue plan. We ask the same question.

If there is a God, and that God is all good, and all that that God created is good – then why is this world in such a mess?

The story always comes back to the free will that humans have to make decisions – to plan and to execute their plan.

Why does one civilization after another implode?

What is the critical mass necessary for enough people turning a corrupt and failing society around?

I don't expect answers in my lifetime. I can only try to make my little area of the universe as good as possible.

Frustration with the way things are can only breed more discontent, negative thinking, and loss of all hope.

We continue to unravel the harm done to each other and the planet. We continue to discover new ways to unscramble the egg and make a new omelet.

October 18

No man can serve two masters... You cannot give yourself to God and money. – Matthew 6:24

We just saw the movie "Wolf of Wall Street." Not a word throughout the film about God. Not surprising. Where money is big time, it is god. Of course we all need money, the currency with which we barter for goods and services.

There are good hearted people in this world who have plenty of money for themselves and their families, and their friends, and live lavishly. Some of these millionaires and billionaires use their wealth to improve the lives of the needy; those who can never hope to have a small fraction of the wealth enjoyed by so few.

How much is enough? How much is more than enough? I'll never know because I know I am not destined for wealth. I seldom buy a lottery ticket and I don't go to casinos. I just don't feel the urge to risk what I do have for the uncertainty of gambling.

Prosperity is about more than money. I am beginning to think prosperity is an attitude. My mother always told me "you are as young as you think you are." Perhaps, I am also as rich as I think I am. God provides.

October 19

He performed those great miracles before our very eyes. – Joshua 24:17

Although Joshua is recounting the protection and care of God during the long journey out of Egypt, we take comfort in knowing our trust in God guides us on our short and our long journeys. This passage could have been written at any time during the history of humans. It could be written today.

Not all who trust in the Lord complete all their travels – only the successful write the letter of thanks. There are no guarantees that we will always say "thanks be to God for a successful journey." Real life is more realistic than that.

As much as we would like to believe that we are invincible because God is on our side, it may happen that we end up getting hit by a car or falling off a cliff. Even though God is on our side and the angels are watching over us; life is unpredictable and real.

All the voodoo, rabbits' feet, and prayers cannot stop some events from taking place. We thank God when we return home from our travels, but that doesn't mean those who didn't make it back were less loved by God.

Even a first place soccer, football, basketball or baseball team can lose a game. God doesn't choose sides or change sides.

October 20

With exultant and sincere hearts they took their meals in common. – Acts 2:46

In days long gone by I heard the promise of my church people that "the family that prays together, stays together." This did not happen for me, because we were not all on the same page at the same time.

Prayer is more than recitation of series of words. Saying something does not always make it so. Affirmations are positive statements we repeat to ourselves to change and encourage better actions.

According to my little Webster dictionary, with over 60,000 definitions, prayer can mean one or more of the following, 1. An expression of devout petition, addressed to God or a deity. 2. A formal set of words used in praying. 4. An earnest entreaty.

I contend that everyone has a deity – either the individual is his or her own highest power or it is something or someone else.

The passage above describes the living, active prayer of communicating with one another, sharing meals, simply being together in love and caring.

Why do we have to make life so complicated? Prayer is a word. Temple is a word. Church is a word.

October 21

Mary treasured all these things and reflected on them in her heart. – Luke 2:19

Luke must have been a close friend of the family to have the mother of Jesus share the circumstances surrounding the birth of her son. Imagine her surprise when a group of shepherds dropped in on the parents of a baby those angels had prompted them to search out.

The fact that the angels told the shepherds they would see the Messiah and Lord is obviously validating Mary's original story about her incarnation by the spirit of God.

This would be outrageous today, to hear about angels appearing to Mary, then Joseph, then Mary's Cousin Elizabeth, and then shepherds. Not priests or rulers, or people of influence who might convince the Hebrew people that prophesies had been fulfilled – but, to people of little influence – who accepted the message and took the journey to Bethlehem to see if it was true.

With the exception of Christmas, most Christians pay little attention or respect to Mary's part in bringing Jesus into the world. And, Joseph is cared about even less. Even though Joseph's heritage, from the house and family of David, was a huge issue in the fulfilment of prophesy, Mary's life and position within the Hebrew faith and tradition cannot be ignored.

October 22

If you go on biting and tearing one another to pieces, take care! You will end up in mutual destruction! – Galatians 5:15

The diversity in the early Christian churches kept Peter and Paul, and all the other original followers of Jesus on their toes to prevent discord and dissention. The common people were hungry for the messages that freed them from the fear and poverty of spirit they experienced under Roman rule, but the message about Jesus was all so new to them.

These early preachers went into faraway places where no one had heard about this Jesus person who these people claimed to be the Messiah – the one who was to come and free them from tyranny.

Communication networks did not exist outside the talk that people heard on the trails, in the streets and in the temples and meeting places. With our current 24/7, instant news being delivered electronically to our homes, cars, and smart phones, it is hard to imagine how the news of Jesus swept through country after country, hundreds and thousands of miles from Jerusalem and the Galilee.

You have to admire the courage and determination of people like Paul who carried the message the distance.

October 23

I am sending an angel before you, to guard you on the way. – Exodus 23:20

Where are the angels when I need them in my life? Are they really watching out for me, for my children and grandchildren, and my friends? I hope so.

When my father died I asked him to be my literary angel. Since I believe my father is still in existence, somewhere, I feel free to ask for his help.

When my youngest son went into the Navy and became a rescue swimmer, I asked my brother to watch over Paul. Since my brother drowned when he was just past eleven, and I was ten, I figured he would make a good angel for my son.

My mother is just my angel – for no other reason than I ask her to be. I know she will be there for me when I go into the next world, just as she brought me into this world. And, I will always be an angel in this world or in my next life for each of my children – except Carol, who has already gone before me, and is now an angel to me.

God promised Moses an angel to guide him on his journey. We know that angels exist because Moses tells us that God sent one for him. It sounds good to me.

October 24

Jude, a servant of Jesus Christ and brother of James, – Jude 1:1

I did not meet any other apostle except James,
the brother of the Lord. – Galatians 1:19

While thumbing through the New Testament one Sunday during Mass, I stumbled upon the epistle of Jude. The passage I read, which follows the part quoted, was a harsh condemnation of all forms of lust and "un-natural vice, and pollution of the flesh, and men consorting with men." He speaks of grumblers and whiners and those who use flattery to lead you off the path. Jude is filled with hell, fire, and damnation in one and a half pages preceding the Book of Revelation.

Who is this Jude fellow of whom I had not heard? The introduction to his brief letter referred me to the introduction to James, whose epistle rests between Paul's letter to the Romans and Peter's first short letter. There, in James' preface it is said James is designated by Paul, not as one of the Twelve, but as the brother of the Lord – as quoted above.

It appears that much of the traveling, preaching, writing of letters – and much later translations and inclusion of what we now know as the New Testament attempts to sort out everyone's relationship to Jesus – and to Jewish tradition. It is somewhat confusing for us.

October 25

Decide today whom you will serve. –Joshua 24:15

Choices! Life is about choices – where to go, what to do, who to talk with, what to say, what to buy, what to sell, how much to sell, how much to charge, whom to love, whom to marry, whom to leave, when to stay, how long to stay.

There are no easy answers to life's questions. So much trial and so much error. Are we always feeling as though we have to defend our choices, always questioning other's choices? It's a puzzlement! Must we always feel like Alice in Wonderland's white rabbit?

We prepare our children to make correct choices by encouraging them to make simple choices at first, and then more difficult decisions. I raised eight children and it was rather frightening at times – how to prepare them to make their own decisions.

When children were old enough to dress themselves, I would put out two sets of clothing on occasion, and they would choose. When it came to their choice of friends or mates, I was totally out of the picture. When they chose their spiritual path – I stood back and prayed.

October 26

See to it that no man falls away from the grace of God. – Hebrews 12:15

I learned to compliment others for the work they do, the care they give, the way they look – and just about that same time I learned how to accept and appreciate a kind word or compliment given to me.

I regret not giving out more words of encouragement and praise to the people in my life – especially my children. But, then, it is never too late to start again to give praise and thanksgiving to young and old, big and small – who thirst for a kind word, a loving gesture.

There is a beautiful song, I have heard played and sung at church – "They will know we are Christians by our love."

We do not have to be Christians to show love in action, we just need to be good people and care about others.

Those who hunger and thirst for a kind, loving word must learn to reach out and ask for love by giving away what they so longingly seek. Children do not know how to do that if they haven't felt it personally. Always give what love you can to the children. They need that nourishment to grow.

October 27

God is our refuge and our strength, an ever-present help in distress. – Psalms 46:2

Many years ago when we were traveling in Australia, we saw a movie about a man who went to court to sue God. Because his insurance company refused to pay for damages to his property they attributed to "an act of God" the man decided to file his law suit and claim against God. It was funny and enlightening.

We blame God, or Mother Nature, for "natural" disasters – a hurricane, a typhoon, and a tornado. I suppose people should know better than to build their houses in flood zones, or near the beaches of the oceans, or in the open fields of the Midwest they later found out, the hard way, were in "tornado alleys."

Since God hasn't issued a warning about a pending "natural" disaster then it seems odd we should blame him (God) or her (Mother Nature) for what happens to us.

We live and learn – and for the most part – ignore the warning signs that God or Mother Nature send us. So, some say, climate change is a force of nature and global warming is a hoax – so, there is nothing we can do.

October 28

He gives strength to the fainting; for the weak he makes vigor abound. – Isaiah 40:29

We gain strength by using the resources available to us, knowing some great power that rules the universe has placed us in our surroundings. We will never know or understand this power that we must, for now, call conscience, intelligence, and insight; sense of sight, sound, taste or touch.

Where is it written that we should receive a daily memo from "Him" to guide us on our path?

How fortunate we are to be alive at the particular time in history where we have a wealth of options available from which to choose. We read about solutions to problems we never knew we had before. Our electronic communications devices deliver messages constantly regarding "How to" have a better life.

I am totally responsible for making choices that make me stronger in mind, body and spirit. Healing is an option. Finding the right healer is an option. Making the right decisions, at the right time is an option for me.

I make the decisions about what food to buy, how prepare it, and how much to eat.

I make the decisions about how much exercise is good for me, and how much exposure to the sun is healthy.

Much as I would like to blame someone else for my extra pounds, and poor memory, and procrastination – I am stuck with me – the buck stops here. Damn!

October 29

Therefore, comfort and up build one another, as indeed you are doing. – 1 Thessalonians 5:11

I remember when "support groups" became fashionable and "How to" books filled the shelves of book stores. We were in a "new age" of discovery. We went to "assertiveness training" seminars, and "parent effectiveness training" and transcendental and enrichment classes of every kind. We started Yoga, drumming, sweat lodges, and all manner of evangelical and meditative practices.

And, then, what happened?

It is as if everything we did and learned during that age of enlightenment was put into a blender, turned to liquefy and poured out into communities all over the country and the world – and diluted.

Gone is the enthusiasm of the Sixties and Seventies when large groups of people were on the same page at the same time, and we were all hell bent to achieve a personal and lasting sense of brotherhood, fellowship and peace.

There was something "blowin' in the wind" that does not seem to be blowing anymore. That sense of working together, camaraderie and love power seems to have faded into "what's in it for me."

Cooperation, compromise, and caring about each other are always fashionable.

October 30

There is no greater love than this: to lay down one's life for one's friends. –John 15:13

To lay down one's life may not always mean dying, it may mean sharing all you are with another person; so that when you are sad they feel for you; when you are in pain they feel your pain; when your heart aches, words are useless because you know that they know what you know.

To me, a friend who has earned that designation knows me better than I can ever know myself. I see myself from the inside out – my friend sees me from the outside and into that place where I live every moment of every day – and all the frightening moments during the dark nights of my soul.

I have such friends – or I could not say what I have just said. God bless them for being in my life. I can only hope that I can be as good a friend to them as they are to me.

Friends encourage, uplift and listen to you. Friends look past our faults and help us correct course when we stray from our true path. Friends help us up when we fall from grace.

To have a friend, I must be a friend – a friend in time of need, a friend to share our laughter and our joy.

My friends know who they are, and they know how much they are loved.

October 31

Together with the Levite and aliens who live among you, shall make merry over all these good things. – Deuteronomy 26:11

Today is a day that once was called All Hallows Eve. It was a day of celebrating life and those who had lived life well.

Halloween has come to mean many things to many people. You can be someone else for a time. You can wear a mask to hide who you really are, or wear a costume to portray who you would like to be – who you can pretend to be – just for the fun of it.

We give treats or we play tricks. Harmless for the most part.

What is this dark side of us that wants to come out and play on Halloween? Why do we let it all hang out for just one day, just one night? We know we are in control and we can put the genie back in the bottle when we have scared enough people – all in fun of course.

One time I dressed up like a terrorist for a party, with a nylon stocking over my head and face. No one knew who I was. No one wanted to talk with me or sit by me. It turned out to be less fun than I imagined. I was grateful when the masquerade was over, and I could be the real me. I guess that's the lesson – down deep, I want to be real – be authentic.

November

November
Novem, Latin for 9.
Catholic countries
adopted the Gregorian calendar in 1582,
skipping 10 days that October,
correcting for too many leap years.

November 1

Blest too are the sorrowing; they shall be consoled. – Matthew 5:4

Day of the Dead. All Souls Day. All Hallows Day. The Day of Remembrance. The day of sadness and celebration.

Remembering the lives of those we love – those people who once breathed the same air and ate the same food, and laughed at the same jokes, and loved us, and sometimes hurt us – they all have earned the right to be remembered.

Of all the things we do in life, we wish we could handle death better –with less pain and sorrow. People don't want to think about their own death, and the death of a loved one tears us apart. Death comes to each of us – ready or not – it is inevitable.

I admire those who make peace with death.

We must learn to deal with death on death's terms, as we have learned to deal with life on life's terms. There are many things in life and in death over which we have no control. We can only live each day as if it were the last day we may spend on this planet. We never cease planning, however.

We are human, after all, and we need to thrive on hope for better things to come.

My life is perfectly wonderful at the moment I write these words, but hope springs eternal – and I believe I will be here as long as I can be here.

November 2

For the spirit of God has made me, the breath of the Almighty keeps me alive. –Job 33:4

In days gone by, I participated in a healing group. We met weekly at the church, and used therapeutic touch with the auras and energy fields that surrounded each of us. We were quiet, or we sang, or we played soft spiritual music. The healing came slowly, peacefully and spiritually.

One of the songs we used for background music was *I Release the Past and Let the Healing Power of Love into My Life.* I still, on occasion, when I am walking, play that in my head or whisper it to myself. Being clean spiritually certainly aids the very cells of the body to sing along.

One of the women in that group was experiencing a blood disorder related illness. She said she asked the physician to arrange for her to see her blood cells under a microscope, so she could identify and nourish her own cells spiritually. It struck me as totally realistic.

During that time I was seeing a cardiologist for the first signs of heartbeat arrhythmia. I had help from the healing group in getting over that episode. Periodically, the arrhythmia raised its ugly head, until I had a pacemaker implanted in 2009.

Now, I touch my little heart starter frequently and thank the God who made me and the spirit that energizes my little battery, and the scientific energy and ingenuity that brought it all together.

November 3

Whenever you pray, go to your room, close your door, and pray to your Father in private. – Matthew 6:6

Jesus, more than once, warns of hypocrisy. He has a problem with those who love to "stand and pray in synagogues or on street corners in order to be noticed."

This is what I learned as a child and still believe as an adult. I was taught to honor the spirit within and not be a show-off. I am shy by nature, and do not look for recognition. I do, however, look for recognition of my work, my writing.

My work is like my children, all dressed up and ready for company. I shy away from those who shout and preach, who make certain all sinners know who they are. Those who demand you come and bow down to them and accept Jesus Christ as Lord and Savior – scare the hell out of me.

I go into my quiet space, into my inner place, where I know God is always present, and I say "hello God, what shall we do now? What do you ask of me? How can I be a kinder, gentler, more loving and tender version of myself? How can I be more like you?"

November 4

A joyful heart is the health of the body, but a depressed spirit dries up the bones. – Proverbs 17:22

We live in a society consumed with altering its individual moods. We are racked with mental health issues and depression. There are very real medical, psychological and physical health problems. We, as a society, consume millions of dollars of pills, both prescribed and abused, to help get us into a better or different psychological and physical space – where there seems to be no room for joy.

We face post-traumatic stress from war, and from personal traumas resulting from violence and so called "natural" causes.

How, in God's good grace, can we be expected to have a "joyful heart?" Don't you know the holidays are coming, and we should get in the proper state of mind? If for no other reason, let us be joyful for the children.

Come on now, pull yourself together!

So you feel like your heart is breaking and you must mend it – get on with life. It is so easy, for someone else to tell us all that. So easy, it seems, to look in the mirror and tell the sad face staring back at us to "buck up" you know the world isn't coming to an end."

We know that depression, sadness, confusion, moodiness, irritability and discontent dry up our bones, our skin, and our brains. We really do seek joy. We keep hoping it will find us.

November 5

He shall defend the afflicted among the people, save the children of the poor, and crush the oppressor. – Psalms 72:4

Peoples of old put great faith in the mountains, or the spirit god who lives far up the mountain and into the clouds – closer to the sun – for peace.

During my more active days I did a lot of hiking on trails in the Columbia River Gorge, on either the Oregon or the Washington side. I climbed or hiked up many mountains, and felt invigorated by the height – and the peace in looking down on the world below. It is a holy, spiritual moment.

At the top of a mountain we find peace – within us. We discover that God is near and far – and in charge of keeping everything running on time – God's time.

The sun appears to come up and go down, depending on where we are standing at a particular time.

For a moment on the mountain top we sense that all is right with the world; there is some justice at work somewhere.

We look for God's help at the top of the mountain. All the time we are enjoying being in the presence of great power we are being empowered. God has called us up the mountain to be anointed, to take what wisdom we have received back down to our real world and "defend the afflicted, save the children of the poor and crush the oppressor" – in us.

November 6

I stay not with worthless men, nor do I consort with hypocrites. – Psalms 26:4

I woke early this morning with my inner voice telling me, "I have many projects to finish." At that point in time the message I gave myself was reflecting on this book, which is far more than a book; it is a living document – for me.

The day or morning that I put pen to page for these comments is actually March 19. So much for perfect order. When I began this project on the first of January, four years ago, I expected foolishly, that I would write one page each day, and be done with it in 366 days. Obviously, living life got in the way of writing about life.

This morning, I think I separated myself from the worthless one within me who procrastinates and makes excuses, and forgets and gets off the path – the hypocrite within.

So, sad to say, I am my own worst enemy when it comes to following a project through to the end – to feel the sense of completion and accomplishment.

Being a writer is a blessing and a curse. Like any talent, writing requires discipline. If I am serious about what I do – and I am – then I am responsible for self-discipline. So, I will shake off the wicked ones who say it cannot be done. I will trudge onward to happy destiny.

November 7

Cast all your cares on him because he cares for you. Stay sober and alert. – 1 Peter 5:7-8

For me, staying sober and alert means that I do not consume alcohol or other mind altering substances, neither legal nor illegal. As a result, I cast all my cares on the God of my understanding, and he/she takes care of all my needs. My faith in a higher power acts as a source of all my assistance. I am dependent on god-power.

I have experienced periods of anxiety, with panic attacks, where I have needed prescription medication and counseling. Whether from a health issue, psychological trauma or unknown causes, I have had to let go and let my God guide me, through the medical professionals.

Any time I cast my cares on him/her there is always a learning curve where I know what tasks I must perform. These tasks are not always to my liking, not something I would have chosen to do, left to my own devises.

He – God – is always there, omnipresent, omniscient and caring. What a good feeling that is for me.

A longtime friend, neighbor, mentor once wrote out the above passage for me when I went complaining and crying at her door. I used that piece of paper as a book mark for months. I finally got the message – God loves me.

November 8

They returned to Galilee and their own town of Nazareth. The child grew in size and strength, filled with wisdom. – Luke 2:39-40

One of the most mysterious and vague passages about the life of Jesus, the one quoted above, leaves us speculating about his true humanity. All Christians concede to the divinity of Jesus, but some of us respectfully question his true humanity – as portrayed in the New Testament.

The so called "hidden years" of Jesus' life lead us to ask about his human curiosity, sense of adventure, and sexuality. If he came from the Father in heaven to be a human among humans, then why are we left wondering about how he spent his formative years? Wouldn't he want us to know what happened during the years from twelve to thirty? That is a very long time to wonder about?

For those of us left wondering about those missing eighteen years, the churches tell us to accept everything on faith that he never left the area now described as the "Holy Land." According to Bible reports his parents fled into Egypt soon after his birth to escape Herod's wrath. If Egypt for a time, why not Alexandria, Athens, Rome, or the land of Buddha during those missing years? We know how travel enriches us; why not Jesus?

November 9

When you stand to pray, forgive anyone against whom you have a grievance so that your heavenly Father may in turn forgive you your faults. – Mark 11:25

Forgiving doesn't mean just excusing the harm or hurt I feel as the result of another person's words or actions. Forgiving is an active and preemptive word with a directive for a life style – a life style of giving everyone the benefit of my being open minded. If I approach every human and spiritual encounter with an open mind and an open heart, I am preempting good and being non-judgmental. I am expecting only good to come from every encounter.

If I am set in my way of thinking then my mind is not open to hear what you have to say – because I am focused on my argument – my truth. God only knows what has happened to civil public and private discourse. We may think we want to have a pleasant conversation, but it soon becomes a television commercial where each person is selling a point of view – a product.

I have spent more than half a century in the communications business – asking questions of people to find out what they are thinking – to hear their stories. When I get out of that role and start to communicate with my point of view alone – I am alone. I am out of character – for me.

November 10

For I was hungry and you gave me food, I was thirsty and you gave me drink. I was a stranger and you welcomed me, naked and you clothed me. I was ill and you comforted me, in prison and you came to visit me. – Matthew 25:35-36

Decades ago, I told a priest he would better serve his congregation if he would deliver his sermons without reading from his prepared script. He tried it one Sunday. His delivery was slower, more thoughtful and more meaningful. He used the above passage for that particular sermon. It became more meaningful for me as well. It was less rote, and I gained new insight.

It is not easy to live a life where you see Jesus in everyone you meet. We are not saints. We are not Mother Teresa. We are human beings with our own set of challenges and plans. We take time out for our daily routine to support our not-for-profit organizations in aiding the plight of the poor – the hungry, thirsty, naked or imprisoned. We seldom go into the trenches and become one with those we serve.

I belong to an organization that does all of the things descried in this passage – but there is a safe distance between me and those we help. I have served meals to the residents of the streets on Thanksgiving. I have taken recovery meetings to the women's jails, and I go through my closet periodically to give clothes and bedding to charities. I raise money for projects for the less fortunate. But, do I look into their eyes and see Jesus? I wonder.

November 11

As a mother comforts her child, so will I comfort you. – Isaiah 66:13

This is not my birthday date. It is really March 7, tomorrow, as I write this page late at night. This just happens to be the day I am commenting on this passage. Nothing in my life is accidental. This is the passage I am destined to write about on this day.

I am honoring my mother tonight. I am imagining how her labor probably started about this time of night, before midnight. I imagine her preparing the dresser drawer that was to be my bassinette. My brother was 13 months old, and he was in his crib.

My parents lived less than a mile from the hospital. There was a ward for four women in labor and after delivery. I was born about 10:00 am on March 7, 1933. I think it was a Wednesday. My parents probably waited as long as they could for my mother to come to the hospital, considering the cost, and waiting for my Aunt Anne or someone else to come and care for my brother.

There was a woman across from my mother in the ward. She named her daughter Marilyn. My mother thought that sounded pretty good. My mother's name was Mary; so Marilyn was a natural derivative.

Although I was an unexpected pregnancy, I know I was wanted and welcomed into a loving home. We endured the loss of my brother when he was just past 11. I guess the mothering part of me has been there a long time.

November 12

Do not judge and you will not be judged. – Luke 6:37

For the past 14 years we have spent our long winter season in Baja Norte, Mexico, along the east coast on the Sea of Cortez. We have many close friends and neighbors, who sometimes extend into the United States. Recently, one of our neighbors was killed in a car crash as his wife was driving him to the States for a hospital emergency. Bruised, injured and traumatized, his wife was jailed.

In Mexico, both drivers go to jail when there is a death, until the authorities can sort out the details. We, friends and neighbors, rallied with great speed and compassion. One couple drove to Mexicali two days in a row to bring food and water to the jail for our friend, because the jails do not take care of such basic needs. She sat up and slept in a chair because of the filthy condition of the cell. Not only had she seen her husband die before her very eyes, but she was alone and suffering that pain in a prison cell.

Fortunately, she was released after one night, with the help of friends making contacts and getting documents in place. There were no air bags in the older car, and her husband refused to wear a seat belt. Judge not. Do not second guess why life rides on such a sharp edge of death. For some situations there only remains the compassion of friends and neighbors who represent a compassionate God.

November 13

Fear not beloved, you are safe; take courage and be strong. – Daniel 10:19

When I was a senior in high school I was struggling with future choices regarding marriage or a life dedicated to God as a nun. I imagine that many young women in Catholic schools consider these options. Some girls profess their desire in grade school or junior high. They seemed to me to get preferential treatment from the nuns and priests. I never mentioned my struggles to anyone until after graduation.

I was in the senior play, and had to walk a mile-and-a-half four times on days we had play practice. I would cut through the church and stop at the altar of the Blessed Virgin Mary to ask for guidance. During the final performance of the play I made a decision to break up with a lovely young man who was a 23-year-old Lutheran. He and his mother came to that final performance and I said hello, with a goodbye in my voice – telling them I was going to the party after the play.

I found out later that he was planning to propose marriage. Instead, he returned to his previous love and I saw the engagement announcement in the paper.

That June, I fell in love with a former high school chum who was on leave from the Air Force. Once again, I knew he was going to propose. I went on a religious retreat. I talked to the priest. He talked me out of my religious vocation because this fine Catholic man was my destiny.

November 14

Your rebirth has come, not from a destructible but from an indestructible seed. – 1 Peter 1:23

I have heard for years about evangelical Christians praising God and being born again in Christ. It sounds so simple, and as I write it – perfectly sensible and normal. Yet it leaves me cold for some reason. Perhaps because every day I wake up, now past 80, I feel reborn in the Spirit. I take my life seriously and I know I live and breathe and will someday die by the grace of a loving and caring God.

Jesus is an historical manifestation of the God of my understanding. He came, by whatever means a loving God saw most fit for him to enter this world. He came to show us how to live with each other and how to relate to this loving God and Spirit of God that lives in each of us.

Not one of us has any more of a direct path to knowing and understanding God. We each search and struggle and experience the joy and sadness of searching – and sometimes experiencing the love of the Spirit of God within us.

I believe there is an indestructible seed planted in the soul of every living creature on this planet. In one way or another that seed will go through a growth and death cycle, and be reborn again in this life or in the next. Nothing that God created can be destroyed – only transformed.

November 15

"I am not worthy to have you under my roof. Just give me an order and my boy will get better." – Matthew 8:8

In Matthew's chapter Eight, he embarks on a series of miracle accounts; from the leper, and healing of Peter's mother-in-law, to the expulsion of demons from two possessed men. Through this series of cures, the disciple offers histories that prove that Jesus was, indeed, a very special man.

The above quote is spoken by a centurion in the Roman army. He has a servant boy at home in pain from a paralyzing illness. The Roman soldier comes to Jesus and asks for healing for the boy. The centurion's words are used frequently in religious services to demonstrate faith in the mysterious workings of God, through humans.

Most often, Catholics recite a version of this passage during the consecration of bread and wine at Mass. We state the fact expressed by the centurion that we are not worthy to receive Jesus/God into our lives and bodies.

The beauty of the centurion's story is that Jesus offers to come to his home to cure his servant, but the centurion declines his offer and tells Jesus to just say the word and it will be done. He tells Jesus that he is a man of authority, with troops – all he has to do is give an order – and it is done.

November 16

In giving alms you are not to let your left hand know what your right hand is doing. – Matthew 6:3

When I prepare my tax information for the CPA, I list all of our contributions in terms of dollars and in-kind donations. It seems so small, and seems to make no difference in lowering the tax. I wonder sometimes why I bother. My left hand certainly knows what my right hand is doing.

I hope my alms are more than the mere listing of donations. I hope my alms come in many forms through acts of love and kindness. I love the idea so prevalent today of "paying forward" acts of kindness. Sometimes those acts of kindness involve money to help some struggling soul survive. Most often these random actions of kindness go unnoticed. Sometimes these acts are so heroic they cannot go unnoticed.

We need to know the goodness that is happening every day, and in every way. We need to know these good people are doing good things every single day. The media, especially television, come under constant criticism, especially by politicians who don't agree with the coverage of their issues.

How else do we hear about a 10-year-old girl pulling her grandfather out of the lake when he has had a stroke, and dragging him three miles through the woods so her grandmother can call 9-1-1, and save his life? How else would we know about this heroic, loving, act of kindness? Alms, indeed!

November 17

Forgive us the wrong we have done as we forgive those who wrong us. – Matthew 6:12

I explained to a woman grieving the loss of her husband that I grieved the loss of my first husband through divorce. After 25 years of marriage and parenting eight children we found it necessary to part ways for the good of all concerned. Dreams of a lifetime together were shattered – and we were wounded deeply, but moved on.

Forgiveness does not come easily, but it must come. Forgiving me for what I did or did not do was hard, but absolutely necessary for me to live with myself. Forgetting is another matter, but there can't be true forgiveness without letting go of the haunting memories that eventually cease being spoken.

Forgiveness is the basis of all great religions.

A recent best-selling book about the death of Jesus left out one of the reportedly spoken last words of Jesus as he was dying on the cross. "Father, forgive them for they know not what they do," was left out because, the author said, it was not possible that anyone could have heard those words.

Whether or not those words were heard by human ears, the premise is imperative. We must forgive or we die a spiritual death – a death from which we may never recover.

November 18

There is hope for your future. – Jeremiah 31:17

God grant me the serenity so that the decisions I make come from a peaceful place, free of malice or ill intent. May I accept the things I have tried so hard to change, so often, it hurts. Give me courage that I cannot find within myself, to change what I must change to survive and live. And, God, in my constant state of confusion and doubt please help me to know the difference – and do the right thing.

After all is said and done; there is hope.

I was taught at one time that Judas hung himself from the tree on the hill after he gave Jesus up to those who would eventually put him on the cross to die. Judas lost all hope, according to what has been written. Since then I have also talked with priests about suicide – the last best hope of a desperate soul to leave this life. I am told and believe there is a reunion with God at the time of death and no one knows what transpires at that moment.

Whether we believe in a real, living, breathing god or not, most of us are willing to err on the side of believing there is such an entity, and we believe in mercy. St. Paul claims there is faith, hope and charity – charity being the most important.

Personally, I believe hope must lead us to our end – although, without love, there is no hope.

November 19

I give you thanks that I am fearfully, wonderfully made. – Psalms 139:14

At some point in my daily commentary on bible passages I knew I would have to address the burning issue of today regarding birth control and abortion. I'm not sure people understand when I say I am both "pro-life and pro-choice."

I believe women have allowed themselves to become slaves to their sexuality. We have been taught it is a sin to have desires and to seek satisfaction in sexual relationships. Yet, men seem to be given a free pass; it is expected that they will be forgiven for sewing their "wild oats," because their very nature demands sexual release.

Women who object to those advances are often suspect; it is said they really consented, but changed their minds after. If pregnant, women carry the guilt and the responsibility of carrying to term or terminating the pregnancy.

I have carried and delivered eight children. Eight pregnancies times nine months. I have carried and cared for all eight – and buried one – the most ungodly event in my life.

But, who am I to say any woman or girl must feel what I feel or do what I did. I had my reasons for doing what I did in my life. Would I do it again, knowing what I know now, probably not? Today, I have a different attitude about prevention, and responsibility.

November 20

Little do you realize how wretched you are, how pitiable and poor, how blind and naked! – Revelation 3:17

Some biblical passages seem to stand alone, not really needing my commentary; this passage is one of those.

Revelation – the last book of the New Testament is used to scare the hell out of Christians – and Jews, as well, should they care to read it. The authorship is uncertain, but the message is clear. There will be a day of judgment – whether that day comes for each of us as individuals when we die – or if it comes to the entire race of human beings in one fell swoop at the end of the world as we know it. It will come, somehow, sometime.

We live again in an age of worshiping at the altar of wealth. Entire civilizations have been destroyed and disappeared when they became greedy, arrogant and self-destructive. They had plenty of everything except concern for their fellow human beings. There was, and appears to be in the United States of America that same lack of moral authority, integrity, civility and deep spirituality.

Really! How could the Supreme Court grant human status to corporations?

November 21

Then you will know the truth, and the truth will set you free. –John 8:32

John devotes this entire chapter to the argument Jesus has with a crowd of Jews who disputed his expressed origin, as one sent by the Father. They pleaded their case as descendants of Abraham, and never having been "slaves to anyone." They claimed to already be free, and not needing the "truth" of which Jesus speaks.

We must all, at last, be true to who we believe we are. The Jews believed then as they do now that they already had or have the truth, and Jesus adds nothing they want or need to their set of beliefs. There were, however, many Jews who saw who their fellow Jew was, and believed in the truth of which he spoke. He touched them deeply, and they followed him.

The historical, living, breathing Jesus was clear that "as the Father has sent me he also sends you." Jesus tells us we are just like him. We have also been sent by the Father. We all are children of the same God. We must stand in our truth, and be free of fear and doubt, and move forward in a life of honor – a life of making our Father proud of us; and, our Divine mother as well. For, have we not been told God is all that is, male and female?

God chose to become man but he needed a woman to make that happen. So, is not that woman also the anointed one?

November 22

Wait here, my daughter, until you learn what happens. – Ruth 3:18

When I am quick to judgment I need to remind myself to wait until I see what happens next. Being a planner has its good and not so good side. I don't always have all the answers I need to make a decision. I don't want to pester people for their information unless they are ready.

Everyone has a schedule. Sometimes they don't want to think about what I want to think about. Sometimes I talk too much, ask too many questions, and give unwanted or unneeded advice or information. Sometimes I just need to be quiet, and write in my journal, and wait to see what happens next.

Ruth was a widow. Naomi was her mother-in-law. Naomi sent Ruth to work for Boaz. Boaz in turn acquired the land that belonged to Naomi's deceased husband, and with it acquired Ruth. No wonder Naomi told Ruth to wait to see what would happen next – a home for Ruth.

I wonder why this short biblical story is named for Ruth and not Naomi – for she seems most capable of running the show. Ruth primarily gets credit for having a son to continue the lineage to the House of David.

Things often work out when we let someone else run the show.

November 23

When he comes, however, being the Spirit of truth he will guide you to all truth. – John 16:13

John writes as one who knew Jesus well, and records his words for future generations. The one who is to come is called the Paraclete – the Spirit of Truth, the advocate, the intercessor.

Jesus makes it clear that he must leave the apostles so that the Paraclete may come to them. This is where we become introduced to the Trinity – the concept that our teachers told us to not even try to understand because our intellect can't handle it.

Civilization seems to be all about putting names on people, places and things. Most people take the church people at their word – that they have the knowledge and the Spirit of Truth, therefore, we must listen to the anointed ones because we are incapable of understanding these deep matters.

On the other hand, how do we know that we do or do not have the Spirit of Truth within us? If Jesus said "the Kingdom of God is within you" – does not that Kingdom include the Spirit of Truth?

Are we not really more enlightened than the leaders and teachers would have us believe? Do not always turn over your power just because someone says they know more than you do.

November 24

Trust in the LORD and do good, that you may dwell in the land and enjoy security. – Psalms 37:3

During the time the Psalms were written, or collected, or told and passed on from one generation to the next – the land referred to is Jerusalem or Palestine as it was then named and known.

Writers or authors of the Psalms could be Moses, Solomon, David, or some unknowns. These songs or verses were gathered together and put in categories – and they are beautiful thoughts that can be taken apart and thought about, and meditated upon. They are frequently sung at services, and in responses.

When Jesus came along, being familiar with the Psalms as part of his Jewish tradition, he included some of those thoughts in his teachings. He was called Master and Teacher by his followers. Some of the above thoughts appear in the Sermon on the Mount, spoken to the crowds by Jesus. He was huge on "trust in the Lord."

The land that Jesus talked about was the life hereafter, or herein. Old and new testaments, known as the Bible, both believe that the heart's request is to live forever in heaven with God.

November 25

I will prepare for them peaceful fields for planting. – Ezekiel 34:29

As we age we are concerned with preparation for peaceful places. Currently, my children are dealing with trying to find a realistic, affordable and comfortable assisted living or home care arrangement for their father. He suffered a disabling heart attack and stroke, and cannot stay permanently in his own home without assistance.

I stand back, away for the winter in Mexico, and read the emails and make a few phone calls. My job is to stay well, and not give my children any cause for concern about me or my comfort.

We all live a life of survival, meeting our basic daily needs and doing what we can to meet the needs of those close, or not so close, to us. Essentially, we are each concerned with what is closest to us. We concern ourselves for a time with the world's problems, its floods and famine, but on a daily basis it's all about us.

The pains in our own heads and in our own bodies that keep us awake at night and nag us during the day – that is what our landscape is made of. We want peaceful fields, and we want them now, every day. We do not suffer well. We long for our comforts of mind, body and spirit.

November 26

In him who is the source of my strength I have strength for everything. – Philippians 4:13

Sometimes I face a blank page and wonder what I am doing, why I am bothering about recording my various moods and thoughts. At times, I remember lines from a poem my father liked to recite about *I'm nobody, who are you, are you nobody, too?*

There are days and nights when I search for that inner strength – that strength that comes from my Source – my God – my inner Spirit. We can fool ourselves and fool others for just so long; until we finally admit that without God I am nothing – "I am nobody."

The first book I wrote was about me as a traumatized 10-year-old when my brother drowned. The book title, *Little Girl Lost: A True Story of Tragic Death* describes that sense of being "nobody." When people read the book they tell me they cried. I say, "I cried when I wrote it."

When I write about sometimes feeling like "nobody" I know that you who read these words will understand and identify. It's not a sad place; it is simply a place, a place to pause and reflect on why we feel like "nobody" sometimes, and why it is alright to feel that way.

We know the Spirit will fill us up – and we will be somebody, again, very soon.

November 27

Let him who has ears heed the Spirit's word to the churches! – Revelation 2:17

This sometimes quoted passage from the last book of the New Testament has words that some have tried to decipher. These chapters appear to be letters to the various churches headed by various disciples and apostles and followers of Jesus.

The "hidden manna" is said to be the "food of life" and the "white stone" is a symbol of victory and joy; and the "new name" is the rebirth in Christ. (p.303, New Testament, footnote 2, 17; The New American Bible. St. Joseph Edition 1970.)

These strange passages make me wonder if the people writing them are resorting to some kind of code to cover themselves from being arrested and punished. They obviously knew who they were writing to and what they were trying to convey. Were they afraid of being found and being put in jail or executed?

Fear is such a normal feeling. Sometimes we have to talk ourselves down from our fears, and we do it with words of encouragement, positive thoughts, and words of cheer. These were real people with the need to encourage each other. Perhaps many left the fold because of the fear they must have felt about losing their lives, their families, their fortune or their future.

Keeping the faith can be a challenge anytime, anywhere, which is why people need people to keep going all day every day.

November 28

I will give thanks to you, O LORD my God,
with all my heart. – Psalms 86:12

I looked for a passage that reflects Thanksgiving Day; beyond the turkey with all the trimmings and being with loved ones – although, all that goes with the holiday and it is important. I am grateful we are in Mexico, with the sun shining, and workers repairing the roof and ceiling from heavy rain damage.

Thanksgiving, the holiday, belongs to the United States of America, because of the long held tradition of coming together in peace and harmony among the first settlers with the indigenous people who called our "new land" their "homeland forever." It is a nice pause in our other tradition of taking on new territory and calling it our own.

The early settlers may have starved or frozen to death without the resourceful efforts of the natives. They were in a new land, with new crops, new weather and new terrain. These strange people in a strange land were Pilgrims. Now the people who have become estranged in their ancestral land *are* the Native Americans.

Thanksgiving is celebrated every year, often ignoring the very meaning of why we celebrate. It is more than the beginning of the biggest shopping season of the year, leading up to the biggest celebration of the year, "The Exchanging of Gifts Day."

November 29

I will give you treasures out of the darkness. – Isaiah 45:3

An inspirational thought is a treasure coming out of a dark place of searching for answers to life and living. Being grateful for these momentary treasures encourages more treasures. Finding a truth hidden among the questions and doubts that plague us – these are the treasures of which life is made.

A phone call from a friend, a note in the mail, a smile from a stranger, the joy of a child playing with a puppy; the little things that give us a moment of pleasure – these are the little treasures that move us through our days.

Holding our lover's hand walking on the beach, comforting a baby, tasting fresh baked bread with butter and jam – these are a few of my favorite things – as the song goes. Most treasures are not hidden from view by any force of nature or human effort – most treasures are in broad daylight, right in front of us all the time.

The month of November is generally gratitude month because of Thanksgiving, but we don't need to wait for November to discover the treasures in our lives – the people we love – the places we like to go – the feeling we like to feel – the sunrises – and the sunsets – the treasures of our awareness of love, of life and of living.

November 30

They will soar as with eagles' wings; they will run and not grow weary, walk and not grow faint. – Isaiah 40:31

I sometimes grow weary of me – the amount of time I spend maintaining my strength, health and ability. When I was working and when I was involved in raising my children, I didn't have time to think about me – I simply kept going because I could not afford to fall behind. I lived far more on trust and nervous energy.

I was never bored in those days, because I was always busy. Now, with this thing called retirement, I want to be busy again, so I don't have to dwell on how I am doing or what I am doing. I say I am never bored, but there must be some reason why I feel restless, irritable or discontented sometimes. Granted, it is mild, but it is there nonetheless.

I am renewed constantly in the Spirit. My pacemaker keeps my heart beating at the regulated rate, and I am grateful to be alive. Some days, that is enough. Other days, I write what seems to be inconsequential drivel like this, and call it work.

Not every word out of the mouth of man or woman can be a gem.

December

Decem
Latin for 10.
Now the last month of the year,
but once the tenth month in the
Julian (Roman) calendar,
when March was the first month.

December 1

I say that my plan shall stand, I accomplish my every purpose. – Isaiah 46:10

I believe that all religions and pre-historic, spiritual communities have their prophets and prophesy. We know primarily the words that have been written in the books of the Old Testament, or Hebrew Bible, the writings of the Greeks, the pharaohs, and the ancient wise ones of the Orient.

I assume all ancient and prehistoric religions and spiritual communities have their version of the beginning of the times in which they lived. If there are many versions of creation how can any of us know for certain which is the one and only, true story of creation?

Actually there are two versions of creation, one right after the other defining the creation of man, in the Hebrew Bible. And then, there are huge gaps in other stories in the Bible. Could these gaps be filled in by other peoples, other times, and other places?

The history of civilization in the world is always told from the point of view of their "known world," from the participants' and the survivors' point of view.

Is it wrong to assume that this "one true God" spoke to other classes of people in other parts of the world at the same time? If we believe that all human beings are children of the same God, then how can we possibly deny them access to that same God and the right to their words of and about their god.

God's plan stands but the purpose may or may not be clear to humans.

December 2

I will set my Dwelling among you, and will not disdain you. Ever present in your midst, I will be your God, and you will be my people. – Leviticus 26:11-12

Many years ago I studied a little book about the practice of the presence of God. It spoke volumes to me. My spiritual goal equates to the constant awareness that I am not alone on this sometimes cold and dark planet.

As a child I was taught that God is everywhere, and that means wherever I am, God is. We are one in the Spirit.

The words quoted above were spoken to the leader of the people coming out of Egypt – and slavery. Are not these words spoken in the hearts of all men and women escaping the bondage of self, and seeking the guiding presence of a power greater than themselves?

People who live with mental depression deny themselves the freedom to escape, because the future is dark, cold, frightening, and uncertain. The way out seems to appear after the escape, when the realization of how bad it really was becomes incredibly clear. While in the midst of a crisis the mind is unclear and the answers do not come fast enough.

No one knows what we are going through – mostly because we isolate and try to avoid talking about what really bothers us. There is a breakthrough that we seek – however, we are not sure we will recognize our saving grace when it appears. The amazing insight after the escape from the dark side is that there is a presence, named or unnamed, that was there all the time. That presence, I prefer to call God.

December 3

He awoke and rebuked the wind and said to the sea, "Quiet! Be still!" – Mark 4:39

In a large motorized boat on the Sea of Galilee in Israel, the operators cut the sound of the motors and the quiet was deafening. Jesus seemed so present, calming the storms that rage inside of us – inside of me at times.

During that silence on the sea, our group of pilgrims began to sing. When we paused, pilgrims in another boat at a distance began to sing in response. We were listening to the calming voices. There was no storm.

I need only think of that precious moment in time, and a beautiful calm sets in. If I could, I would give that precious moment to those in need of calming their stormy waters within. If I can, I will give it to you, now – because, I believe in the power of words to transmit calming and healing energy. It may be called prayer.

Often, people asking for prayers for themselves or others ask for positive thoughts or positive energy to help resolve the issue or heal the pain and suffering. A prayer by any other name is still a prayer – and, always welcomed.

So, from me to you, just open your heart and your mind to God's love, and the Spirit who calms all fear and doubt, and heals all ills.

December 4

In your mercy you led the people you redeemed. – Exodus 15:13

We bought or sold a dwelling each year, for three years in a row. It is exhausting moving once, but three times is even more grueling, even though one of the places was our winter home in Mexico. There, we left it fully furnished, but still had a "few" things to make room for in our car on the way to our permanent residence in Oregon.

I believe our homes are our places of holy dwelling. We put so much of ourselves into our holy dwelling places that the most difficult decisions are about what to leave, what to take, what to give away, and what to throw away.

We accumulate many "things" in our many lifetimes of moving from place to place.

Life was so simple for the Israelites – leaving Egypt with a few belongings.

Times have changed. As long as individuals and corporations continue to produce lovely, serviceable, useful "things" we will continue to buy them, display them, store them, pass them on to our children, donate them to Goodwill or St. Vincent de Paul, carry them out in the trash, and appreciate the opportunity to accumulate more things to which we give some degree of meaning and memory.

It would have been impossible for the Israelites to carry our loads on their desert journey. It is difficult as well for us to give up our many things.

December 5

Love is patient; love is kind. Love is not jealous, it does not put on airs, and it is not snobbish. Love is never rude, it is not self-seeking, it is not prone to anger; neither does it brood over injuries. – 1 Corinthians 13:4-5

It is difficult trying to add or enhance Paul's description of love. These few attributes describe near perfection.

I could take just one – love is kind – to commit myself to learning a more perfect way of living.

I have a perfect example before me, every day, my husband Harry. He is the kindest person it has ever been my pleasure to know. Every day, his example lights my path to being a more loving and caring person. He would, and will, blush, and deny that he is what I say about him. But that does not change the fact and the truth of what I say – he is the kindest person I know. I thank God for putting him in my life.

Acknowledging the kindness of others is in itself an act of kindness. There is no competition. It is not a team sport. It just is what it is. There is a quiet movement in the country regarding random acts of kindness – doing something for someone without being noticed. If I have been the recipient of someone's random act of kindness toward me, then I say thank you. I don't know who you are or what you did, but I thank you for doing it.

I think that if we concentrate on the kindness aspect of love then we will not be jealous, put on airs or be snobbish. Kindness will block anger and brooding. We will be all the better for being kind.

December 6

Love does not rejoice in what is wrong but rejoices with the truth. There is no limit to love's forbearance, to its trust, its hope, its power to endure. – 1 Corinthians 13:6-7

Continuing to follow Paul's description of love, we aim for higher states of consciousness.

Turning on the news gives us immediate cause to be critical of people and circumstances. Most of what we see or hear is political – drawing our attention to whom and what deserve our attention and our criticism.

I constantly try to balance my need to know what is happening with how to maintain my sanity and have positive thoughts about the future of civilization.

"There is no limit to loves forbearance, to its trust, its hope, and its power to endure." I cannot find a better way to express love, except to say to St. Paul: "Thank you for giving us pause to reflect on the simple things in life that give us so much pleasure.

Paul was speaking to members of the spiritual community that began after Jesus finished walking on this earth. They were people getting first or second hand information about the Christ and what kind of a life he lived, and what kind of a life they were expected to live as his followers. They were closer to the source than we can ever be. He was one of them.

December 7

When I was a child I used to talk like a child, think like a child, reason like a child. When I became a man I put childish ways aside. – 1 Corinthians 13:11

As a child, with my parents and brother by the radio on the morning of December 7, 1941, we heard the words of President Roosevelt telling us this was a "day of infamy." The Japanese attack on the United States Navy fleet of ships in Pearl Harbor introduced me to the concept and violence of war. When we went to the double feature movies on Saturday, we saw the news reels about the war in Europe, the Pacific Islands and Japan.

My child's eyes saw the headlines in the newspapers and my child's ears heard the news reports on the radio as my mother listened for information about her brother's troop activities.

But it was a few short years later that my world really shattered – when my brother drowned. My child-self withdrew from the evil around me, and also withdrew from some of the good. The love of God was hidden from me, and I hid from the love of God. How could this God be so cruel – taking my brother because he was so good? I was left behind because I was not good enough. That was the day I became less a child and started putting my childish ways aside.

Years, decades later, I became friends once again with the God of my understanding. My mother/father God had not deserted me as I suspected – but carried me through all of life's traumas.

December 8

The Holy Spirit will come upon you and the power of the Most High will overshadow you; hence the holy offspring to be born will be called Son of God. – Luke 1-35

If we believe this passage it heralds the most important event known to mankind. The angel tells Mary what is about to happen in and through her. Once Mary gave her consent "the word of God became flesh." God entered the heart, soul, mind, body and womb of a woman. She became divine – the divine mother through whom God became human form.

If we believe that God created the entire world as we know it, and God created man and woman, then why not believe that God entered the womb of a woman. If God is all powerful and all-knowing and ever present – if God is God then God can do whatever God wants to do. However, since God gave humans free will, God sought the permission of the woman.

This may be difficult for some to believe, but believe we must if we want to call ourselves Christians – followers of this woman's son – the Son of God. It is no wonder some of the Jews of his time rejected Jesus as the fulfillment of their own prophesies that he was the one promised by the God of Moses and Abraham to restore them in the love of God.

This incredible story, this unlikely event, is what we cling to – God became man and walked the earth. Being God, he could have come into the world in a variety of ways, but, so the story goes – and so I believe – God came into our world through a woman.

December 9

We know that God makes all things work together for the good of those who have been called according to his decree. – Romans 8:28

The teachers tried to tell us that we had responsibility for making our own choices, and that only God knows the outcome. It always comes out the way God knew it would, because God knows everything. We are almost totally in the dark.

When an event happens, over which we have no control, we say "It must be God's will" or "It happened like it was supposed to happen."

In either case we eventually have to let go of our part in the event. We accept whatever happens as part of the divine plan for us, or for the other people in our life. Sometimes we are simply innocent bystanders. It is not always all about me.

What a mystery. What may seem like the wrong outcome for me may be a better outcome for someone else. Life works well for us sometimes and not so well other times – according to our plan. But then, we are not totally privy to God's plan. Hard as we try we cannot get into the mind of God.

Predestination is real for God, but we are not supposed to believe in predestination because we have a free will and make our own choices. Go figure, sometimes it feels like a pinball machine.

December 10

"And know that I am with you always, until the end of the world!" – Matthew 28:20

These are Matthew's final words attributed to Jesus after the resurrection from three days in the tomb; after 40 days of walking and talking with the remaining 11 apostles and other disciples; and prior to his ascending upward into the clouds and into the heavens to be reunited with God the Father.

The chief priests, after consulting with the elders, worked out a plan explaining the disappearance of the body of Jesus from the guarded tomb. According to Matthew, the chief priests gave the guards money to repeat the story that the apostles stole the body while the guards slept.

One evening at a street fair in Palm Springs, California, we passed a booth with the banner "Ask a Rabbi." I asked the Rabbi about Jesus, and the Rabbi said "if there was even a person who existed."

I couldn't have a discussion or argue with a Rabbi who rejected even the premise that there was a real person named Jesus. Nor, can I argue with an atheist who says there is no God – that is their final word on that matter.

If Jesus did not even exist, then millions of people are willing to risk having the greatest and most beneficial hoax ever known to man played out in their lives.

I choose the real Jesus as my teammate, and my team leader.

December 11

You may not demand interest from your countrymen. – Deuteronomy 23:20

As I recall, *The Merchant of Venice* play by William Shakespeare had something to do with the demanding of payment of a loan with a pound of flesh. The judge said Shylock could take a pound of flesh, but not a drop of blood. This story is similar to the account of cutting a baby in half to settle an argument between two women claiming the child as their own.

We may have come a long way with how we settle matters of dispute in the courts, but maybe not. Justice may be blind, but human beings who run the court system are not necessarily so.

How do we explain the overwhelming number of inmates who are people of color – and people of wealth seldom do time. Perhaps people of wealth and substance can afford a better defense than a court appointed attorney.

If you cannot demand interest on your loan to a countryman then how can you possibly make a living running a bank?

This verse came from the law given to Moses. It began to be enforced when the wanderers reached the Promised

Land that was previously occupied by other countrymen. The wanderers were now the countrymen.

But then, I could have it all wrong as this passage leaves itself open to misinterpretation, and, I cannot claim that God has spoken directly to me.

December 12

Enter his gates with thanksgiving, his courts with praise. – Psalms 100:4

I know that life works better for me when I dwell on the good that happens in my life. When I am grateful, more good comes my way. When I stop analyzing my own problems and the problems of my family and my friends I feel better. I turn my concerns over to God and say thank you for the opportunity to be of service. By expressing my gratitude I accept the good that God provides.

I once knew a man who sang a little ditty to the tune of "Oh, Christmas Tree." However, the words he constantly repeated were "Oh, thank you God." On occasion, when I'm walking, I think of that tune with its repetition of "Oh, thank you God."

The Psalm above is like so many other Psalms of thanksgiving that call us to prayer of acceptance for the blessings in our lives. Why doesn't this feeling of contentment with how life is going come more easily, more frequently?

I have lived long and lived well, so much better than so many. And, for now, I can still think thoughts and write words, and speak to my friends and loved ones. The obvious blessings are the ones we take for granted – our human faculties, our total humanness.

December 13

Woe to the shepherds who mislead and scatter the flock of my pasture. – Jeremiah 23:1

Jesus often refers to the sheep and the shepherd, and he is also referred to as the Good Shepherd – and we are his sheep.

Although the passage above was attributed to a prophet who lived 600 years before Jesus, they spoke the same language about the sheep and the shepherd. Why would anyone want to lead the sheep away from their caretaker, and scatter them into the cold? Sheep huddle together on cold nights to keep each other warm, and the shepherd is kept warm among them.

We guess that Jerimiah, and Jesus as well, is telling us to be careful of those wolves in sheep's clothing who tell us, or preach to us, and misdirect us to go this way or that way – and, although it doesn't feel right we do it anyway.

Most false leaders or shepherds are exposed for their poor advice and wrongful leadership. We want to follow the true shepherd of our flock. We can only remember what Jesus told us, that he knows his sheep and his sheep know him.

Our spiritual lives are lived at such a deep level that no one can separate us from the love of our God and the care of God's son, and our true friend, the Good Shepherd.

December 14

The LORD let his face shine upon you, and be gracious to you! – Numbers 6:25

This passage reminds me of the "Irish Blessing." Perhaps that blessing was inspired by readings such as these.

Humans speak words of peace but perform acts of violence, acts of war. Everyone is always concerned about self-protection – protection of their families, their property and their goods. So many are willing to go to battle, to kill, to be free and to protect what they have.

Everyone knows war is senseless. But we do it anyway because not enough people in enough countries have figured out how to design weapons for peace, for profit.

We like to blame God for acts of nature and ask God to hold back the floods and hurricanes. Maybe God is asking something of us, humanity, and we have turned a deaf ear to the pleading for peace; just as a mother pleads with her children to "stop your fighting."

Sometimes we listen to the voice of the God of wrath and punishment in the Old Testament, and then we listen to the voice of God speaking words of love and peace – such as the above passage.

If we ask God, "What do you ask of me?" Are we willing to listen? What if God said "Put down your guns?" Would you listen?

When St. Frances of Assisi asked Jesus what he was to do, Jesus asked Frances to be an instrument of God's peace. So!

December 15

Why do the wicked survive, grow old, become mighty in power? – Job 21:7

Throughout the Book of Job, he laments and cries out to God "Why me?"

Are we so different from Job – the man I have long called my friend – and sometimes mentor? There is a Job in each of us, we can't deny that. We try so hard to do the right thing, to say the right word, to be good. We don't understand all the craziness in the world. We don't understand why bad things happen to good people, or why the "wicked survive, grow old, become mighty in power."

This is where re-incarnation makes sense. The thinking that we might have to come back to this earth in another body, with a different lifestyle – one we look down on in our current life – that's a sobering thought.

If a man in this life may come back as a woman, and vice versa. If a person is a perpetrator of a crime in this life, then he/she may be a victim in the next. If we knew we had to change roles in another life, would that give us pause to think about the poor beggar on the street?

Maybe those who grow old in one life died early in another life. We can live our life "as if" we may have to do a repeat performance in a totally opposite life style. We may have to walk in someone else's shoes, sandals, boots, moccasins, or have no shoes at all.

December 16

Some friends bring ruin on us, but a true friend is more loyal than a brother. – Proverbs 18:24

Loyalty means many different things, and friends come in many forms, at many levels.

My mother must have read Proverbs and Psalms a lot, because, I hear her voice in so many of these Biblical wisdom discoveries. She said I should consider myself fortunate to have one really good friend in a lifetime. I am indeed blest with wonderful friends.

Since I lost my best friend, my brother, when I was only 10, I nurtured friendships with neighbor girls, school chums, and women in the neighborhood when I had young children. I have one girlfriend from second grade. We live states apart, but try to see each other when passing through. We care, but we are not in a position to help each other out when we might like. Fortunately, we each have daughters who come to our aid in time of need.

I observe how my adult daughters have become friends, and offer their experience, strength and hope to each other on many occasions.

A true friend doesn't need to hear all the background and detail when a situation comes up. That friend is a short cut to getting to our issue. What a blessing are true friends, and family members who are there for us as well.

December 17

He will rejoice over you with gladness, and renew you in his love. – Zephaniah 3:17

Zephaniah was one of the original "Dooms Day" prophets, lamenting the day the Lord "will completely sweep away all things from the earth," in this second to the last book in the Hebrew Bible.

Renewal, revival, recovery – three of the "Rs" for re-educating ourselves at every crossroad we encounter. If we love ourselves enough we will acknowledge our own self-worth, and we will take the time and care to keep moving forward.

Our bodies have a way of reminding us that we need to attend to some ache, pain or discomfort. We ignore these warnings at our own peril. We may not always recognize a "soul" ache, or a rupture of the spirit. We tend to concentrate on our moods and our feelings – and we may neglect the root cause. Our soul is missing something.

If you listen to "soul" music you know how deep the hurt as well as the joy can be buried inside. The soulful sounds come from deep inside and find expression in sounds, like music.

I love the Gospel music, with its soulful sounds. The whole body gets into the soulful music of the old time "negro spirituals." Sometimes music can lift us up when no other word of encouragement and enlightenment can do so. God is in our midst, and He loves soul music.

December 18

When you seek me with all your heart, you will find me with you. – Jeremiah 29:13-14

When I was looking for love in all the wrong places, I knew there was a better way, a better place to look – but, it took time. I made plenty of detours on the way to finding the love of God – the love that was always there – waiting for me. There were plenty of clues, plenty of time, plenty of opportunity.

St Augustine said, "The soul is restless until it rests in Thee Oh Lord." God does not move closer or farther away from me. God is always right where I started from and right where I finish my search.

I didn't even know what I was looking for. So, how would I know when I found it – love? We search for God like a child looking for the Christmas presents' hiding places. What pleasure we experience finding something that was hidden, something wonderful that had been lost.

We are told to seek God with all our heart. If we are meant to love the Lord our God with our whole soul – and love our neighbor as our self – we have a lot of work to do.

Because God is everywhere, we seek the love of life.

December 19

Wisdom from above, by contrast, is first of all innocent. –James 3:17

Innocent = free from wrong
Peaceable = not quarrelsome
Lenient = mild
Docile = easily taught
Impartial = without prejudice
Sincere = honest
Sympathy = shared feeling

Wisdom is next to godliness. It is often referred to as "she." Some call Wisdom the female side of God – the mother of all good. Each of the attributes of God named by James creates a building block of spiritual power. Perfection is less than possible. When we refer to ourselves or others as perfectionists we know we are referring to an effort to achieve the impossible. We can only achieve the perfection as defined by human standards.

Achieving perfection is impossible in this life, by the standards set by God. We still work toward that worthy goal, knowing we will only know perfection in the next life.

We pray for wisdom to know the difference between what is possible and what is impossible for us to achieve. We do the best we possibly can do, and leave the rest to God to do the impossible.

December 20

Who will separate us from the love of Christ? Trial, or distress, or persecution, or hunger, or nakedness, or danger, or the sword? – Romans 8:35

We are promised that nothing will separate us from the love of God. No matter what things or events trouble us, or how dismal life may seem, our faith tells us that God's love is everlasting and all present and all powerful. We cling to that promise, even though we are hanging on by a thread of hope. Words are easy, reality is hard – but what seems real to us may be an illusion.

I never know when I have exhausted my belief in the promise of God's love. I never know when I have lost all hope. My mind holds on for dear life – no matter what.

My mother would say, "Where there is life, there is hope." I have to believe that is true, because my mother said it, and I trust her.

Paul speaks of the love of Christ, and Jesus taught that He and the Father are one. We are told to ask the Father anything, in the name of Jesus, and it will be given to us.

Is God a genie? Make three wishes and we are done? We do not count our prayers of request, and fortunately, my God isn't calculating my requests either.

But, on the other hand, the song goes "I count my blessings instead of sheep." So, I need to remember that blessings make a much more comfortable pillow for my head at night – rather than the lumpy, bumpy pile of requests.

December 21

Given my preference, I should like you to be as I am. Still, each one has his own gift from God, one this and another that. – 1 Corinthians 7:7

When I was a child in about the fourth grade, I began to compare myself to others. My best girlfriend was artistic, and her drawings were always posted above the blackboard. Her grades were always straight "A" I couldn't draw horses' hoofs or human feet. I knew I wasn't an artist. I couldn't imagine anyone wanting to be like me. It seemed to me I was always somewhere in the middle – average.

One place I excelled later in life, was my fertility – that which the Bible and the Church praised.

After our first child was born we had a priest friend over to our house for dinner. He asked when we would have our next child. We were certainly trying. The doctors told me I wasn't ovulating, and chances were slim that I would get pregnant. Well, to the surprise of many, I went on to carry and deliver another seven babies. I excelled to the satisfaction of my church.

I do have other gifts. I have built a career as a writer. Probably average. When people ask about my career, I say I am a writer. They say they wish they could write. I say, everyone can. But, do I want everyone to do what I do? God, no! There are plenty of exceptional writers already appearing on the television talk shows with their new books, and my Kindle is crowded.

My success is average, my gifts average – the average in me speaks to the average in you, and says "Thank you, God for my averageness."

December 22

I will entrust to you the keys of the kingdom of heaven. – Matthew 16:19

Many battles have been fought over this passage – giving Peter authority over the community of Christ's early followers. Those who broke away from the Roman Catholic Church headed by the Pope, successor of Peter, believe themselves to be every bit the true followers of Jesus.

So much of formalized religion is based on a previous passage, when Jesus asks his followers, "Who do you say I am?"

Peter, after being given the keys to the Kingdom of Heaven denied even knowing Jesus when asked by curious people witnessing the punishment being brought upon the innocent man about to be crucified.

Those who have followed Jesus down other spiritual paths than that of the Pope in Rome believe themselves to be true followers of the Christ sent to live among humans by an all-powerful God. It is a truth that lives in the hearts of all good people answering the question, "Who do you say I am?"

My mother was brought up in the Orthodox tradition (the one that geographically and formally split from the church based in Rome), my father was Roman Catholic.

When East met West my parents fell in love and married. I honor both spiritual heritages.

When asked, "Who do you say I am?" I say I follow the Christ – the one who lived before ecclesiastical power structures were built.

December 23

I command you to open your hand to your poor and needy kinsman in your country. – Deuteronomy 15:11

In this chapter, Moses reiterates the rule as to how God's people are to treat their own kinsmen. There is a "relaxation of debts at the end of every seven-year period." They may press a foreigner on debt payment, but must relax the claim on friend or neighbor.

Out of this rule comes the part about "there should be no one in need." The people are told not to harden their hearts when one of their own is in need.

Jesus, who was a Jew and knew scripture to the extent he was called master and teacher, preached inclusivity, not exclusivity. Jesus did not say we shall only help our relatives, friends, and neighbors, but that we are all one family. He said, "Whatever you do to the least of these you do unto me." And he told the story of the Good Samaritan to make the point.

When I was growing up I heard "charity begins at home." I understood that to mean, take care of your own first. That is where charity, love, care for others begins – however, according to Jesus, it does not stop there. We are meant to reach out to those I need by enlisting the help of our friends and family.

The fact that there are so many faith-based charitable organizations gives proof that we are meant to include all needy – to each according to his need – in our circle of caring.

December 24

I will turn darkness into light before them, and make crooked ways straight. – Isaiah 42:16

Isaiah prophesied the coming of one who would reunite mankind with God. He foretold of one who would "turn darkness into light." Jesus called himself the light of the world.

When I was a child, our family tradition was to celebrate the Birth of Jesus on Christmas Eve. We decorated the tree together on my brother's birthday, the week before. We turned on the lights to symbolize the coming of Jesus into the world. I remember the peaceful feeling with only the tree lights on in the darkened living room.

Some Christians believe all the decorative lights represent the light of the world – Jesus – lighting up the darkness.

Children are still taught about being good little girls and boys if they want Santa to come and bring their heart's desire. The expectation and the joy take over the atmosphere of the day, of the season, of the giving and the receiving. It's the Christmas Spirit that people talk about as either having it or not having it. Does it come in the egg nog, in the gifts under the tree, in buying and wrapping gifts for those we love?

Sometimes that Spirit of Christmas just comes because we want it to come; we want to feel good about being alive, and having a day set aside to just feel good about the gift of life.

December 25

Many have undertaken to compile a narrative of the events which have been fulfilled in our midst, precisely as those events were transmitted to us by the original eyewitnesses and ministers of the word. – Luke 1:1-2

The "word" refers to Jesus' entrance and presence in the world. And who were the "eye witnesses" referred to by Luke? Mary, the mother of Jesus was the primary witness to the birth of her son.

Luke is sometimes referred to as a physician of his day. Some of us believe he was a confident of Mary, mother of Jesus, by the way he tells her story of receiving the announcement from the angel that she was to be the mother of the Christ child. He relays Mary's words, and Mary's memories surrounding the visit to her cousin Elizabeth, and the birth of Jesus. She no doubt told him about visits by the shepherds, the angels, the three kings from the Orient, and about the flight into Egypt. Only Mary could give the details necessary to write what Luke has written.

Luke says of Mary that she "treasured all these things and reflected on them in her heart." (2:19) He tells of how he "carefully traced the whole sequence of events from the beginning." (1:3) He was a careful journalist, interviewing the only living human being who could possibly give him the true story about Jesus, the woman who carried, birthed, and ultimately buried her first born son.

Some will argue that Mary was the mother of other children – perhaps – perhaps not. We do know, that above all humans she is the spiritual Mother of us all. We can't get much closer than Mary to show us how to talk to her son – for she knew him best of all others.

December 26

Many are the plans in a man's heart. – Proverbs 19:21

How do we judge our own success?

We set goals, and we reach beyond our known ability to achieve those goals – and we, rightfully, feel good about our success.

Sometimes we may be recognized for our successes with certificates, pay raises, and acknowledgements by both peers and superiors. But the sweetest reward is the sense of accomplishment in achieving what we were never quite sure we could.

Life is a journey, not a destination. Maybe someone else said that, but I have said it many times over the years. Heaven may be a destination, or it may be part of the journey. Why wait? We certainly experience episodes of hell on earth – why not experience episodes of heaven as well? Jesus said that "the kingdom of Heaven is within" us. God is everywhere.

I have always had many goals, many projects, and I will accomplish whatever I have the time left to accomplish. I know no limits with my planning. I will move forward, because I cannot go backward. If God wants me to accomplish all that I plan then I will have as much time as I need to get done what I am meant to do. It's all on God's time anyway.

December 27

Work at your tasks in due season. – Sirach 51:30

This advice is as current as any advice about getting the job done. Patience is a virtue, along with persistence. When we know in our heart of hearts that something needs to be done, we believe it can be done. No one knows this any better than an artist, a writer, an engineer, or any other person with an idea searching for a way out.

Creativity has traditionally been referred to as an attribute for the arts and artists. However, creativity is an attribute of great importance to every human being. Everyone wants and needs that sense of accomplishment that comes from making something happen – where you know it happened in a unique way because it was your idea and your effort that made it happen.

We call birth a co-creation because we know we are not totally in charge of making human life happen. God creates; humans co-create, when we speak of reproducing other humans. I believe that if that creative process is interrupted then God still has the power to bring that soul into the world. I have no proof, only the thought that with God all things are possible.

When I looked at the passage above I had a thought or two about what it meant to me. When I started writing, I had no idea where I was going with this commentary. There is tremendous trust involved in the development – or creation of an idea. It is a thought process available to every human being.

December 28

He rested from all the work he had done. – Genesis 2:3

What a strange concept – that creation was work for God, from which he needed to rest. And, why did creation take place in six days? Only man, in his infinite state of ignorance could assign human time references to an almighty and all powerful entity. This God of whom we speak could have created the entire universe in an instant – or over an evolutionary period of decades, or centuries, or millenniums.

Why is man so eager to put God in a box? Every day can be a day of rest, renewal, regeneration and reward. Every day is a profound gift of living and breathing. The people who abide by the creation story in the Old Testament believe Saturday is the seventh day of the week, and begin their observance at sundown the previous day.

People of the New Testament brought about by the life, death and resurrection of Jesus honor Sunday, the first day of the week, as their day of worship. It is said, and written, that Jesus rose from the dead on the first day – thus, that is the day his followers have chosen to rest, worship and renew.

Does it really matter to the Christian God, or to the Hebrew God, or the Muslim God, or the Hindu or Buddhist

God – which day we hold as holy? What probably matters most to the God of all religions or non-religions is how we treat each other; how we get along and love and respect each other and the creation we all share.

December 29

The LORD said to Eliphaz the Temanite, "I am angry with you and with your two friends; for you have not spoken rightly concerning me, as has my servant Job." – Job 42:7

It's not fair! Friends try to intervene and they are rebuked, not only by Job, but also by the God who has allowed the devil to torment their friend Job. Let this be a lesson to us all that there are times when our most well-intentioned thoughts, words and actions are unwelcomed. We learn so late in life that our advice and our opinions, or perception of the other person's problem and our proposed solution is none of our business.

Job's three friends tried – each on several occasions – to bring Job out of his misery. They were doing the best they knew how – but they didn't have all the facts. They didn't know about God's involvement, until God rebuked them for misjudging their friend.

We have to remember that the story of Job is written by the man who is named Job. No one else could have all that insight. Everyone involved in the story is misunderstood by the others. It was a total breakdown in communication. There were so many words spoken – so little light shed on the problem at hand for Job; until he finally figured it out for himself.

There is no explaining why bad things happen to good people, or why good people become bad people and do bad things. No matter how hard we try, we will sometimes fail to say the right thing at the right time. We can only try to do the best we can to help others work through their problems, their suffering and their pain.

December 30

Do not return evil for evil or insult for insult. – 1 Peter 3:9

The early Christians had several churches, depending on where each of the Apostles and Paul, the late-comer, were located. Peter was considered to be the elder of all the various churches, and James was also considered to be a heavy hitter.

Much of the time, Peter was trying to keep peace in the family of churches and among their leaders. There were Jews who followed Jesus, and non-Jews – or Gentiles. Sometimes they complemented each other and then again they might disagree regarding traditional practices and the new ways of working together.

Peter asks for simple courtesy and civility among the followers. He addresses their common purpose – to keep the Christ teachings intact. He implores the people to be loving, friendly and teachable.

Most of the requests or lessons were no doubt delivered in person on many different occasions. It may have been a letter delivered by someone else – but the message was one that Peter delivered and meant for all to hear or read.

We don't know if Peter's wife or family accompanied him on his journeys as far as Rome. We do know, or so we have been told, that he died in Rome, spreading the good news that Jesus was the savior promised by God and the prophets of old.

December 31

I know that your strength is limited; yet you have held. – Revelation 3:8

John, the Apostle, claims he was visited by an angel who assisted him in bearing witness to the words written in these letters to the churches of Asia. They believed the end of the world as they knew it before Jesus was rapidly coming to an end. They were preparing themselves for the return of Jesus once again. This book speaks for Jesus, telling his followers, "I am coming soon. Hold fast to what you have lest someone rob you of your crown." (3:11)

Centuries later, the Christian world waits for the return of Jesus. Millions of followers have not grown weary of the waiting. They continue to disagree among themselves as to what Jesus really meant by his presence, his teachings, his miracles, his death and his resurrection.

What did Jesus really say and do? Will faith see us all through to the end of our lives on this planet and into the next world – the Promised Land?

As we come to the end of another year, we know with near certainty there will be a tomorrow. We know that tomorrow will become another today – and that's all we will be responsible for – one day at a time – building bridges and bridging gaps in relationships – and filling potholes left on the highway of life by previous occupants of our world.

Today is just one more day that soon will be part of our collection of yesterdays.

Afterthought

A reminder, to those who are just starting a daily meditation practice, or are well on their way, that "any holy book" will serve the purpose of reading, reflecting, responding and resting. The process is the purpose – to simply begin, trust, and relax into your search for unification with the divine living within you.

If you have found anything in my writing that you wish to repeat or quote, feel free to use whatever I have been so freely given. It is only words, and I don't own the meaning of the words.

We move methodically from hour to hour, day to day, and year to year. However, our lives are really seamless. Even our sleeping is a continuous thread woven into our lives.

For some reason, it gives humans comfort to take apart, separate, and mark passages of time. It is, after all, only time, and space, and energy. The only thing we have any control over is how we use that time, space, and energy. May we use it well.

Author Biography

Marilyn Catherine McDonald has been a professional writer since 1967. She received her undergraduate and graduate degrees while raising eight children. Then, as a single parent she returned to the work force for the first time in 25 years and climbed the corporate ladder. She worked in the fields of corporate communications, advertising, public relations and publication production. She has served as an officer in several professional communications organizations. In addition, she volunteered as a suicide-crisis hot line counselor, a Court Appointed Special Advocate (CASA) for abused and neglected children, and a recovery counselor to women in prison.

A 25-year marriage to the father of her eight children ended in divorce and was followed by 22 years of single parenting. In 1999, she married Harry Taylor, the widower father of her son-in-law, Dee. Her husband Harry is a 26-year Air Force retiree and they travel every chance they get by land, sea or air to countries near and far. They have been all over the Pacific Northwest and the Southwest, as well as Alaska, Hawaii, Florida, and Canada. They spent an entire month in Australia and New Zealand, and have been to Japan, Singapore and even Pago Pago, American Samoa. For five weeks during the summer of 2003, they traveled by automobile visiting dozens of cities in Europe, including the city of Prague. In 2006 they traveled by train stops across Germany,

Austria and the Slovak Republic to join a Danube River tour from Budapest, Hungry to Bucharest, Romania. After which they traveled by plane and train to Warsaw and Berlin. They went to Egypt in 2010 and Cuba in 2013.

As a result of their love for travel, Marilyn did newspaper and magazine travel writing for 10 years, while working on book length projects. After spending 15 winters in San Felipe, Baja Norte, Mexico, they sold their home there and are once again mostly, full-time Oregonians.

A Writer's Soul

by

Marilyn Catherine McDonald

While yet a child
I discovered thought.
Then
I discovered words.
Then
Thoughts and words
Became one.
I discovered the miracle
Of thinking about
My own thoughts,
And
Putting words on paper.
I became a writer.
I made my living as a writer.
My life as a writer
Makes me
Who I am.
I write because I must.
I write because I can.
Writing is my gift
from God,
And, my gift to you.

16249445R00272

Made in the USA
San Bernardino, CA
25 October 2014